More praise for *My Hea*

"*With stunning bravery and un.* ___ *, award-winning* journalist and mother Amy Silverman creates an engaging, surprising, and, at times, shocking memoir that is unparalleled in its research, precision, and enormous helpings of determination. **My Heart Can't Even Believe It** *is a remarkable journey through the territories of science, truth, and above all, love. Amy demolishes the status quo and insists on nothing but the best opportunities for her daughter Sophie. Like the unforgettable Sophie herself, this book will resonate with readers for a long time to come.*"

—Laurie Notaro,
New York Times best-selling author of **The Idiot Girls' Action-Adventure Club**,
and **Autobiography of a Fat Bride**

"**My Heart Can't Even Believe It** *is entertaining, enlightening, and emotionally devastating. Amy Silverman has managed to write a book that addresses history, medical science, parenting, and her own daughter's Down syndrome with fearlessness and wit. I have not stopped thinking about it.*"

—R. Bradley Snyder, author of **The 5 Simple Truths of Raising Kids**

"*Raising a child with a disability is not for the faint of heart. Amy Silverman's honest, funny, and heart-warming account of her family's journey is a must read for anyone who not only plans to endure something hard, but believes that rising above it is their destiny.*"

—Keith Harris, father of Tim Harris, restaurant owner, social-media icon,
and inspirational speaker, who also happens to have an extra 21st chromosome

# MY HEART
## CAN'T EVEN
## BELIEVE IT

# MY HEART
## CAN'T EVEN
## BELIEVE IT

## A STORY OF
## SCIENCE, LOVE, AND
## DOWN SYNDROME

## AMY SILVERMAN

Woodbine House

Drawings on title page and in chapter 12 ("Portrait of Sophie as an Adult") by Annabelle Stern

Chapter 7 is based in part on the story "Educated Guess," which originally aired on the radio show *This American Life* on June 27, 2008.

Chapter 11 is based in part on the story "Lucky Day," which was originally published in *Brain, Child: The Magazine for Thinking Mothers* (www.brainchildmag.com).

The following chapters are based on stories first published in *Phoenix New Times*, a Voice Media Group publication: chapter 4 (from "Up the Down Staircase," November 25, 2004); chapter 12 (from "The New Segregation," May 15, 2014); chapter 13 (from "Dying Poets Society," June 22, 2000); and chapter 14 (from "Game Changer," May 6, 2015).

Library of Congress Cataloging-in-Publication Data

Names: Silverman, Amy, 1966- author.
Title: My heart can't even believe it : A Story of Science, Love, and Down Syndrome / by Amy Silverman.
Other titles: My heart cannot even believe it
Description: First Edition. | Bethesda : Woodbine House, 2016. | Includes bibliographical references.
Identifiers: LCCN 2015049969 (print) | LCCN 2016010424 (ebook) | ISBN 9781606132746 | ISBN 9781606132753 ()
Subjects: LCSH: Children with mental disabilities. | Child rearing--Psychological aspects. | Down syndrome--Patients--Family relationships. | Mother and child.
Classification: LCC HV891 .S565 2016 (print) | LCC HV891 (ebook) | DDC 362.3/3092--dc23
LC record available at http://lccn.loc.gov/2015049969

10 9 8 7 6 5 4 3 2 1

FOR RAY

# TABLE OF CONTENTS

lllll

# INTRODUCTION

I stood alone in the Phoenix airport on a hot June night, giggling. I had just discovered the going-away gift my barely ten-year-old daughter, Sophie, had left on my phone, in the form of thirty-nine self-portraits and a two-minute video. The photos were all close-ups of her face—slightly crooked bangs, more-than-slightly-crooked teeth, smiling, frowning, goofy-with-her-tongue-out. In the video, Sophie alternately sings one of her favorite songs, "Gangnam Style," and begs me to take her along on this work trip to New York City, but mostly she talks about how much she loves me. This is a familiar refrain, and one that for me never gets old. Not yet, at least.

"You are the best mom I ever had," she often tells me. On homemade cards, in handwriting only I can read, she writes, "I love you because I love you because I love you."

And this time, on the tiny iPhone screen: "I love you so much my heart can't even believe it."

I stopped and stared at the phone, not noticing as my computer bag slipped from my shoulder to the airport carpet, the editor in me pausing to say (almost aloud), "Hey, nice line!"

Sophie has no internal editor. What you see is what you get. If she likes you, be prepared for an onslaught of love. If you rub her the wrong way, get ready for the cold shoulder. Sometimes her lack of an inner censor gets us in trouble (like when you don't really want the whole world to know you've just finished the lice treatments), but more often, there's a lesson in Sophie's lack of inhibition. I didn't officially become an editor till Sophie was born, but I've been editing myself my whole life. A lot. I didn't realize that until I had her.

But although I've come to love all the things that make Sophie different, I wasn't always so Zen about the whole thing. Far from it. In fact, Sophie is the first person with Down syndrome I ever met. Which wouldn't have been so awkward if she wasn't my daughter.

My husband, Ray, and I named her early in the pregnancy: Sophie. It means wisdom in Greek. After the diagnosis, I wondered aloud if we should consider a new name, because at that point, in a lot of ways, I didn't have an internal editor, either. But I had a lot of questions, once I got over the shock of having a kid who isn't perfect. And eventually I approached finding the answers the only way I knew how: as a journalist. In fact, I have spent the last decade trying to figure out what I could about Sophie and what makes her unique. Although it did take me a while to get there—for a long time I was so focused on the day-to-day of raising my daughter that I only gathered the books, articles, names of other parents, and documentaries, sticking them in a big Rubbermaid container and shutting the lid tight, eyes covered.

"Do you realize," Ray asked once, early on, "that really, Sophie shouldn't be alive?" Genetically speaking, he's right. Every part of her is different than every part of us. Every bit of the matter that makes her who she is. And who she isn't. Sophie's our own little science experiment. As it turns out, she has taught us more than I could learn anywhere else—on topics ranging from heart valve configuration to federal education law to (corny but true) the meaning of life. That from a girl (me) who once stuck a button on her bulletin board at work that says, "If at first you don't succeed, you'll be a loser and a burden on society for the rest of your life." The button's still there, buried under family pictures and other mementos of a busy, mostly happy life. I haven't changed completely. But things are different now. This is a book about how.

# I

## CURLS

When my daughter Sophie was a few days old, the pediatrician scribbled a name on a prescription pad and handed it to me. A geneticist. When you have a baby with a genetic disorder, they send you to see a geneticist. I didn't think to ask why. I figured this guy would look at Sophie—maybe test her blood—and tell us all kinds of things, like how smart she'd be and whether or not we'd have more kids with Down syndrome. Sort of like a fortune-teller.

It took four months to get an appointment, and by the time we got in, I'd already figured out that those questions don't have answers. I really only had one question left for him: Do people with Down syndrome ever have curly hair?

In our house, hair is a big deal. Specifically, hair that curls. When Sophie's older sister, Annabelle, was a few months old, her straight brown hair fell out and she was bald. For weeks afterward, Ray and I watched her head carefully for signs of curls.

Perhaps Ray and I are so obsessed with hair because both of us had transformations when we learned to let our curly hair be curly. For me that happened my junior year in college, when I spent a semester in London and got a spiral perm—going to the other extreme from my previous hairdo, which had required hours with the blow-dryer, round brush, and iron. Okay, so with the perm I looked like Dee Snyder from the heavy metal band Twisted Sister, but that was stylish in the late 1980s, and finally, I felt good about myself. I dated cute boys all summer.

Ray won't tell me exactly when his mother stopped blow-drying his curly hair straight. I asked once, and he got a funny look on his face and said, "You're going to write about this, aren't you? No way am I telling you anything."

No matter. When I met Ray, he had dark, curly hair and everyone told us how cute it was that someday we'd have a little baby with curly hair.

We did. By the time I was pregnant with Sophie, Annabelle's hair had grown in and she had a full head of perfect blonde ringlets. Old ladies in Target would stop me to ask if I used a curling iron on my two-year-old's hair. No, just an entire bottle of No-More-Tangles. When Annabelle's hair was wet, it stretched almost to her butt. She loved to shake her curls. She knew they made her special.

But what about Sophie—so tiny in her carrier, with straight black hair and a feeding tube up her nose, chromosomally challenged and days away from open-heart surgery?

Would her hair ever curl?

Years later, I still can't believe the words came out of my mouth as we sat there in the geneticist's office. From the look on his face, neither could he, a sweet older man with a booming practice and a packed schedule. In the time it took us to get in to see him, Ray had done his own homework on the topic of Down syndrome. His side of our bed was piled with books; more than once, I'd caught him staring at baby Sophie—silently sizing her up next to whatever new fact he'd just discovered, hesitant to tell me much.

Before the doctor joined us in the exam room, we met with a genetics counselor who gave us some history. "Down syndrome was first identified by a man named J. Langdon Down in the seventeenth or eighteenth century," she began, reminding me of the public relations people who call newspaper reporters to pitch well-worn story ideas, practically singing them off a script.

"Actually," Ray said gently, "It was 1866." After that, Ray did the talking, and the genetics counselor took notes.

After Sophie was born and we got her diagnosis, Ray and I took very different approaches, which is weird, since he and I are both journalists, each of us in the habit of soaking everyone and everything for information on any given topic. Ray jumped into his research, but I retreated into the bliss of ignorance, particularly for those first fuzzy months of Sophie's life. When I was a little girl—and even now, sometimes—when I'd hear a noise at night, I would pull the covers over my head, confident that if I couldn't see it, it couldn't hurt me. Ditto for adulthood. When I had the chance to take the tests while I was pregnant (and even when they told us there was a better than average chance Sophie had Down syndrome), I didn't. And now that she was here, I still didn't want to know. I didn't want to know what was lurking around the corner, in the dark.

Instead I focused on the day to day. I decided I could only live with my baby and learn to love her and get her what she needed. And even though she was just four months old, she'd needed a lot, so far—a feeding tube, therapy three times a week. Echocardiograms, rows of pill bottles, a mini-hospital set up in the nursery. Scariest of all, a few days after this appointment with the geneticist, she was scheduled for open-heart surgery.

I survived by taking deep breaths and focusing only on the immediate. If Sophie wasn't going to be like the rest of us, if she wasn't going to be like Ray and Annabelle and me, that was okay. I just didn't want to know about it in advance.

Except for Sophie's hair. I wanted to know about her hair.

The day before Sophie was born, I had an ultrasound. The technician never saw the hole in her heart, but she pointed out my baby's hair, floating in the amniotic fluid. It was beautiful.

And so was Sophie when she arrived, right down to her full head of straight hair. As lovely as it was, however, I won't say her hair didn't cause a pang. Selfishly, instinctively, I wanted her to be just like us. And so, I wanted her to have curls. Not the kind you get from a perm or an iron, but real curls—snaggled-at-the-back-of-the-neck, need-to-be-coaxed-with-conditioner, on-the-verge-of-dreadlocks, don't-touch-I'm-in-the-critical-drying-stage curls.

As we sat in the geneticist's office that day, I had yet to read any of the books or surf the websites or talk to the parents whose names we were given regularly, but somehow I knew before I asked that Sophie's hair would never curl, and I knew that there were so many things about Ray and me that I already saw in Annabelle that I'd never see in Sophie.

The doctor stared at me. Then he explained that people with Down syndrome do not have curly hair. "African-American hair might wave a little," he said, "but otherwise, no."

(Over the years, I've found out that the doctor wasn't 100 percent correct. From time to time, I have encountered people with Down syndrome who had curly or wavy hair. These tended to be the children of parents with much curlier hair than Ray and I have, though. And these examples were few and far between.)

Sophie would never have curly hair. I have to admit that I felt a little cocky for having figured it out—but mostly, I just felt sad. And dizzy, both literally and figuratively. Having this baby hadn't just thrown me off kilter; it had knocked me over and I couldn't figure out how to get up. Not that you'd have known by looking at me. (I don't think so, anyway.) I was going through all the paces that a new mother takes, feeding Sophie, clothing her, rocking her, keeping her alive. Cooing at appropriate moments. But I didn't feel like she was mine.

And now it felt like she'd never be. The hair was a symbol of all the ways she would continue to be different from us. She wouldn't love the books I loved, wouldn't "get" subtitled art house movies or defend socialism to a roomful of capitalists, and she'd never have curly hair. I looked down at her, strapped carefully into her carrier in her sweet pink-and-white onesie with her straight hair, and knew what I had to do. There was no other option. I picked up the infant carrier with this foreign creature inside, and we went home.

In a lot of ways, Sophie and I grew up together. And as she got older and I morphed from a spoiled, self-centered brat—one who used words like *retard* and switched lines at Safeway when I saw a bagger with special needs —into the mother of a kid with Down syndrome, I had more questions.

How was Sophie going to fit into the world? Not just my world and our family's world, but society in general?

This was the big, unanswerable question. I had smaller ones, too. Like, how come it used to be okay to describe a person with Down syndrome as mentally retarded, but suddenly it wasn't? Did people with Down syndrome ever get depicted in pop culture simply as themselves—or was the story always about how they had a disability? How would school work for Sophie? Would she be able to talk? To read?

Would she be able to have sex, get married, have kids? Would she always live at home? Would she only be able to find work bagging groceries? And while we were on the topic, why did it seem that all people with Down syndrome bag groceries? Can't they do anything else?

Why do people with Down syndrome tend to be so happy all the time? (And later, why are they so stubborn?)

Okay, so some of those questions weren't so small, either. But big or small, they all shared equal space in my head, particularly late at night when too many Diet Cokes kept me awake.

Finally, curiosity won out over fear. It was not an overnight process; far from it. For so long, Sophie was my daughter who had Down syndrome. She was cute, I knew I should love her, and I did love her, in some basic way. But she wasn't just my daughter in the same way Annabelle was. It was never that simple, not for many years. I was so busy worrying about the parts that I didn't let myself consider the sum. When Sophie was born, I abandoned the luxury of simply sitting back and enjoying my kid. Instead, I made doctor appointments and looked for therapists, fought with school administrators, and admonished people who used the word *retarded*.

And then one day around Sophie's seventh birthday, I woke up and realized she was no longer my daughter with Down syndrome. She was my kid, and I loved her and not because I was supposed to. I can't tell you exactly what did it. Time, I guess. And the fact that she was walking and talking, making friends, expressing opinions. Sophie had become her own little person—something I'd long ago decided would never happen. I was wrong. She had ideas and opinions—sometimes even stronger than those of her peers. One day I walked into her second-grade classroom to volunteer; the kids were learning how to use computers. Every other kid was on the correct screen, learning a basic function. Sophie had found her way to the Target website and was shopping for Olivia the Pig merchandise. The teacher smiled and rolled her eyes, and I suppose I should have scolded Sophie. But I couldn't. I loved every bit of her in that I-can't-stop-staring-at-this-kid-don't-you-see-how-amazing-this-kid-is way.

On Sophie's seventh birthday, I wrote this on my blog:

*Last night, I wandered the aisles of Target looking for some last-minute presents for Sophie to open. I felt the excitement well up in me as I imagined her opening various items and wrote a Facebook status update in my head:*

*"I'm ALMOST as excited about Sophie's birthday as Sophie is."*

*It was true. I was giddy, considering just which water guns to buy (Ray's idea, and I'll admit, a good one) and I practically fell over when I found a stuffed Olivia the Pig. Then I had kind of a weird thought. I'm addicted to Sophie. It's an odd thing to say about a person, but it's true. I look forward to the moment she bursts into our bedroom way too early each morning; I crave the touch of her soft cheek when she cuddles up against me. I relish the (too rare) days I sneak away from work to pick her up early from school; there's nothing like the feeling when that unfiltered joy comes charging full-speed, when she sees me waiting.*

*Don't get me wrong, she's not just this little ball of kid to cuddle, she's got a lot more going for her than that. She surprises us every day. But at the heart of that kid is, well, her heart. Always will be. And I'm addicted to it. I'm addicted to Sophie. I'm addicted to love. The unplugged, unconditional kind.*

*I never, ever would have expected to have fallen in love with a child with Down syndrome. Until Sophie, I didn't even know what Down syndrome was. Suddenly, it's seven years later…. And I don't know about the future, but I know what seven looks like. It looks pretty darn good.*

I finally had a real relationship with Sophie. And that allowed me to begin figuring out her place in the world. It was wonderful, but it was also painful, since I'd fallen so hard for this kid and now I had to face the fact that she'd be lucky to live into her sixties, and that even if she did live a long life, it might not be a happy one. Where would she live when she grew up? What would growing up look like, in Sophie's case?

And so it was that I was finally ready to take out the reporter's notepad and start asking hard questions. I'd already been reporting around the edges—collecting books and articles, taking notes, even doing the occasional interview. But now I began in earnest.

First up: Just what exactly *is* Down syndrome? The genetics counselor (and every doctor I've talked to and book or article I've read) explained it so simply: In the vast majority of cases, something goes haywire during conception (probably having to do with an old mom, according to the "expert") and the fetus winds up with an extra twenty-first chromosome.

This explanation is usually accompanied by a worn-out Xerox copy of twenty-two pairs of squiggly black lines—and one set of three squiggly lines.

Um, yeah, sure. Got it. Now, what the hell is a chromosome again? This isn't the kind of thing that is addressed during the length of a typical doctor appointment, and it's sort of awkward to have to admit that you weren't paying attention that day (week/month/year) in high school biology. Besides, even though it's all about biology, it turns out that deciphering Down syndrome is also a lesson in anthropology and history, with a dose of psychology thrown in.

At an early stage in my research, I mentioned my quest to understand Down syndrome to my friend and former coworker, Ando Muneno, who had recently left journalism for the physician assistant program at George Washington University. Eager to help (or maybe just to procrastinate), he set out to answer my questions. He returned dumbfounded.

"If the body is a house," Ando e-mailed me, "then people with simpler genetic disorders tend to have a problem like faulty wiring in the den or oddly colored wallpaper in the kitchen. But a person with DS has plans for two living rooms that the contractor went ahead and built within each other."

In other words, Down syndrome affects pretty much every bit of a person. You can't get away from it. And you can't fix it. Not yet, anyway.

Here's how it works, on a scientific level:

There are fifty trillion cells in a human body, give or take. Each cell contains what's called a nucleus, and inside each nucleus is the genome sequence—all of the genetic material that makes you who you are. A typical genome sequence is comprised of twenty-three pairs of chromosomes.

You get twenty-three chromosomes from your mother and twenty-three from your father, for a total of forty-six. During conception, when the sperm fertilizes the egg, the mother's twenty-three chromosomes come together with the father's twenty-three, mix it up, and then begin dividing into new cells. Each cell contains a matched set, forty-six chromosomes.

Unless something goes wrong. Sometimes chromosomes refuse to split, and you end up with an extra one in a cell—forty-seven chromosomes. That's called nondisjunction. If it happens with any chromosome other than the twenty-first—which is the smallest—the cell development only rarely results in a live birth.

Here's why chromosomes are so important: They include our DNA, the genetic code that makes us who we are. Chromosomes are microscopic, but they are densely packed with genetic material, that twisty rope thing called a double helix that you see in videos and textbooks. Unravel a chromosome and it can contain more than three meters of genetic material.

That is what wreaks havoc with the development of a person with Down syndrome, also called Trisomy 21, which stands for "third twenty-first chromosome." The twenty-first chromosome is the smallest, but it still includes enough genetic material to make a dramatic impact if you have an extra one in each of your trillions of cells. (Or even if you have an extra twenty-first chromosome in selected cells—that's called mosaicism, and is a less common, often milder form of Down syndrome.)

Scientists have only recently begun unwinding our chromosomes to find out what the genes contained in them do. For a long time, we knew that there was an increased chance a person with Down syndrome would get leukemia and early-onset Alzheimer's disease, and a decreased chance that the person would get tumor-based cancers. Now scientists can point to the genetic material in the twenty-first chromosome and begin to say why.

These scientists have actually been able to create mice that have a form of Down syndrome (I've seen pictures, the mice even look like they have it), and so they know a lot about what the twenty-first chromosome contributes—and what can happen when the extra material of a third one is present. For example, a gene called APP is present in large amounts in a person with Down syndrome, and it accounts for Alzheimer's-like symptoms. Gene DYRK affects neurological development, and IFNAR can affect your immune system. COL6A1 makes collagen and can account for heart problems. ETS2, troubles with various organs. And so on.

But what about hair? Why do people with Down syndrome almost always have straight hair?

A few days before my conversation with Ando, I had been having a particularly good hair day—curls approaching ringlets, thanks to an extra rigorous scrunching session in the bathroom—and we were rushing to get out of the house for school when out of the blue, ten-year-old Sophie announced, "I want curly hair, Mommy."

"Why?" I asked without thinking, pretty sure I'd been careful to never talk about hair around her.

"I want to be like you," she said.

I was simultaneously thrilled and devastated. It was a Sally Fields moment—you like me, you really like me, you want to be just like me! And it was also a terrible moment, one I'd been dreading. Sophie knew she had Down syndrome, but it was still an abstract concept for her in so many ways. Suddenly, it was real. Would she notice she wasn't like us? Would she care? I bent over to stroke her stick-straight hair, gave her a hug, told when I was her age all I wanted was straight hair (truth), changed the subject, and ushered her to the car, hiding my stinging eyes.

I thought of this moment as I read Ando's reply to my question about Sophie's hair: "The straight hair thing is intriguing," he told me. "It is a notable characteristic of DS, but so far I haven't read an explanation for why they almost uniformly have straight…hair. Hair is mostly made from keratin which…doesn't appear to be on the areas studied on chromosome 21. I'll have to look into it!"

ℓℓℓℓℓℓ

Ando never did find anything out about curly hair and Down syndrome. And I still had questions. So I cast my net farther—just down the street from my office, actually, to the Translational Genomics Research Institute in downtown Phoenix. The public relations guy gave me contact information for a scientist named Matt Huentelman.

I called. Dr. Huentelman was off to meetings the first two times I caught him, and the third time he wanted to explain things right away on the phone.

Could we meet in person? I asked. "I might need to look at a chart or something." (Plus I really wanted to see inside his laboratory.) He agreed, and I headed downtown on a Friday afternoon, only to find a lanky guy with a buzz cut standing at the reception desk when I walked in the building.

"I'm really hungry," Huentelman said. "Okay if we get something to eat?"

So I didn't get to see the lab, but across the street, over a bowl of chili and a Coke Zero, the scientist did draw me some diagrams and explained chromosomes and DNA several different ways—till the whole thing finally stuck with me.

Turns out, chromosome 21 is the smallest, but it doesn't have the fewest genes. (Nineteen, a relatively small chromosome, has the most.)

And this genetic material explains pretty much everything about us.

"It's why the public should be excited about science," Huentelman said, grinning shyly into his chili. He got me excited about it, too, drawing the picture of a cell as a construction site—with the nucleus as the foreman's trailer (because it contains the blueprints, or DNA) and the construction materials (or RNA, which creates protein) surrounding it. In all, among the twenty-three chromosomes, we have 20–30,000 genes. There's a lot of room for differences—and error. When you have a trisomy, it's as though the DNA was putting itself in a copy machine, and the paper got stuck and the image repeated. That results not in a mutation but what Huentelman called an altered "gene dosage."

In other words, too much genetic material. In one case, he said, that extra material creates the plaques on the brain that causes early onset Alzheimer's.

"Right," I said, trying not to sound frustrated. I knew that already. Here comes a dumb question, I warned him. "Why do all the people I see with Down syndrome have straight hair?"

"It's a great question," he said. "You're behaving like Mendel."

I had a moment of pride. I had learned from some of my earlier research that Gregor Mendel was a scientist who lived and worked in Germany in the nineteenth century. He's considered the father of modern genetics. Scientists didn't actually come up with the tools to map chromosomes and truly understand genetics until the 1950s, but by breeding pea plants, Mendel demonstrated that plants inherited certain traits from their "parents," and that in some cases, something in their makeup prevented them from inheriting traits. This was all based on observation, the way I had observed that people with Down syndrome tended to have straight hair.

In fact, that's how Down syndrome was "discovered" in the first place. For centuries, people had noticed that sometimes their babies had odd features such as almond-shaped eyes and short stature, often died early (undiagnosed heart defects), and had trouble learning. In one ancient culture, the babies were revered because they were thought to look like the jaguar, a deity. Some called them mongoloids because they resembled the Mongolian people. In the mid-1860s, at around the same time Gregor Mendel was experimenting with his pea plants, a doctor named J. Langdon Down noticed that many of the patients in an institution he ran in England had similar features. He wrote a paper about his simple observations. Boom. Down syndrome.

It was as unscientific as that.

Sitting in that café with the cutting-edge genetics expert, I couldn't keep from smiling. I'd impressed the scientist. But Huentelman didn't know the answer to my question, either.

No one was able to tell me why Sophie's hair doesn't curl.

# 2

# ALL EARS

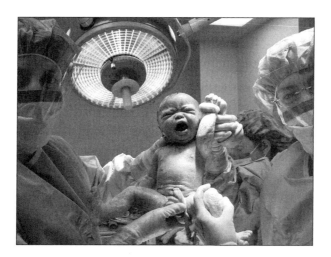

On a cool winter day in 2003, I parked my little silver VW station wagon at a rambling medical complex in downtown Phoenix and found my way through a maze of offices to my appointment for an ultrasound, the nonroutine kind.

I was six months pregnant with my second child and I should have been scared shitless, but I was oddly calm as I waddled toward the elevator.

Half an hour later, the technician clicked off the machine and handed me a rough paper towel to wipe the goop off my stomach.

"I'm not supposed to say anything," she said as I yanked my black maternity T-shirt down and struggled like a turtle on its back to pull my body to an upright position on the exam table in the small, dim room, then stuck my feet back in my red Dansko clogs. "But I know why you're here. And I can tell you without a shadow of a doubt that your baby does not have Down syndrome."

The ultrasound had been a compromise. A week earlier, I'd sat on another exam table in another medical building a few blocks away, shivering in a paper dress as my obstetrician tried to talk me into getting an amniocentesis. A blood test that screens for birth defects had come back showing an elevated risk of Down syndrome, he explained.

To be honest, I really did not understand what Down syndrome was. I think I knew that Corky, the kid from that '80s TV show, had it, and that the baggers at Safeway—the chubby ones with the round glasses who made me uncomfortable, the ones I always avoided—had it, too.

I just knew that Down syndrome was part of the list of things you don't want your kid to have—right up there with spina bifida and Tay-Sachs—and that my unborn kid had a 1 in 214 chance of getting it, according to this doctor. Those seemed like pretty good odds, but the guy looked so serious I got a little spooked. I called Ray and explained the whole thing in a rush, ending with the risk of miscarriage associated with amniocentesis.

"That, and I don't really want anyone sticking a needle in my stomach," I admitted.

"If they find out she has it, can they fix it?"

"No."

"Then why would you get the amnio?" Ray asked. "You're six months pregnant. What are you going to do, get a late-term abortion?"

Well, when he put it like that—no way.

Ray and I had just hung up when the phone rang. It was my father, calling from his cell phone to say hi. My dad and I had never been close, not in an emotional way. He is a good father, pretty nonjudgmental about decisions ranging from the guy I married to the jobs I accepted (including one at the alternative newsweekly when he, an executive at a public utility in the same city, would likely have preferred I work at the mainstream daily paper) and supportive financially. But before that day, I could hardly recall a conversation with him that you'd deem "personal." He'd only recently started calling me at all—thanks to extra time on his hands as he drove to and from the office, newly acquired cell phone at hand.

I'm not sure what motivated me to ask his opinion on such a sensitive subject, but I did.

"Hey Dad, I just heard from the OB/GYN. He says there's an increased risk the baby has Down syndrome. He wants me to have an amniocentesis. But I don't want to risk a miscarriage, and it would be a late-term abortion, and—"

He interrupted. "Well, I don't know, Ames," he said in his deep dad voice. "Those kids are a lot of work. What about Annabelle?"

It was a really good question, one I asked myself about a trillion times after Sophie was born. I've never reminded my dad of the conversation; I don't know if he recalls it. Looking back, I'll admit that I didn't get the amnio more because I was afraid of a long needle and a painful abortion than because I was okay with having a kid with Down syndrome.

As the years rolled by, it was fascinating to watch Sophie and my dad interact. In so many ways, his gruff, quiet demeanor is the opposite of her own. Long after his other grandchildren had abandoned efforts to get on Papa's lap, Sophie still crawled up without asking, sticking her thumb in her mouth and settling back for a cuddle. He played tic-tac-toe with her at the dinner table (I'd have to remind him to let her win once in a while), and she's the only one I ever saw get him to utter the words "I love you" back.

And he's as proud of her accomplishments as he is of Annabelle's. He's quiet about it, but I can tell he's one of Sophie's biggest fans.

That day on the phone, I sputtered around a little and got off the phone without saying much more. I looked down at my (already) enormous stomach. Ray was right. Anyhow, this whole thing was silly. We already had one child: a beautiful, perfect little girl. The only difference between this pregnancy and the last one, I was certain, was the fact that I'd had Annabelle at thirty-four. Now I was thirty-six.

Did you know that they call it a "geriatric pregnancy" when you're thirty-six? They do, and they give you a bunch of tests no one gives you when you are thirty-four. Silly.

I called the doctor. No amnio. Okay, he said, but please, at least get an ultrasound, the high definition kind where they can see everything.

Not quite everything, as it turns out.

I walked out of the medical imaging office into a pretty Phoenix February afternoon and can honestly say I didn't think about "Down syndrome" again till a hot morning in May when I blearily opened my eyes in a bright white room. I couldn't move. It took a minute to realize where I was. The recovery room. I'd just had a baby.

I'd awoken before dawn, in a puddle. My water had broken, three weeks before my due date. So much for the scheduled C-section. Ray and I scurried around, packed bags, met my in-laws in the hospital parking lot, and hugged and kissed Annabelle good-bye. Then I aimed myself through the automatic sliding doors at Desert Samaritan Hospital, a giant bath towel wadded between my legs.

At that point, my biggest problem in life was that my father-in-law had now seen me crossing a parking lot with a giant bath towel wadded between my legs.

Because it was an emergency C-section, my obstetrician wasn't available. A young associate from his practice—a woman I'd never met—delivered Sophie, holding her high in the air for me to see over the blue surgical curtain. Everyone cheered, and the young OB (my new favorite person, after she'd told Ray to quit complaining that I was squeezing his hand too hard as she gave me the epidural) asked if I'd like an extra shot of painkillers. Of course I would.

I suppose it took me a little longer than normal to wake up. And when I did, Ray and a nurse were deep in conversation.

"What are you doing?" I asked.

"We're measuring Sophie's ears," Ray said without a trace of emotion. "It looks like she has Down syndrome."

I felt my stomach drop several stories, even though I was flat on my back. I had to be dreaming, right? This was some sort of drug-induced nightmare. The epidural, maybe? The extra shot? I couldn't run. I couldn't move. I couldn't believe it. So I did what any normal person would do. I closed my eyes and went back to sleep.

I woke up in another room. My hospital room. Sophie was there in a hospital-issue bassinet, wrapped in the hospital-issue blue-and-pink striped blanket, fast asleep. Ray was not asleep.

"OK, so here's the deal," he said as soon as my eyes fluttered. "I've asked all the nurses, and they all think she has it."

I started to sit up, quickly stopped by the pain in my gut. It's not true, I thought to myself. No way. It can't be. I won't let it be. I turned my face to the wall. Ray took off for the hospital library. I stared at the ceiling. All day long, doctors and nurses came in and out of the room—checking on my incision, giving me painkillers, helping me stand up, whisking Sophie off to the nursery and back again—and every time, I asked.

"Do you think the baby has Down syndrome?" I tried to be nonchalant. You know, like I had my hand on my hip, my head cocked to one side. Just curious.

Not 100 percent completely freaking out. Not ready to open my mouth and scream and never, ever stop. I felt oddly detached; this wasn't happening, I was sure of that. When was I going to wake up, look up at Ray in the recovery room, and collect my compliments for another perfect baby? When was this going to stop?

Each nurse looked, and each nurse said the same thing. "Yeah, looks like she has it."

Years later, I stare at Sophie's baby pictures or pictures of other babies with Down syndrome, and I still can't see it. The eyes are a little slanted, the ears a bit lower. Are the features squashed? I really can't tell. Maybe it's a coping mechanism left over from that period of denial.

One of the nurses offered me the number for a support group. The gash on my abdomen was the only thing that stopped me from running out the door. I took the paper but didn't look at it. I didn't need it, right? No one had said for sure that the baby had Down syndrome. No way was this going to happen to me.

But what if it did?

The OB who delivered Sophie came in to check on us, a big smile on her face, a smile that faded completely by the time I was done asking my question.

"Oh, I have no idea," she said brusquely, all the friendliness from the operating room gone, her eyes purposefully avoiding the bassinet. "You'll have to ask your pediatrician." It was as though I'd accused her of something, and looking back, I guess I had. How many babies had this woman delivered? She'd never seen one with Down syndrome? It was that hard to tell? Had she even looked? I felt abandoned. She'd cut me open, looked at my organs, maybe even moved them aside to lift a baby out of me. And now she had nothing to say?

And yeah, our pediatrician. That was complicated. My OB would only deliver babies at a hospital our pediatrician didn't serve. And so instead of sweet Dr. David Alexander, who'd already seen me through almost two years of first-time-mom questions and concerns, I'd lined up a pediatrician we'd never met.

Norman Saba had a good reputation, but—and I'm not proud to admit this—the real reason I chose him was that he was related to the people who own a famous local western wear store in Scottsdale. At least it was a familiar name, and I knew that some of my relatives knew some of his relatives. I figured that might help in a pinch. Dr. Saba was scheduled to come by at the end of the day, one of the nurses assured me. So I waited, staring as the big clock on the wall ticked by in impossibly slow motion. Now I know what people mean by the term "suspended animation." My entire life as I knew it was in the hands of this pediatrician I'd never met, this man who was going to tell me if our baby was perfect or not. Because, to my way of thinking, there were no shades of gray here. My life was either over or it wasn't. Ray came back to the room, and we waited together. We called our parents, siblings, and close friends with the good news that Sophie had arrived, but we didn't say more than that.

We held the baby. She didn't look any different to me—just another crinkled-up, reddish face with dark hair like her sister had when she was born.

There is no way she has it, I told myself. You worry about everything! Stop worrying about this. Everything will be fine.

Ray and I didn't say much to each other. To discuss it would have been to acknowledge it, and neither of us was ready for that. Technically speaking, I still didn't have a child with Down syndrome, and I was going to keep it that way as long as possible.

At 5:30 in the afternoon, a middle-aged man with shiny black hair came into the room. Finally. The pediatrician. He shook our hands and quickly announced, "I know you are concerned that the baby might have Down syndrome. I've heard that some of the nurses think she does. But I have examined this baby, and I can tell you with certainty that she does not have it!"

For the first time all day, I took a deep breath. Those fucking nurses. See? I knew they were wrong.

I sucked wind again when I realized the doctor wasn't done.

"We'll do a blood test," he said, super casual. "Just a formality, just to be sure."

OK, I said, but I am not leaving the hospital until we get the results back. Dr. Saba agreed.

The next day, a nurse stuck a needle in Sophie's scalp and drew blood, leaving her with a giant bandage on her tiny head. The blood was sent to Utah; it would be three days till we had the results.

An eternity.

We waited. I watched TV and held the baby, my jaw set tight. Ray went back to the medical library and returned in tears. I wouldn't let him tell me what he'd read. This was all going to be over soon.

We plastered on big smiles for our families. No one suspected a thing, not even Trish, one of my closest friends. When I was in labor with Annabelle, Trish stayed up all night in the hospital with Ray and me. She's got two older kids of her own; she's the one I always call when I have a question. She showed up this time with a stuffed leopard and held Sophie for an hour. I watched Trish's face, figuring if anyone would figure it out, she would. Nothing.

Years later, Trish admitted that when she'd gone home that evening, her husband, Tony, had asked her how the baby was. "She's adorable!" Trish said. "She does the cutest thing where she sticks her tongue out."

Tony walked into the bathroom, where Trish was brushing her teeth. "That baby has Down syndrome," he said.

Another friend came to visit. She oohed and ahhed over the baby, then settled in for a gossip session. She and her husband and kids had just returned from a trip with another family. "You know their son has Down syndrome," she said, shaking her head. "It was just terrible." The boy was eight, she explained, but wasn't potty trained and couldn't talk. I sat there with what I could only hope was an appropriate look on my face, wishing so hard that she'd leave. Oblivious, my friend chattered on.

This has to be what hell is like, I thought after she left.

Three days later, Dr. Saba was back in the room. This time, he'd brought an associate along. Neither man could meet my eye. I shook my head hard, trying to wake up. But this was no nightmare. It was my life, my new life. I knew it before he opened his mouth.

"Well, it turns out she has it," Dr. Saba told the linoleum, after an uncomfortable pause.

Ray and I both stared at him. This has to be a joke, I thought. He has to be wrong. I have to wake up.

*I have ruined our lives. I had a sick baby, a baby who is going to make us miserable.*

I wanted to cry, but I couldn't, because I couldn't breathe. This white-hot ball I've never felt before or since was suddenly lodged in my throat.

I swallowed hard and watched the doctor watch the floor. On some far-away level, I knew that it wasn't his fault that Sophie had Down syndrome, but I wanted it to be. I desperately wanted it to be someone else's fault.

Finally, Saba looked up and smiled. "The good news is that I've examined her thoroughly, and there's nothing wrong with Sophie's heart. That's wonderful, because heart problems are very common in Down syndrome."

The associate cleared his throat.

"Oh, we'll do a test on her heart before you leave the hospital," Dr. Saba said. "Just a formality. Just to be sure."

I actually believed Saba when he said Sophie's heart was okay. I think my own heart couldn't handle any more right then.

After the doctors left, someone was kind enough to close the door to the hospital room, and I opened my mouth and wailed. Screamed, grabbed the covers, cried for Sophie, for Annabelle, for Ray, but mostly for myself. My life was over. Totally over. I was one of those people, those people you feel sorry for, those people I wrote about in stories for the newspaper.

I cried till the corners of my eyes were chapped, till my throat hurt, till I thought I was done, and then it would start all over again. And then, finally, I stopped.

It was time to call our families. And that started a whole new round of tears. This was the part I'd dreaded the most since I'd opened my eyes in the recovery room and noticed Ray measuring Sophie's ears. How could I tell my parents? How could I disappoint them like this? People in my family didn't have imperfect babies. But I had to tell them sometime, and the longer I waited, the worse it was going to get.

I called my mother, who had been over to see Sophie earlier in the day—several times since she was born—and had noticed nothing.

"So, we have some news," I said quickly, ripping off the Band-Aid. "They did some tests and Sophie has Down syndrome."

I couldn't hear anything on the other end, but I knew she'd gasped. I had practiced what I would say; I had a quip ready to lighten the mood. There's an oft-told story about my birth, how my grandmothers huddled outside the nursery window and ooh-ed and aah-ed over my feet, poking out of the swaddling to kick and point, just like a ballerina.

This was a big deal because my mother has danced her whole life, eventually running a ballet studio in Phoenix. I never danced, but promised my mother I'd have a girl who would, and Annabelle didn't disappoint: from birth she, too, was pointing beautifully arched feet, destined for the ballet barre.

"So here's the thing, Mom," I said really quickly. "It's going to be okay. You know how we've always known Annabelle would be a ballerina? Sophie will just have to do modern dance."

I chuckled weakly. Nothing on the other end of the phone. I never asked, but I've always assumed that my mom was sobbing too hard to speak.

We both cried for a while until finally she pulled herself together, and we hung up so she could tell my dad. I called my sister next.

"I'll be right there," she said.

And she was. Several hours later she flew in from Denver, and when she walked into the hospital room, she was carrying her own six-week-old daughter. Jenny is my only sibling, and growing up we'd never been particularly close. Almost five years apart, we were never in school together, never shared friends or interests. We were in each other's weddings, but really just by default. And then we got pregnant at the same time with our first children. Ben and Annabelle were born weeks apart, so it only made sense when we turned up pregnant together again. I hadn't yet met Kate, pink and round and healthy in the infant carrier.

Looking back, I guess I should have felt jealous of Jenny and her perfect baby. But I didn't. I was happy to see my niece. And as for my sister, it's hard to describe the relief I felt when she came through that door. It was weird—it was like for the first time in our lives, I suddenly understood what it felt like to truly need her. Ray was there, yes, but he was grieving in a way only he and I could, and he needed space. My mother was a wreck. Jenny was my rock. I don't remember what she said or what we did. Only that once I saw her, I knew that as horrible as things were, on some level they were going to be okay. I'll never forget the image of her walking through that door. Or her first prediction, delivered wryly: "Well, at least Amy will always have someone to get a pedicure with."

It's true. I've taken her from birth, practically, and Sophie is always up for a pedicure. I think she enjoys it so much because I can't chase her when I'm in the chair, feet soaking. She takes over the nail salon like the littlest tech ever, greeting each customer and advising her on her nail polish selection—whether she wants advice or not. (I have learned to tip well.)

The next morning, we packed up our things and Ray brought in the new car seat. Just before leaving the hospital, we walked down a hallway to a dimly lit room where a barrel-chested man in surgical scrubs ran a wand over Sophie's chest—sort of like the ultrasounds I had when I was pregnant, but this was called an echocardiogram.

I didn't know it then, but he was looking for a hole in her heart.

The room was quiet, except when the tech documented each measurement with a loud click on his machinery.

"Can you tell us anything?" I asked, as he finished up, wiping the baby's skin and turning to leave.

"No," he said, turning back for a moment but not catching my eye. "We're not allowed. The doctor will call you with the results."

You would think that I would have suspected something from the tech's attitude. But denial is a powerful drug, and I wasn't ready to go cold turkey.

So we went home.

The next day, the phone rang.

Ray ran to grab it, then walked slowly back to the doorway of the nursery where I was standing, watching Sophie sleep.

It's a snapshot tucked in the scrapbook of my memory—that tiny baby, that sweet little nursery I'd obsessed over: lavender gingham crib bedding, a soft yellow glider that had rocked Annabelle to sleep on so many fussy nights, and a wall hanging from the Land of Nod catalog that tied all the colors together. I'd been so pleased that the terrycloth cover on the diaper pad was an exact match to the pale violet paint on the walls.

The look on Ray's face as he held on to the phone, his skin ashen.

This time Dr. Saba hadn't had the nerve to break the news himself. He had his associate call to tell Ray that our baby had atrioventricular septal canal defect. A hole in her heart.

"Our baby has to have heart surgery," Ray sobbed. I was frozen, like you feel in a dream when you're trying to run from an attacker, but your limbs won't move. We looked at Sophie, still asleep in the crib, so tiny and perfect. Scratch that. Not perfect.

She wouldn't need the surgery immediately, but soon. We needed an appointment with a pediatric cardiologist, quick.

For Ray, it was a breaking point. But looking back, for me, it was almost a relief—like that blissful shot of pain you get when you stub your toe really, really hard.

Don't get me wrong. It was terrible. Beyond terrible. A *Twilight Zone* episode, a horror movie—or, at least, a Lifetime made-for-TV movie. But here's the thing: Everyone can agree that it's a tragedy when a baby needs open-heart surgery. Down syndrome? That one's muddy.

Having a baby with a heart defect is a medical crisis. But having a baby with Down syndrome is an existential crisis.

What are you supposed to say when one of your best friends calls and tells you that her baby has Down syndrome? I still don't know. I definitely didn't know then. I sure didn't know how to break the news to anyone.

As soon as I could drive after the C-section, I'd fib and say I was going to Walgreens, and I'd get on the freeway and drive really fast and call my friends on my cell phone and tell them, one by one.

"Hey!" the friend would say, "I got your birth announcement! Congratulations! Cute picture! How's Annabelle liking having a little sister?"

I'd hit the gas, taking the Broadway Curve on the I-10 a little faster.

"Well," I'd begin. "We have some bad news. Sophie has Down syndrome."

Silence. Sometimes there'd be sniffling on the other end. This happened maybe half a dozen times before a friend stopped me, midsentence.

"You know, it's not a bad thing," Becky said. "I've worked with kids with Down syndrome, and they're some of the sweetest, most loving people I've ever met."

Um, they are? I had no idea. That's how little I knew about Down syndrome. I didn't even know the most popular stereotypes.

After that, I reworked my speech.

"Well," I'd begin, "we have some news. Sophie has Down syndrome."

And then before the friend could say anything, I'd jump in with, "and she needs heart surgery."

Then we'd cry together. I'd hang up and move down my contacts list. It was always better if I could break the news first, before they said anything. Because inevitably, before they knew Sophie had Down syndrome, they said the wrong thing.

My friend Rob in New York left a voicemail. "Hey! I heard the baby was born. I found her the cutest onesie. It says, "Smarter than President Bush.""

Awkward.

"I hear you have two kids?!?!" my favorite grad school professor e-mailed. "Please share details: I want names, ages, IQ scores."

Ouch. I wrote back with the truth and never heard back.

My favorite reaction came from my friend Laurie. I'd called her during one of my drives and broke the news straight out—before I realized it was helpful to toss the heart surgery in there as a chaser. She gasped and started crying, saying, "Oh no, oh no, oh no, oh Amy, I'm so sorry."

I thought nothing of it. Frankly, it seemed like an appropriate reaction to me. But her response obviously haunted Laurie, because later that day, I got an e-mail.

*Listen, I'm really embarrassed about our conversation this morning about Sophie. I didn't know what to say. And I've been thinking about her and you all morning, and I just want you to know that I said the wrong thing. I mean, when I said that I was sorry about Sophie and Down syndrome, that just came tumbling out. Since then, I've realized it was a stupid thing to say, because Sophie is going to be fine. She's just going to be Sophie.*

Laurie continued, saying what good parents Ray and I would be, what a good big sister Annabelle would be. And this is how she concluded:

*Now this may not be an appropriate story for right now, I don't exactly know what's appropriate and what's not, but you are one of my dearest friends, and I think you'll understand. My neighbor Jean has a daughter, Paula, who has Down syndrome. Paula is about 40 now, she works at the library, and she and Jean are always together. One day, I saw them both walking home from the library, and they were holding hands, but they were swinging their arms back and forth. And I watched them for a while, and I thought, "Wow, when's the last time I held hands with my mom? Probably not since I was five, six. When's the last time I held hands with my mom like that? Probably never." And I remember thinking, Jean is so lucky to have Paula and Paula is so lucky to have Jean. It seemed to me at the time that Jean got all of the wonderful, little tender moments of being a mother, and she just got to hold on to them a little bit longer than other mothers.*

*Okay, that's enough of an emotional outpouring for this blackhearted girl. But know that I'm here, know that I'm thinking about you, and know that I can't wait to meet our sweet Sophie. I bet she's just a doll.*

Not long after that e-mail, Laurie came to the house with two Baby Lulu outfits (the expensive ones, not the kind you can buy at Costco) and an apple Danish from the best bakery in Phoenix.

But my favorite baby gift from Laurie came in a different form. At the time Sophie was born, Laurie was putting the final touches on her third book of essays. (You might have heard of her, Laurie

Notaro—she wrote *The Idiot Girl's Action Adventure Club* and several more.) She actually went through that book proof, page by page, and took out the word *retarded* every time it appeared.

"Well," as she later explained over chicken-fried steak at our favorite soul food restaurant, "almost every time. In some places, there just wasn't another word that worked."

That cracked me up. I was only beginning to understand how I was going to have to change my own vocabulary. I was realizing how ignorant, how insensitive I had been, and how I could no longer afford that luxury.

Not long after Sophie was born, Laurie and her husband moved to Oregon. But Laurie came home often, and we flew up to visit. Sophie and Laurie are best friends; they have the kind of bond you see among fraternity brothers. Sometimes that's the level of humor these two display.

"Take a picture of my butt, Mommy," Sophie ordered one day during the summer she turned eleven, turning around (fully clothed), waiting. Seemed harmless enough, so I did. Turns out, Sophie and Laurie were in the middle of a text war. They'd already called each other "fart face" and "potty mouth." Sophie was upping the ante.

Sophie: (IMAGE OF BACK OF SOPHIE'S DRESS)
Sophie: "Face"
Laurie: "Did you just call me a butt face?"
Sophie: "Yes."

By the end of the conversation they were debating whether Laurie should be a butt face for Halloween—or a smelly armpit.

Laurie never used the word *retard* in a book again, as far as I know.

I was raised by liberals. My mother was a McGovern delegate, and she volunteered for Common Cause, even in conservative

Arizona. We would never, ever make fun of a black person or scorn a Mexican. We were good people—agnostic Jews who believed in the Golden Rule.

But did that apply to the developmentally disabled? I'm honestly not sure. I only have one family story that has anything to do with that.

My mom loves to tell my birth story. As she gets older, Sophie asks to hear it (along with her own birth story, and Annabelle's) over and over, so I know it well.

I was her first baby. She was three weeks from her due date, and it was almost Halloween. She and my dad were at the movies, and suddenly she had an overwhelming craving for candy corn, so he got her some. The next day, her friends threw her a surprise baby shower. They lived in a small apartment complex—think Melrose Place but not as swanky—and there was a giant gong by the pool. To get my mom's attention, someone banged on the gong. It scared the crap out of her; she swears that's when her labor began, though to this day she's not sure whether to blame the candy corn or the gong.

Sophie loves the story. She doesn't know the part my mom and I stopped telling after Sophie was born. A few weeks before I was born, the phone rang. My mom picked it up. It was a strange woman.

"Mrs. Silverman?" she asked.

"Yes," my mom replied. "Who is this?"

The woman explained that she worked at the state institution for the mentally retarded.

"We have a space open for your baby, David Silverman," she said.

Quickly my mom explained that the woman had the wrong number and hung up. But she was haunted by the call.

David was the name she'd chosen for me if I'd been a boy.

"Ooooooh," we'd all say when she told it, like it was a ghost story. Too close for comfort. For the record, I told it at least as many times as my mom did.

I like to think it's more that we were ignorant than horrible. None of us had ever been around anyone with developmental disabilities. It just wasn't in anyone's vocabulary in our family.

The question wasn't whether or not my sister and I would go to college. It was where. Ditto for grad school. To be honest, I was more of a smart ass than smart—the kind of kid everyone thought got better grades than she did.

"Hey, why weren't you at the National Honor Society meeting?" my high school classmates would ask. I'd just laugh. I was barely passing my classes, but I edited the school newspaper and won debate tournaments. An underachieving nerd.

I couldn't let anything be easy—although, by all accounts, my life certainly was. Phoenix in the 1960s and 70s was a blank slate, huge planes of land razed to make way for strip malls and matchy-matchy housing developments. From an early age I watched Bob Newhart and Mary Tyler Moore on TV and longed to live someplace like Chicago or Minneapolis. Someplace cold with tall buildings and lots of people.

Phoenix was hot and the Bermuda grass that grows everywhere made me itch. I could not wait to leave. So I did. I went to Los Angeles for college, worked for two years on Capitol Hill, and then—deciding I preferred writing about politicians to being one—I applied to graduate school.

I got my first choice. Columbia University in New York City. I would be Meg Ryan in my own Nora Ephron movie; I was Diane Keaton, Mia Farrow. Valerie Harper!

The dream ended nine months later, on graduation day. My parents didn't tell me I had to come home; I chickened out all by myself, terrified I wouldn't be able to find a job during what, in retrospect, was a pretty mild recession.

It was more than that. Something pulled me back to Arizona— the safety of family, the familiarity of surroundings. After two years of working at a small daily paper, I got a job writing for *New Times*, the alternative weekly paper in Phoenix. It was a lot like the *Village Voice* (in fact, years later the company that owned *New Times* would own the *Village Voice* for a while) and for more than a decade, I got to write long stories about whatever I liked.

It was really hard, and kind of awesome. I wrote profiles of politicians, stumbled onto all sorts of dirt about John McCain (then just a U.S. Senator; it was years before his presidential bids, though I wrote about those, too). I wrote about government corruption; an abortion doctor who wore a gun at work; a woman wrongly accused of Munchausen by proxy.

I spent years telling other people's stories. Meanwhile, my own unfolded.

The night before I started my job at *New Times*, I met a young ad salesman at a staff party. This was strictly a gathering of editorial employees; he crashed. I liked that. It took him almost a year to ask me out. It was worth the wait.

Ray was born and raised in Queens. His parents moved the family to Arizona after his father—a member of the New York Fire Department—was forced to retire early because of lung damage from smoke inhalation. Ray loved Phoenix, had no intention of ever leaving. I stayed, too.

By all accounts, it's a mixed marriage. Ray was raised Catholic; I'm Jewish. He's a Republican; I'm a Democrat. He loves guns and cats; I can't stand either. That, my mother says, is how she knew it was true love: I was willing to move in with a tabby.

Perhaps the biggest difference between us: Ray craves adventure, while I prefer to stay lower to the ground. Literally. He has flown planes and jumped out of them. He loves to climb mountains—the kind of climbing you do with ropes and screws. I don't particularly like to fly *in* a plane, and I'd never put on a climbing harness. But (aside from the death-defying part) I love this about Ray, and I hoped he'd pass it on to our kids.

Turns out, we were in for an adventure neither of us had banked on.

That first summer, our world revolved around Sophie's heart.

You can't fix Down syndrome. There's no pill, and even the therapies Ray learned about couldn't start for a while. Our regular pediatrician, David Alexander, slapped on a bright smile and told me we wouldn't notice anything for a while. Sophie would just be a typical baby who'd slowly fall behind, as the milestones ticked by.

"I have a patient who's doing so well!" he told me on our first visit. "Mainstreamed in a third-grade class, keeping up with his peers."

I held on to that comment for years.

For now, it was about the heart. Dr. Alexander pressed the stethoscope to Sophie's chest and agreed the whooshing of the hole was hard to hear—but it was there. Next we visited a pediatric cardiologist. I relaxed into my role as "Mother of Heart Patient" rather than "Mother of Kid with a Mess of Problems and a Future Bagging Groceries."

They couldn't operate for four months. Sophie had to get stronger. The cardiologist warned us to keep an eye on how much formula she drank; in my state of denial, I didn't realize that meant she could starve.

For the first couple weeks, our baby did fine. I rocked her in the big yellow glider, feeding her formula, watching bad movies on cable late into the night. I hadn't had any luck breastfeeding Annabelle, although I'd dutifully pumped for months, giving her a couple of ounces of breast milk a day. I never tried with Sophie; she got the bottle treatment from the start.

But by the end of the third week, Sophie wasn't eating much, even from the bottle. And she was sleeping a lot. A lot more than Annabelle had slept at her age. Annabelle had been colicky, a projectile vomiter. Sophie was so calm it was scary.

And dangerous, as it turned out. On our second visit to the cardiologist, we discovered that Sophie had lost weight. They whizzed us across the parking lot at the Phoenix Children's Hospital complex and I found myself in another dark room, like the one where that first echocardiogram had taken place.

Halfway through the test, the cardiologist looked over at me. I realized I was frozen in place, eyes wide. "Don't be afraid," he said. "It'll be okay."

*Easy for you to say, I thought, trying to smile. Inside I was screaming. No, it will not be okay. It will not ever be okay. Even if you save her, if you make her heart strong, it won't be okay. My baby has Down syndrome—don't you get that? Why are you even bothering? Do you doctors really even care about these babies, or is this just some charity thing you feel like you have to do?*

*Is it some sort of charity thing that I feel like I have to do?*

I thought about running out of that dark room, leaving this baby I obviously couldn't keep alive. Instead, I stayed as still as I could, staring at the screen because I was too afraid to look at my child.

We wound up on the fourth floor of the hospital, sharing a room with a kid with an undiagnosed stomachache. Sophie had a diagnosis, along with her heart condition: failure to thrive. When babies are too weak to eat, it turns out, there's a fairly simple remedy, the cardiologist explained: a tube is placed up one nostril and fed carefully down the throat and into the stomach.

Um, okay. Actually, no fucking way. As in, no fucking way am I sticking a tube up my baby's nose and into her stomach.

But guess what? They won't let you leave the hospital till both parents can do it.

Ray did it the first day. I prolonged our stay, refusing to even try. If you stick that tube in the wrong way, it goes into the baby's lungs, and she drowns in formula. You test for this each time you feed her by injecting air into the other end of the tube. If it makes the right sound, you're good.

I was not okay with this. It seemed like a better idea to just stay in the hospital for the next thirteen weeks, till it was time for the surgery. There's pretty art at the children's hospital, and a good cafeteria with soft-serve ice cream—but no one, from Ray to the insurance company, thought that was such a hot idea.

Looking back now, I realize that keeping Sophie in the hospital was my way of keeping her at arm's length. This wasn't *my* baby who had a hole in her heart and a tongue that stuck out, who might never walk or be potty trained, who might never be able to engage in a grown-up conversation. Why was she my problem? Why couldn't someone else take care of her, of this feeding tube thing? What had I done so terribly wrong in my life to deserve this? And why did these nurses and doctors keep calling me "Mom," a title I so totally didn't deserve? I had failed; I had made a broken baby. And while I never seriously considered leaving her behind for good, I had no desire to take Sophie home with a feeding tube up her nose—not if I was the one who had to put it there.

In the end, a giant nurse in Fu Manchu scrubs who continued to call me "Mom" even when I told her my name was Amy ("Um, lady, I'm not your fucking mom, okay? I get that you don't remember my name, and that's cool, but why does every nurse and most every doctor in every hospital insist on this incredibly condescending practice? Or am I just that insecure about being someone's mom?!") bullied me into doing it.

So I stood over Sophie's body in the giant bed with this narrow tube and, gritting my teeth, gingerly poked the tube into her impossibly tiny nostril, turning several times to the nurse to insist that there was no way I could do this, hoping that just trying was good enough. But it wasn't. I couldn't run from this. I wasn't shaking, but I couldn't breathe past that giant, white-hot lump in my throat. I was so positive I'd kill her, that I'd stick that tube right in her lung and fill it with formula. There was no way I could do it—and then, somehow, I'd done it, threaded the tube up her nose, down her throat, and into her stomach.

I looked down at the bed, expecting the baby to choke, to die right there. It was my fault that she had Down syndrome, that she had a bad heart, that she couldn't eat right. It would be my fault when she died. But she didn't die, didn't even breathe funny. She just looked at us. The nurse cheered and smacked me on the back. I gave her a dirty look, collapsing into the recliner that had been my bed for days.

I never did it again. But it was enough to get us sent home.

And suddenly, Sophie's heart problem came to life in a very real way. Her pretty purple nursery became a mini-hospital room, with a cabinet filled with syringes, measuring devices for the formula, medical tape to keep the tube secured on her cheek. During the day, we fed her on a schedule, with a very specific protocol: checking to make sure the tube hadn't slipped from her stomach to a lung, filling a plastic beaker with formula, attaching it to the tube, then holding it aloft so gravity could slowly feed the baby.

We didn't just do this in the nursery. After the initial shock wore off and I realized if I didn't buck up I'd be spending the entire summer in the house, I started taking Sophie—and her accoutrement— everywhere. To see *Shrek* at the morning movies at the mall, to the Science Center (where we looked like a real-life experiment), and even to the beach for a week.

At night, Sophie was fed a slow drip from a continuous pump that would run out at 2:00 or 3:00 a.m., signaling with a super loud, beeping alarm. When Annabelle was an infant, I'd spent nights rocking her, singing "Hey Jude" and versions of Three Dog Night's "Joy to the World." It was how we bonded, I realized later, as I rolled out of bed to change Sophie's feed bag. Sophie slept peacefully, didn't even stir when the alarm went off.

Some nights I'd change the bag and then stay in her room, sitting alone in the glider while she slept, watching movies on HBO, cheesy tearjerkers like *Life Is a House*. I'd sob each time Kevin Kline built his dream house and then died of cancer, but I couldn't muster up any tears for Sophie. Not that I didn't feel plenty sorry for myself. I did. This was all so complicated. Why couldn't she have something simple, like cancer? I didn't know much about Down syndrome by then, but I knew enough to know I wasn't supposed to be feeling sorry for myself. I was supposed to be glad that I had a baby, that (relatively) simple heart surgery was going to make her well, that we already had all kinds of therapies lined up to make her strong.

I was definitely not supposed to wish my kid had cancer instead. But back then, before she was Sophie, when she was just this tiny, sallow baby with a feeding tube up her nose, I'd sit in doctor offices and hospital waiting rooms and size up other families and wonder if I'd rather be in their shoes. I know they were doing the same with me. *A feeding tube?* Horrible.

But you see enough of those little red wagons toting bald little kids in hospital gowns, too weak to walk to the hospital cafeteria, and eventually, your perspective changes. One day I realized that these parents were fighting to keep their children alive, while I was mourning a kid who'd never been born, a baby without a heart problem, and, more than that, a baby without developmental disabilities.

As we waited for Sophie's heart surgery, I went through the motions—making the appointments, confirming that Annabelle could stay with her grandparents. My maternity leave ended the week before the surgery was scheduled. I scrounged together a few more vacation days. On some level, I suppose, I was concerned about the surgery going well, about the doctors fixing the hole in Sophie's heart. I certainly acted that way in front of everyone, from Ray to the strangers who came up at the mall to ask about the feeding tube.

But really, my own heart was numb.

# 3

## THERE'S A HOLE IN MY HEART THAT CAN ONLY BE FILLED BY YOU

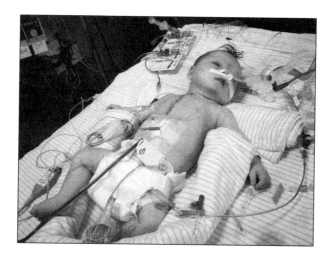

My extended family is not particularly close. We don't gather for birthdays or Thanksgiving, and there's no guarantee of attendance at weddings or even funerals. But there's one thing that will bring the Silvermans together, and that's a relative in the hospital.

Some of my earliest childhood memories are of walking through the sliding doors of Good Samaritan Hospital in downtown Phoenix, feeling a whoosh as the hot outside air mixed with the icy air conditioning, ushering me inside a grown-up, important place. I loved the gift shop at Scottsdale Memorial Hospital, particularly the flower arrangements you could order that looked like a clown or a shaggy white dog. I didn't know how they did that, but I knew that if I was ever in the hospital (I never was, not till I had babies), that's what I wanted. Years later, as an adult, I was poking around that same gift shop and noticed something in the back of the refrigerator case. A clown flower arrangement! It didn't look as good as I remembered, just a carnation in a cheap vase, decorated with googly eyes and pipe cleaners. But that wave of nostalgia was a huge rush.

Here in the hospital, at the bedside of an elderly grandparent or great aunt, I'd see cousins, aunts, and uncles I hadn't seen in months (or longer), tape my homemade card on the wall, and head down with other visiting family members for what I considered to be an exotic meal in the cafeteria. Even my father, not the most sentimental of souls, often showed up for visiting hours, which tended to involve minor injuries and illnesses. Nothing too serious (I was not brought along on those visits, anyway), and as far as I know, no one in our family ever had a baby with any kind of significant health issue.

Until Sophie.

On the day of the heart surgery, I found myself in a large, dimly lit room filled with tables and chairs, several of which were occupied by members of my extended family. My grandfather, the patriarch of the Scottsdale, Arizona Silvermans, was there. Even Great Aunt Charlotte, his sister, showed up, and the two of them hadn't spoken in years. This was a big deal; no one dared sneak out to grab frozen yogurt downstairs, and small talk was at a minimum.

Ray and I had been up before dawn that day, giving Sophie one last dose of formula through the feeding tube and packing for the hospital. By then, we were experts at taking care of an infant with a Serious Medical Condition. The sweet nursery I'd decorated so carefully had been transformed over the last few months into something much more clinical, even though I'd tried putting the syringes and tubing packages into cute baskets to keep things looking homey. I pushed the feeding pump aside, hoping that would be the first thing to go when we returned home, grabbed the overflowing diaper bag, and headed out to the car.

After we'd signed in, our first stop at Phoenix Children's Hospital was pre-op, where each patient is assigned a tiny room and given a once-over—blood pressure, temperature, "vitals"—the final all-clear to be cut wide open.

It's also where parents say their good-byes.

Like many children's hospitals, Phoenix Children's has a wonderful art collection, hung just where you need it, as it turns out. There was only one piece of art in the small exam room that barely held Ray, me, the baby, and the diaper bag—a framed painting of a woman in white scrubs handing a large, bright red heart to a small boy in a bed.

I am not a religious person—far from it. But as I've gotten older, I've increasingly been on the lookout for signs, and no more so than on this day, in this stark, fluorescent-lit place, with this baby I couldn't figure out, about to undergo an operation I couldn't begin to describe at the time.

"There's a hole in her heart," was as close as I could come to a medical explanation when anyone asked for details.

My throat caught as I leaned in closer to read the wall text and confirm the artist. I nudged Ray.

"Look," I said, pointing to the wall. "Rose Johnson."

Johnson was a well-known local artist, particularly known to us. Not only was she a frequent contributor to *New Times*, but I'd hired her to illustrate our wedding program several years before; she'd literally camped out on the lawn at the old hotel we'd chosen as a wedding site to capture the height of the palm trees and the curves of the Mediterranean architecture. She even designed a wedding logo, intertwining our names, cactus (for Ray) and roses (for me) around a wedding cake. I had the logo made into a gigantic stamp, and I stuck that image on everything from bakery boxes to goody bags.

I stared hard at the image of the woman and boy till I could see it with my eyes closed. A heart, of all things! Rose Johnson!

I got Sophie out of her infant carrier, the last time I'd lift her by the armpits for several months, careful not to pull out the feeding tube. I smoothed the tape over her face and ran my fingers over her stick-straight hair, trying my hardest to really connect to her, pretending for Ray, myself, the world.

Ray wasn't paying attention to me. He wasn't pretending. He was teary. He held Sophie close, and we both cooed and gurgled and made all the typical baby noises. Then we said, "See you later!"—careful not to use the word *good-bye*. A nurse put Sophie on a giant gurney and she rolled off into the distance, white fading into white down the hospital corridor, just like in the movies.

About half the babies born with Down syndrome have a congenital heart defect, which means that the heart develops incorrectly in utero, leaving misshapen valves or other problems that might need to be fixed surgically or might resolve themselves on their own. Of all babies with Down syndrome born with heart defects, about half have what Sophie has—atrioventricular septal defect, also called AV canal.

This one requires surgery. It's not uncommon, but it is serious.

I wasn't wrong when I described AV canal as a hole in the heart. The heart can best be described as two pumps with four chambers. The right side pumps to the lungs, the left side pumps to the body, and never the two should meet—unless you have an AV canal defect, in which case the walls between the chambers did not grow in the middle, leaving holes in the atrial septum (at the top of the heart) and the ventricular septum (the bottom). In that case the stronger left side (stronger because it has to pump blood to the whole body rather than just to the lungs) will pump some of the oxygenated blood back into the right side, where it's pretty useless and forces the heart to work harder to provide oxygenated blood to the cells.

None of this is an issue, health-wise, before birth. In his 2004 book, *Walk on Water*, Michael Ruhlman writes that the heart's fate is decided very early on. He describes how cells come together to form the complex muscle:

"The little creature growing around it is not even a fetus yet (at eight weeks old, it's still called an embryo), and this ingenious pump—four chambers, four valves, arteries, veins, and a conduction system—is the size of the head of a pin," he writes.

But, Ruhlman adds, "Defective hearts get along beautifully in the womb, it turns out, happy as demented little pearls."

Despite its complicated apparatus, the heart works as a single pump in utero; the fetus gets oxygen from the mother's placenta, Ruhlman explains. That changes at birth; the heart suddenly has to pump the deoxygenated blood to the lungs and oxygenated blood to the body. And that's when a defect like AV canal becomes a problem.

Several ultrasound techs missed Sophie's hole in utero (finding a congenital heart defect is often how Down syndrome is discovered in the first place, before birth). Then, once she was born, that pediatrician didn't hear the whooshing that signals a congenital heart defect, particularly one as significant as Sophie's. But the guy who performed the echocardiogram when Sophie was five days old saw it clearly.

Four months later, she was in surgery. As Ray would write at the end of that day in an update to our friends and family, the surgeon patched the hole in Sophie's heart with a piece of her own heart tissue. "In closing the hole, the structures of the valves were complete, allowing the valve 'flaps' to work properly," he explained.

It was a little more involved than that.

After Sophie was whisked away, a team took over in the operating room. She was put under, and the surgeon picked up an electric tool and sawed her chest down the middle. This is called a sternotomy, and observers have described the acrid smell of burning flesh and bone as the saw cuts through the sternum.

Next, Sophie was placed on a heart-lung bypass machine, which made the heart and lungs work and provided oxygenated blood during the operation to keep her alive.

Then her heart was stopped with "carioplegia," an injection of potassium that also protected the heart muscle during the procedure. And then, in a bloodless, beatless environment, the surgeon went about repairing the hole. He opened the pericardial sac, which holds the heart, and removed tissue to patch the hole.

Once the repair was complete, the bypass machine was turned off and the surgeon closed our baby's chest.

The risk of death in AV canal surgery is under 5 percent. But considering we only had a 1 in 214 chance of having a baby with Down syndrome, everyone in the family was looking at odds a little differently that summer.

And as complicated as my relationship was with my younger daughter at the time, I knew one thing for sure: I didn't want Sophie to die.

*lllll*

We waited. Someone showed us out of pre-op and into a waiting area. Family members trickled in and out. No one said much.

A couple hours in, a man in blue scrubs emerged through giant double doors. It took me a few moments to realize it was Dr. Lupinetti, the surgeon himself. Smiling, he informed us that Sophie was on the heart-lung machine and doing fine. He lingered, so casual, and I smiled and nodded and wanted to scream, "Why the fuck are you out here talking to us?! Get back in there and do your job. Keep that baby alive! Fix her! And while you're at it, get rid of that Down syndrome thing. Give me my life back."

Instead, I just stared at him, blinking.

After several more hours, we were led to a new waiting area, the dim room with the tables, which was a space reserved for family members of patients in the pediatric intensive care unit, the PICU. That's where Sophie would be soon, an orderly told us, and disappeared.

My aunt, my uncle, my grandfather, his sister, my parents, Ray's dad (his mom was at home with Annabelle), Ray, me—we all continued to wait, shifting on the hard plastic chairs, silent, staring at the carpet. And then the door opened. We all looked up in unison, expectant.

It wasn't a doctor or an orderly or another family member. It was Paul Rubin. Paul and I had worked together for a decade; he was at the paper when I started, already a seasoned journalist, and was a mentor from the start. I studied his stories—except for one that I couldn't bring myself to read—trying to figure out how he did it.

The year before Sophie was born, Paul had spent months haunting the cardiac unit of Phoenix Children's, profiling a pediatric cardiac surgeon named Michael Teodori. Paul knew from experience (or maybe from asking the nurses) that Sophie would be out of surgery shortly, and he wanted to be there to introduce us to staff he knew at the PICU.

That was gracious of him, considering I hadn't even read his story. I couldn't. The profile was published when Annabelle was fourteen months old—and as a new mom, I hadn't been able to bear stories about kids with scary health problems.

"C'mon," Paul had said one afternoon as I stood in the doorway of his office, hands over my ears, play-shrieking, waving my hands and begging him to stop describing how he stood on a stepstool and looked down into the chest cavity, watched the surgeon literally hold a baby's heart in his hand.

I'd had no idea that day that I was already a couple of weeks pregnant with Sophie.

After Sophie was born, after the blood test and the Down syndrome diagnosis and the echocardiogram and the news from the pediatrician, I called Paul, sheepish but terrified.

"You know that surgeon you profiled?" I asked in a small voice. "Can you call him?"

Paul promised to call Dr. Michael Teodori, and he did. But the surgeon had been in a terrible car accident the previous year; he'd eventually make a full recovery, but at that time was still in rehab. His colleague, Flavian Lupinetti, performed Sophie's surgery. Teodori was there. He stood and watched; it was the first operation he'd observed since his accident, Paul told me later.

When Lupinetti finally did come out to announce that Sophie's surgery was over, it was a success, and we could see her, Paul stayed behind with the family while Ray and I went in. At one point I looked up and my dad was standing by Sophie's bed. I was shocked; my father's not the type to hang out near super-sick infants and bloody incisions. Paul had convinced him to come in and see her.

Nobody convinces my dad to do anything. But nobody had told Paul that. Paul cracked jokes with the nurses and made them promise to give Sophie the royal treatment.

But he couldn't change the fact that there was my baby, splayed on her back on a full-size hospital bed, a tube down her throat and dozens more (or so it seemed) coming out all over her tiny body. And eventually, Paul had to leave.

The family was long gone by then. Ray had gone to pick up Annabelle and sleep at home. I sat on a purple vinyl bench, shivering in the hospital chill, and stared at the nurse standing over Sophie. The first night after open-heart surgery, you get your own nurse, and Sophie's kept herself busy, carefully untangling and rearranging the tubes sticking out of the baby. I watched her work, mesmerized, until the nurse stopped and looked up, embarrassed, apologizing for her OCD.

"Oh no, no need to apologize," I stammered, feeling guilty for staring.

Really, though, there was nowhere else to stare. Finally, I curled up on the vinyl bench with a hospital-issue blanket and tried to sleep.

lllll

If Sophie had been born before the 1960s, she almost certainly would not have survived past a few months.

Pediatric cardiology is actually one of the oldest medical specialties, but without imaging to see the heart's parts and diagnose a condition both before and after birth, doctors were literally blind.

The study of congenital heart defects dates to the seventeenth century; for a very long time, it was all done postmortem. Scientist/artists made beautiful, intricate illustrations of the hearts of dead children. Anatomists studied stillborn babies with heart abnormalities. A young child who turned blue and then died was infamously dubbed "blue boy"—later, doctors learned that he had a congenital heart defect.

In 1816, as the story goes, a French doctor invented what would become the stethoscope because he was embarrassed to press his ear to a female patient's chest—the accepted form of examination. By the end of the 1930s, surgeons were doing what was called "closed heart surgery," which was incredibly risky because not only were surgeons working blind, they had not yet figured out how to stop the heart without killing the patient. Instead they cut a small hole in the side of a beating heart and reached in with a finger to try to make repairs. Operating rooms were kept very cold, and other means were used to chill the heart, but that only slowed it down. And there was still blood everywhere.

Michael Ruhlman, author of *Walk on Water*, muses that the profession was started by crazy people.

"Imagine the questions people must have asked before the first open-heart surgery," he writes.

The first successful open-heart surgery was performed on a five-year-old girl in 1952 at University Hospital in Minnesota. According to G. Wayne Miller, the author of *King of Hearts*, published in 2000, the child was the daughter of a carnival worker and had been sick her whole life. Doctors suspected she had a valve defect. But there was no way to know for sure without opening her up.

As one pediatric heart surgeon told Ruhlman, "They had a license to kill because the patients were dying anyway."

In 2003, when Sophie had her first heart surgery, Mark Zuckerberg had yet to launch Facebook, and the iPhone wouldn't be released for years. But I had a friend who knew how to build websites, and each day Ray and I would go downstairs and write an update on the hospital library's desktop and then e-mail it to Ruth, who would post it. Mostly Ray would write the descriptions and I'd transcribe them, adding parentheticals, things I thought were funny or touching.

**August 28, 3 p.m.**

*Sophie is recovering slowly and, they tell us, doing really well. She has a full-time nurse whom she keeps busy. There are many adjustments going on, nothing very serious—all typical for a baby who has just undergone the AV canal procedure. Watching the doctors and nurses take care of Sophie is like watching a team of chefs: a little fluid drained here, another drug added there—we'll spare you the sometimes-gory details. She has been on a pacemaker, but the doctors are hopeful that won't be permanent. Sophie is being weaned off the ventilator today, meaning it has been providing less support for her breathing, but it will likely be in place until at least tomorrow. She looks comfortable in her sedation surrounded by Beanie Babies (don't tell Annabelle) and a jungle of tubes and gear. The initial recovery phase has been a bit more stressful than we expected, but the doctors say nothing out of the ordinary is happening. We'll keep hoping it stays that way.*

That website is long gone, but Ray's mother printed out the entries and put each page in a plastic sleeve and the whole thing in a binder, preserving the memory. Which is good, since I don't remember much about that time in the hospital. Ray says we sanitized those web entries—a lot.

**August 29, 4 p.m.**

*Sophie is still on the ventilator and they hope to take her off tomorrow. Her temperature and heart rate were up last night and through the day, and the doctors and nurses are working to get both down, with some success. We have posted her smiling picture above her bed, so everyone knows how cute she is!*

**August 30, 2 p.m.**

*Ray reports from the hospital that he saw the first smile since the operation. Sophie is much more alert today, looking at a balloon and around her room. They took out her main chest tube this morning, then had to put another small, unrelated one in—but the good news is that it improved her health dramatically and they're weaning her off the ventilator. Her temperature and heart rate are much lower (a very good thing) today, and the doctors and nurses continue to adjust everything— now we've decided it's like watching someone make a Long Island Iced Tea.*

## September 1, 10 a.m.

*Sorry we didn't post an update yesterday—the hospital library was closed. Sophie is doing incredibly well! After a false start Saturday, they took her off the ventilator Sunday and she is breathing very well on her own. Her vocal cords were temporarily shut down (a normal reaction) so it was strange to watch her open her mouth to cry—and have nothing come out. (Wonder if they can patent that?) But today, Monday, her voice is back a bit and she's got a cough that the nurses assure us is a good sign. The dry erase board by her bed no longer has a list of medications, and the chest tubes, pacemaker wires, and most of the other tubes are gone. She's just got an IV in her hand and the feeding tube, which we're accustomed to. The surgeon was thrilled with her progress this morning and says we'll be going home soon. (Not TOO soon! we begged.) Amy was able to hold Sophie yesterday and today, and she's as cuddly as ever.*

## September 2, 4 p.m.

*She had a great night and today ate two meals almost exclusively by bottle—fed by Amy and Ray. It's a little stressful to hold a post-op baby, but clearly harder on Mom and Dad than Baby. She still has the IV, and will go home with the feeding tube but other than a quickly healing scar is the same old Sophie, but already with more energy.*

## September 3, 9 p.m.

*Well, Sophie's passed the one-week mark in the PICU at Phoenix Children's Hospital, and we're now old friends with several nurses. (And we think it will be hard to tear Dick Silverman, Amy's dad, away from the hospital cafeteria, when it's finally time to pack up and go.) As of this morning, we thought we were headed upstairs for a day before going home tomorrow, but Sophie had other plans. Just as Amy walked in* with farewell cookies for the staff on Wednesday afternoon, Sophie's heart began to race and she had to be treated for what the doctors call "jet." The short story is that she's fine, but now on yet another medication and stuck in ICU for a couple more days, most likely, for observation. We had been nervous about going home, so this only makes things a little more tense, but the staff assures us this is very common and nothing to be worried about. Sophie's room is comfy, her bed packed with stuffed animals and her door decorated with artwork by cousin Ben.

## September 4

The ICU folks tell us Sophie will remain there for at least a couple more days. This morning her heart sped up again and the doctors believe it's not the "jet" they thought yesterday but instead "SVT." Don't ask me (Amy) to explain it, but apparently SVT is better than jet. But it will mean some additional monitoring, and more medication. We'll update you as we learn more—I'll try to talk Ray into putting together one of his super-duper technical reports, which the nurses say are quite accurate and impressive.

## Friday, September 5, 3:30 p.m.

Sophie looks fabulous today! She had a long-overdue bath, and after great consultation and debate, the nurses put her hair in a tiny ponytail (very Pebbles) tied with a bow.

Her SVT continues. It started up again right after the doctors made their rounds this morning, and continued for about an hour. They are tinkering with her medications. We will most likely be here through the weekend.

## Monday, September 8, 11:30 a.m.

Sophie is better and better every day. Yesterday the nurse pulled out the feeding tube—for good, we hope!—and she's been "nippling" really well. She seems pleased to have one less thing attached to her and is all smiles. Sophie's happy, but the rest of us are going stir crazy in the hospital. It looks like we're here for at least a couple more days, because

*Sophie's heart keeps racing—the same SVT problem has been popping up every day or so. We're in a holding pattern, while the doctors continue to tinker with medications.*

### Tuesday, September 9, 1 p.m.

*So far so good....Sophie hasn't had more than a blip on her rhythm radar since Sunday night. We could be out of here by tomorrow.*

### Wednesday, September 10, 10 p.m.

*Elvis has left the building! Late this afternoon, we packed up a little red wagon with two weeks' of belongings, and Sophie came home. We're nervous, as you might imagine, but happy to have our little family intact. This evening, Sophie was fussing a bit, lying on a blanket on the floor, and Annabelle took me (Amy) by the hand and ordered me to leave Sophie's room. I spied, of course, from behind the door, and watched Annabelle stroke Sophie's hair and tell her, "Don't cry, Sophie, Annabelle's here." Then Annabelle put her head next to Sophie's, looked up at the ceiling with her, and sang "Twinkle Twinkle Little Star." Sophie quieted down.*

*It was pretty cool.*

### Thursday, September 18, 7:45 p.m.

*We've been home for a week, and so far so good. The doctors have cut back on her medications, and the feeding tube is gone—for good, we hope, although we're keeping the machinery around just in case. We still have doctor appointments quite often, and can't pick Sophie up under her armpits for a while, but life is pretty darn normal around our house. She's even waking us up in the middle of the night, a change now that she's not on her all-night "irrigation drip" feeding system. Sophie is much, much more active and demanding with the increased energy from her happy heart—and that makes us happy, too—although tired. Annabelle's heart is also happy! She tells us often about the good old days when she was a baby—but now, we are told, she's a big girl. We agree.*

The high temperature, the second chest tube, the long stay all hinted at a much more serious time than we described. But the worst was the ice.

That "SVT" we wrote about? It stands for supraventricular tachycardia, and it is the most common form of arrhythmia, which is a fancy way of saying a racing heart.

With SVT, the heart may increase from a normal 100–150 beats per minute in a child to as many as 300 beats in that same time. It occurs in the upper chamber of the heart, and it's dangerous because it makes the heart less efficient and can result in damage to the brain or body.

Pacemakers and medications can control it—and in the end, medicine helped regulate Sophie's heart—but Ray and I chose to not mention to friends and family the other method of treatment the staff at Phoenix Children's Hospital employed when our four-month-old's heart raced.

A large bag of ice to the face.

Really. As soon as they'd notice on the monitor that her heart rate had increased, someone on the hospital staff would place a large bag of crushed ice over Sophie's entire face for a few seconds, in effect shocking her heart back into its normal rhythm.

That which doesn't kill us makes us stronger, right? It worked every time, and finally we were told we could go home. With instructions to keep a bag of ice in the freezer.

"No fucking way," I whispered to Ray. "I did that feeding tube once, but no way am I doing that."

"We don't have a choice," he replied, keeping his eyes on Sophie.

I had already been terrified to leave Phoenix Children's. I am a Silverman, and the truth is I loved the hospital. I loved the cool air, the salad bar in the cafeteria, the nurses. In the hospital, two weeks is like two years, and by the end of Sophie's stay, I pretty much knew the life stories of the entire PICU staff. We were exchanging mixed CDs. I had fallen into a routine, sleeping on the bench at night, going home to shower, coming back, and during downtime standing over that giant bed reading back issues of *The New Yorker* aloud to Sophie—I figured at that point the sound of my voice was good enough, why not kill two birds? It was comfortable.

More than that, the hospital was safe. Sophie was going home with a gigantic, still-raw scar down her chest—*the chest they'd cut open with an electric saw just two weeks ago*—and a stack of prescriptions, several of which had to be compounded at a fancy pharmacy across town. There was no heart monitor at home, no friendly nurses; we were supposed to look for signs of SVT ourselves. What if it happened in the middle of the night when we were asleep? What if I couldn't bring myself to put the bag of ice on her face? What if it didn't work?

I cried that last day, as the nurses helped me pack up the Beanie Babies and vases of flowers. But as much as I hated to leave, I had no intention of returning. Ever.

"You'll be back," said one of the nurses, a sweet, older Norwegian woman with a lilting voice and a continuing fondness for my colleague Paul. "I can tell you're the type. You'll come back to see us."

"No way," I thought as I hugged her tight, promising to visit soon to show Sophie off. "Not unless I have to."

Turns out, I had to.

By the time she turned three, Sophie was long done with heart medications, and her six-month appointments with the cardiologist were due to become annual visits.

At three she still slept in a crib, and potty training was two years off, but Sophie was walking—just barely, in orthotics to keep her wobbly ankles stable. And by the time she was three, Sophie had preferences—for the color purple, the television character Elmo, apple juice, and her sister Annabelle.

I was attached. To be honest, I still thought of Sophie mostly as my kid with Down syndrome rather than just my kid, but we had bonded hard since those first few sick months.

I didn't think much about the heart surgery anymore, although there was a reminder down most of Sophie's torso, a long scar, along with a couple of white spots where the chest tube went in. And her bones grew back together with a huge bump. It didn't really occur to me that this would be an issue for Sophie, that she'd ever be self-aware enough to consider this scary, death-defying thing that had happened to her when she was so young.

One night before bed, I put Sophie on the changing table, as I always did. I took off her diaper, and she pointed down and said, "Owie." She was a little red, so I put some Desitin on her butt.

As I was doing that, she pointed to her bare chest, right where the bump was. "Owie, owie," she said, tracing the scar with her fingertip, then looking up at me, clearly waiting for an explanation.

There's no cream for that, I thought.

Pulling her in for a hug, I told Sophie her heart was sad, and we made it happy, just as we had told Annabelle at the time of the surgery. She nodded, satisfied, and hugged me back.

Months went by. Sophie began attending preschool—a program that mixed kids with special needs with typical kids, sponsored by our local school district. Each morning I drove her to the end of our block to wait for the bus, which terrified me and thrilled her. She had a cute magenta-and-khaki backpack from LL Bean, embroidered with her name, and although it was the smallest size they had, it pretty much stretched from her head to toes when she put it on. I'd help her on the bus and off she'd go to Ms. Janice's Morning Monkeys— to learn how to sit for circle time, memorize letters and numbers, and remember to put her backpack away in her cubby.

Annabelle began kindergarten that year, and our little family fell into a routine of relative normalcy—packing lunches, planning trips to the beach, keeping up with ballet classes for Annabelle and physical, speech, occupational, and even horse therapy for Sophie. There was talk almost year-round of what the girls would be for Halloween.

By the time she was four, Sophie was screaming "OH MY GOD!" when something excited her, and "BUY IT!" when she'd see something she wanted in a store. She wasn't only walking, she was running—

careening through the mall like a wind-up toy, skidding across the waxed floors, catching herself just when I thought she'd surely fall.

She still had the bump on her chest, and looking back, I realized that summer that she'd taken to climbing into my lap or Ray's, taking my hand or Ray's, and placing it gently on her chest. She'd settle in, sneak her forbidden thumb in her mouth, and sigh.

I wonder if she knew something we didn't know.

One hot July morning, Ray took Sophie for what had been billed as her last six-month checkup with the cardiologist. After that, it would be every year. It felt like a formality, Ray taking Sophie to the doctor that day. I was about to peel out of a grocery store parking lot—hoping to make it to work before the icing melted on the cupcakes I'd bought for a colleague's birthday—when my cell phone rang. I answered quickly, not noticing who was calling.

It was Ray. "Are you sitting down?" he asked, his voice tight.

"I'm driving!" I replied, annoyed.

"Sophie needs heart surgery again."

I pulled into a parking spot and stopped the car.

"No." That was all I could think to say. "No."

She had a valve that was leaking badly. It happens.

Flavian Lupinetti had moved out of town, but Michael Teodori was back at work. I called for an appointment. Teodori was busy. He cancelled twice, then still had no answers about a date for surgery. I wasn't too worried; we'd been told the surgery just needed to happen in the coming months. September turned into October. I got out the Halloween decorations and hung them up. The girls had chosen their costumes—Annabelle was going to be a vampire, and Sophie a bat—but I was ready for Halloween to be cancelled. Obviously surgery would take priority.

One night, the phone rang. It was Dr. Teodori. I held my breath—and my tongue. What kind of mom sacrifices her kid's health for a dumb holiday? He was quiet for a moment, and I imagined him looking at the calendar, figuring out anesthesia, an operating room. Then he had a question.

"Do you celebrate Halloween?"

"Well, yes, we do," I answered, "but of course…."

He cut in. "Well, I have an opening on October 29, but let's do it on November 7, instead, so Sophie can go trick–or–treating."

I wiped away tears, loving that man.

Sophie was still young enough that she really didn't understand the implications of the surgery, and for that I was grateful. The mom of one of her preschool classmates made her a quilt with photos of each of the members of the Morning Monkeys on it; she still has it, although it's been washed so often the photos are barely visible.

I got my first iPhone for my birthday the week before the operation, and one of the first photos on it is of Sophie, post-surgery, grinning. She woke up asking for apple juice. Paul Rubin showed up at the hospital several times during the few days we were there. Sophie was thrilled; she was understandably a little cranky after surgery, but never with Paul. For months afterward he told the story of how she reached up from her hospital bed and grabbed his finger, refusing to let go.

Ray remembers that she had one episode of arrhythmia, but otherwise there were no complications. The biggest challenge was untangling her bed-head hair when we got home; I went through an entire bottle of olive oil.

Ray and I both cringed when it came time for that first six-month appointment after the second surgery and celebrated when Sophie was cleared to see the cardiologist just once a year. But I don't think either of us will ever take another doctor's appointment for granted.

Open-heart surgery like Sophie's costs well over $100,000 a pop.

In twelve years of doctors' appointments and insurance claims, no one has once raised an eyebrow, mentioned how costly it was to save a little girl with an intellectual disability, a kid who will never contribute to society in the way the rest of us are expected to contribute. Not to my face, anyway.

From Sophie's earliest days, I wondered what the doctors and nurses were thinking. Are all kids with congenital heart defects treated equal, regardless of their chromosomal makeup?

And Sophie's earliest days aside, what about the earliest days of open-heart surgery? I developed a theory, that kids with Down syndrome—half of whom, remember, are born with heart defects—had to be either the first or the last babies operated on in those early days of pediatric cardiac surgery. I wondered, since there was a good likelihood a baby would die in surgery in those early days, were the kids with Down syndrome sought after as guinea pigs of sorts? Or were they simply ignored, not worth even trying to save?

I secretly hoped that the former was true, that babies with Down syndrome were the guinea pigs—that in some small way they saved the lives of others by allowing surgeons to learn by cutting into their tiny, misshapen hearts.

I combed the best books written on the topic of pediatric hearts and found almost no references to Down syndrome; instead there was a lot of discussion of the treatment of heart problems associated with rheumatic fever.

So I started asking around. Even putting the guinea pig question aside, it's delicate business, asking someone who's taken the Hippocratic Oath if he and his colleagues would rather not bother with a baby who doesn't have much of a chance of driving a car or attending Harvard. I began with Mike Teodori.

When I reached him by phone in the summer of 2015, Teodori had just announced his retirement from his current job at the University of Arizona in Tucson.

Teodori was as soft spoken and thoughtful as I remembered, and he said no, he never considered his patients with DS to be different from any others.

"I don't think we ever thought that way," said Teodori, who had practiced in Pittsburgh before coming to Phoenix. "For me, one of the good things about America is that everyone gets a chance to get treated."

That did not surprise me. Teodori did recall that in the mid to late 1980s, there was a study in Great Britain that suggested that it was not wise to try to attempt a complete AV canal repair because the mortality rate at the time was high (10 to 15 percent), and even when a child survived, the repairs didn't always go so well in the early days, whether the baby had Down syndrome or not.

Teodori was much more interested in hearing about how Sophie was doing these days—both heart-related and in general—than speculating over the role of kids with Down syndrome in the history of pediatric heart surgery.

"To me, the most amazing thing is that everybody has their dreams and aspirations of what they want their kids to do," he said. "I'm so impressed that the families can somehow integrate the child [with Down syndrome] into their life and have a better life than they would have."

Regarding any kid with a heart defect, he cautioned: "If the family's perception is that their kid is broken, then it doesn't matter whether the surgery is good or bad, and somehow it never plays out very well. But how the family deals with the whole problem and how to help them is probably one of the most fun parts of heart surgery."

I left the conversation with Teodori feeling warm and fuzzy but still wondering about those earliest days.

I kept asking around, and finally ended up on the phone with Dr. Joel Brenner, who has been practicing since 1972, currently at Johns Hopkins Children's Center in Maryland. Brenner is a cardiologist but not a surgeon.

"I sweat too much," he told me.

I liked him instantly. Also because he was ready to give me some evidence, even if it wasn't the evidence I thought I wanted.

It's a tale of two studies.

In the early 1970s, Brenner explained, a study was done by the New England Regional Infant Cardiac Program, a population-based examination looking at children under a year in age in the New England area referred by medical professionals for surgery related to congenital heart defects. This was in the days before echocardiograms; only the babies with the most serious heart disease were referred. Five percent of the babies referred for surgery for congenital heart defects had Down syndrome.

A decade later, the Baltimore/Washington Infant Study was conducted. The age criterion was the same, Brenner said, but some of the inclusion criteria were different. Still, he said, the results were different enough from the earlier study to lead him to draw some important conclusions. More than 10 percent of the children in the Baltimore/Washington study with congenital heart disease also had Down syndrome.

The percentage of babies born with Down syndrome between the 1970s and 80s certainly didn't double, Brenner said.

"The difference is the referring," he added. "Resources were limited, experience was limited, and it was thought to be a very high risk group."

Brenner worked on both studies. "To me, that was probably the most telling demonstration of the change in medical attitude. Societal attitude is really almost secondary."

So in the beginning, no, it wasn't kids with Down syndrome.

"I never looked at kids with Down syndrome as being the guinea pigs," he said. "The kids who had that anatomy and had that operation at the beginning were the kids who taught surgeons to do a better job."

Fair enough. Pretty cool, actually. And as it turns out, kids with Down syndrome are involved now in some important research about congenital heart defects.

Cheryl Maslen, a researcher at Oregon Health and Science University, is studying people with Down syndrome who have atrioventricular septal defects—as well as people with Down syndrome who have no heart defects at all—to see if she can find genetic differences between the two groups.

"Clearly, having trisomy 21 isn't sufficient to cause it," she says of the heart defect, because not everyone with Down syndrome has it.

And yet about half of kids born with Down syndrome have a heart defect, compared with less than 1 percent of the typical population. Why is that?

"We would like to know, and that's what we are focusing our study on," Maslen said.

She has a theory. The belief is that it's not actually the third twenty-first chromosome that's causing the defect. But the extra chromosome could sensitize the development of a heart defect if there are weaknesses in other genes on other chromosomes.

"We're all different; we all have genetic variation that makes us who we are in total," she said. "Kids with Down syndrome also have that variation, so we need to start looking outside of chromosome 21."

She and her colleagues are comparing the two groups, she said, and have about six hundred people in the study.

The research is not only about the heart.

"I don't want this to sound insensitive, but not every kid with Down syndrome makes it to birth. The in utero losses are enormous," she said. It could be that the babies with Down syndrome who do survive and thrive have protective factors in their genome. Scientists want to know about that, too.

Maslen recalled that her mother's best friend from kindergarten (they are still BFFs in their late 80s, she added) had a child with Down syndrome. The families vacationed together, celebrated holidays. "We were brought up to know that Candy was different and sensitive and we couldn't tease her...or roughhouse her. We were raised to be protective and respectful of her," Maslen said.

It wasn't until Maslen was in a high school science class that she learned about Down syndrome and realized that's what Candy had.

Candy lived into her sixties and died in 2013. She's not the reason Maslen decided to research Down syndrome, the scientist said, adding that she came to that through an interest in heart defects and what causes them and learning "what an amazing resource kids with Down syndrome are because of this."

The work is far more complicated than it sounds, Maslen warned. There are billions of variations and many factors that affect heart development. She's been working in this field for twenty-five years; the advances in genetics in the last few years have amazed her.

"I'm now all of a sudden able to do all of the things I wanted to do twenty years ago," she said, adding that it's still hard to find funding for studies, and to convince people to participate. For a study like hers, which isn't invasive, it requires filling out paperwork, procuring medical records, having blood drawn, and returning a saliva sample.

I signed Sophie up that day.

# 4

# MEET THE HUFFS

After the first heart operation came a helmet for Sophie's flat head, outpatient surgery for clogged tear ducts, and, while she was under, a hearing test.

In the early 2000s, the custom-fitted helmets were all the rage and not just for kids with Down syndrome. Back-sleeping cut down on the rate of sudden infant death syndrome, but it caused other issues, like a flat head that was a problem for cosmetic reasons and sometimes actually caused real physical damage. The helmets were an alternative to scary, invasive surgery.

The helmet rubbed hot spots on Sophie's scalp like the ones our golden retriever got on his back from licking himself, and the three tear duct surgeries didn't work, but her hearing was good.

Not much else came naturally during Sophie's first three years of life. And so Sophie had physical therapy three times a week and occupational and speech therapy once a week each, and another therapist, called an "early interventionist," was assigned the task of teaching her how to play. Sophie had this horrible metal contraption called a stander that we had to strap her into for a few minutes at a time, so she could one day bear weight on her feet by herself.

Even with all that, we settled into a routine. By the time Sophie was a year and a half old, she wasn't walking or talking or even up on all fours, but she could commando crawl with the best army recruit, and she'd figured out how to press the buttons on her musical toys, swaying to the songs, beaming.

In some ways, Sophie was an easier kid than Annabelle. That second summer, we took the girls to San Diego for our annual trip with my extended family. Annabelle, three and a cranky toddler, refused to step foot on the beach, announcing, "It stinks!" Sophie sat in the wet sand, cracking up as the water lapped her toes. She let me make her into a dribble castle.

That doesn't mean I'd totally adjusted to the idea of having a child with Down syndrome. At bedtime, I'd sit in the nursery with Sophie on my lap and read her board books with titles like *Moo, Baa, La La La,* and my eyes would wander from the page, landing on the paperbacks I'd put on her shelf before she was born, like the young adult classic *A Wrinkle in Time* by Madeline L'Engle. I'd cringe, thinking about how Sophie probably would never understand one of my favorite stories.

Ray and I avoided the topic of what would happen when Sophie was an adult, although I thought about it all the time, and I bet he did, too. But there was a topic we had to face, and that was whether to have a third child.

By the time Sophie was closing in on two, I knew for sure that I didn't want to trade her for a typical kid. But I was also certain that I didn't want another child with Down syndrome. I didn't want to put another child through the risks (even with her heart defect, we'd been relatively lucky with Sophie's physical health), and I was quite sure my mental health couldn't take it.

I also knew, with equal certainty, that I could never terminate a pregnancy simply because the fetus had Down syndrome. No way, not at any point in a pregnancy—not now that I had Sophie—and that's coming from someone who's staunchly pro-choice.

To make matters more complicated, I wasn't sure I wanted a third kid at all. I had vomited my way through every single day of my two pregnancies. I liked having two kids, one for each hand. But Ray wanted a third. He'd always wanted three.

So we talked about it, as the clock ticked me past thirty-seven, thirty-eight, thirty-nine years old. I pictured a tote board like the one on the Jerry Lewis muscular dystrophy telethon I had watched as a kid, the black and white numbers shuffling with new numbers, the odds increasing each day that I'd conceive a baby with Down syndrome. Or something else.

I was worried about the odds but had to admit they were still in my favor. And I also had to admit that I'd never heard of another family that had more than one kid with DS. Could that really happen?

Then I opened the mail one night, and there, in the Sharing Down Syndrome newsletter, was an article about the Huff family.

I don't know why I read that newsletter, because typically I let them stack up on the mail table. Early on, a friend had hooked me up with a friend of a friend with a newborn with Down syndrome, and that mom had come over with barbeque, brownies, and a list of local therapists and doctors. Beyond that, I had been fending for myself. I had no interest in joining a support group.

No one mentioned that to Gina Johnson. Johnson runs Sharing Down Syndrome, one of two Down syndrome support groups in metro Phoenix (more later on why there are two Down syndrome support groups in metro Phoenix), and one of the nurses at the hospital had given Ray her number when Sophie was born.

I had no idea he'd called Johnson, let alone arranged for her to drop by the house on a Wednesday evening. Sophie was about two weeks old. We were home; in fact, I already had visitors —a couple of work colleagues who'd stopped by with one of those frozen buckets of margarita mix (just add tequila!) and a bottle of wine. Add that to the Percocet I was already popping, and let's just say that I wasn't really company-ready. Not company I'd never met. Not Gina Johnson.

I heard her before I saw her.

"Where is that baby? I want to smooch on that angel baby!"

She swept into the dining room, an older lady with a gray bob and an armload of gifts, including a book about the ABCs featuring photographs of older children with Down syndrome and a ceramic angel, both of which gathered dust for months on a low shelf in the living room till I tossed them in the Goodwill pile. She sat down with us at the table, turned down the offer of a drink (I'd later learn she's a devout Mormon), and pulled out photographs of her son, David, in his tuxedo at the prom.

"Well," I said to Ray later, "neither of us went to our prom. So I guess that's something."

I couldn't look at the photos of this sweet-faced, chubby young man with Down syndrome, couldn't look at Gina, couldn't look at Sophie, now nestled in Gina's arms. When one of my tipsy colleagues told a long, loud story about how her own fifteen-year-old daughter was an asshole, I did my best to end the evening there.

I didn't encounter Gina again for a long time, but we did make it on to her newsletter mailing list, and once a month we'd receive word of births and deaths, Easter egg hunts, and picnics. Sometimes she'd profile a family with a unique story.

The Huffs' story was certainly that. The young couple lived in Gilbert, a suburb of Phoenix, and they'd had three children—all with Down syndrome. The newsletter sat on my desk for weeks. I couldn't stop thinking about the Huffs. How had that happened? What was it like? Would it happen to Ray and me if we kept having kids?

The mom in me was asking questions, and so was the journalist. I handed the newsletter to Paul Rubin, the one who had profiled the heart surgeon, hoping he'd bite. He didn't. I took the newsletter back and let it sit for a while longer.

Finally, I e-mailed Gina Johnson and asked for an introduction to the Huff family—and, with their permission, pitched a story about Down syndrome, including both my experience and the Huffs', to my editor. He said yes, and I began spending time with the Huffs, ultimately writing a story that began:

*Tyler was barely born when Kevin Huff looked down between his wife Shawnie's legs and noticed that their third child had Down syndrome.*

*It's hard to pick out the signs of Down syndrome—the almond-shaped eyes, the low ears, the flat nose—on a squishy newborn face. But Kevin and Shawnie had practice. Their other son, Braxton, and daughter, Tia, were born with it, too.*

*As Kevin recalls, he looked at Tyler's face and said to Shawnie, "I think he has Down syndrome."*

*"We just started laughing. We couldn't stop laughing," Shawnie says.*

There had already been a lot of tears. Braxton, the Huffs' firstborn, had died of pneumonia when he was a little more than a year old. His heart was healthy, but at birth his esophagus did not reach his stomach, and his short life was filled with hospital stays and operations.

When I met the Huffs, Tia was almost three; she'd had heart surgery at four months and had recovered. Tyler was eight months old and also healthy. (Braxton would have been six.)

The idea that your kids will stay childlike is in many ways whimsical, but it's also sad. There was certainly something melancholy about Kevin and Shawnie Huff. It's hard to tell, not having known them longer, if they were always that way.

Now they were at a crossroads. The Huffs wanted more children, but they did not want more children with Down syndrome. And as Mormons, they would not terminate a pregnancy. The doctors had told them they'd almost certainly have another baby with DS if they conceived again.

One option for Kevin and Shawnie was in vitro fertilization. Her eggs would be harvested and fertilized with his sperm. Before being implanted, the fertilized eggs would be tested. Only the ones without an extra twenty-first chromosome (if there were any) would be used. The Huffs were okay with this method, even though some hard-core abortion opponents are not. But it costs at least $10,000 each time.

"That's why we're very undecided," Shawnie told me, adding that they were considering adoption instead.

Why did the Huffs need a normal kid? I wondered. Didn't they have enough to deal with? Shawnie said that with Tia and Tyler, she knew she'd never have children who abuse drugs or come home late or throw teenage temper tantrums (actually, Tia could throw a pretty impressive tantrum already). But Shawnie also knew that in some ways, she'd likely always be raising Tia and Tyler.

"Probably, our kids will never get married. Probably, we will never have grandkids," Shawnie said.

Kevin said that he wanted to put some normal kids into the mix.

"I always think about what society would be like if every family had a child with Down syndrome and raised them at home," he said. "We need to have people to take care of, so that we're empathetic."

But how to get that typical kid?

"The whole ethical decision is just different for us than it is for anyone else," Kevin said.

"We're spiritual people," Shawnie added.

They were praying for an answer.

I don't pray, but I wanted answers, too.

One of my questions was this: Where is prenatal testing taking us? With surgery saving hearts and therapy improving minds, Sophie was no longer part of a dying breed. In fact, all indications were that she'd have a pretty awesome life. Not like mine or Ray's or Annabelle's, in a lot of ways, but not bad.

Yet at the same time science was making life better for people with Down syndrome, it was also making it a lot easier to ensure they were never born. Was Sophie part of what would ultimately become a never-to-be-born breed?

The short answer: maybe. For several years now, the birthrate of babies with Down syndrome in the United States has held steady at about 1 in every 700 births, or 6,000 each year, according to the Centers for Disease Control and Prevention.

The CDC officials I contacted didn't have earlier statistics, but some experts I spoke with estimated that the number of babies born with Down syndrome was much higher before prenatal testing became possible.

I often go days or weeks without ever seeing another person with Down syndrome out in the world, or "in the wild," as I like to say. It's not so much because they are institutionalized anymore, or because they are dying at birth—I think it's in part because they are not being born. I run into people all the time who, like me, have never met a person with Down syndrome. Most of Sophie's teachers at school have never had another kid with Down syndrome in class. She was the first at her dance studio and at most of the summer camps she attended as a kid.

One day I dropped by the pediatrician's office to pick up Sophie's annual prescription for therapies. I'd called it in, and it was waiting up at the front desk. I was almost out the door when I realized the nurse practitioner had written "Trisomy 23" on the prescription pad.

And that's a medical professional. I tried not to judge her; the most common genetic defect just isn't so common anymore.

The science is moving quickly. I bet that 1 in 700 figure will change soon. In fact, I hate to say it, but I'm quite certain that if I got pregnant with Sophie today—knowing as little about Down syndrome as I knew when I had her—it's pretty likely I'd be heading for an abortion, simply because an early diagnosis is so much more common and less invasive than it was a decade ago.

Some history:

I got pregnant with Sophie at thirty-six in 2002. As with Annabelle two years before, the OB ordered what's called a triple-screen, a blood test given at fifteen to eighteen weeks. The test screens for several things, including increased risks of spina bifida and Down syndrome. My triple-screen came back showing that instead of a 1 in 219 chance (the usual odds for a mother my age) of having a baby with Down syndrome, my chances were 1 in 214.

Those sounded like pretty good odds to me, but the obstetrician's voice was tight over the phone, as he tried to talk me into an amniocentesis. As I've already mentioned, I turned it down, particularly after I got the all-clear from the (obviously not super-skilled) ultrasound tech. By the time the results of the triple-screen were in and the doctor had made the time to call, I was six months pregnant—and not interested in a late-term abortion. Or the risk of miscarriage. (One in 200, slightly worse odds than having a baby with DS.)

If I'd been a little older or my OB had been more aggressive, he might have suggested a CVS, or chorionic villus sampling, a test given earlier, at about eleven weeks, which involves taking tissue from the placenta. But because the risk of miscarriage is increased with that one, I probably would have turned it down, too. And it's got a fairly high false-positive rate.

Today, scientists have all but perfected a blood test given in the first trimester. It has a 99 percent accuracy rate for detecting Down syndrome, and a 0.1 percent rate of false-positives. If it had been widely available in 2003, Sophie would probably not be here today—a thought that gives me chills but doesn't make me any less pro-choice. It's a personal decision. But it is why I am writing this book—because it kills me to think that I might have had an abortion simply because I'd never met another person—adult or child—with Down syndrome. I had nothing but the vaguest notion of what the diagnosis meant or what it could mean.

The implications of prenatal testing are about as complicated as it gets. And the history is fascinating.

It did not begin with the amniocentesis, although that was the first available test for Down syndrome, made widely available in the late 1970s.

Soon after J. Langdon Down identified what he called "mongoloidism," doctors, scientists, and families began to search for signs of where it came from. Later, the "simian crease," a crease across the palm of the hand, was identified by Down's own son as a common mark of what would ultimately be called Down syndrome, and studies were done to try to trace it throughout families. Sometimes that worked, although it didn't predict Down syndrome, pointing to one of the most confusing parts of all of this.

People with Down syndrome have distinct characteristics, but they also share genetic traits with their parents. The two exist concurrently. Because Down syndrome is a last-minute mutation at conception, there's no way to trace its inheritance, not in the vast majority of cases, anyway. (The Huffs are likely a different story.)

Amniocentesis was available long before it was possible to test for Down syndrome. Doctors were drawing amniotic fluid (the fluid around the unborn baby) from the uterus beginning in the late nineteenth and early twentieth centuries. It was first done to relieve pressure when there was too much fluid; doctors also sometimes added fluid if they believed there wasn't enough. Later, it was possible to predict the baby's sex using amniotic fluid and then to prenatally diagnose conditions such as hemophilia and muscular dystrophy.

But it was not until 1959, when a French scientist named Jerome Lejeune discovered that a third twenty-first chromosome causes Down syndrome, that it was possible to test the fluid and reveal that forty-seventh chromosome.

By the late 1970s, the amnio was increasingly popular and frequently ordered for women over thirty-five, who tended to be the ones having the babies with Down syndrome.

Even the more primitive versions of prenatal testing would have told the Huffs that they were having babies with Down syndrome, but there may be no amount of testing that will ever tell them why.

Braxton, Tia, and Tyler Huff were all born with the most common form of Down syndrome, nondisjunction trisomy 21. Having one child with that form of Down syndrome increases a couple's chances of having another to 1 in 100, unless their odds are already higher due to the mother's age. Still pretty good odds, so the Huffs didn't think much of it when they got pregnant with Tia. Then an ultrasound revealed that she had a large hole in the lower chamber of her heart. The doctors increased the chances to 50/50. Shawnie says she was worried before Tia was born that she'd be disappointed if her daughter was born with Down syndrome, but that when the time came, she wasn't upset at all.

In a way, the Huffs were relieved.

One of the hardest things about losing Braxton, Shawnie and Kevin agree, was losing the community that had grown around him and around them. They were very active in Sharing Down Syndrome, and even as young and as ill as he was, Braxton had several therapy sessions a week, which meant companionship and empathy for the family. Suddenly, the doctors and therapists were gone, and things got awkward with the support group; there wasn't much point in going, with Braxton gone. That was horrible, because the Huffs don't have much family in town, and already they had grown apart from their old friends.

Shawnie has a friend on the East Coast. The two were so close, she planned to name Braxton after her friend's young son. When Shawnie called to tell her friend that Braxton had Down syndrome and was ill, Shawnie recalls that the friend assumed that the Huffs wouldn't name Braxton after her healthy child. (They still did.)

When Braxton died, Shawnie says her friend told her she was lucky.

"It's weird for us to talk to other people, because we don't fit into their world," Shawnie said.

The Huffs are an anomaly even in the Down syndrome community, because they've had three children with it. Rick Wagner, their genetics counselor at the Arizona Institute for Genetics and Fetal Medicine in Chandler, had worked in the field since 1978 and told me when I interviewed him in 2004 that he had never seen a case of a family having three children in a row with trisomy 21. Wagner said he believed that either Shawnie or Kevin has mosaicism, meaning that only some of the body's cells are affected, rather than all of them. In this case, Wagner said, either Shawnie's ovaries or Kevin's testes are affected. They've had blood tests, which did not indicate translocation, but even a biopsy might not reveal the cells, since they're not present everywhere, according to Wagner.

In any case, the Huffs don't really want to know.

Kevin and Shawnie had been married seven years when we met. It's his second marriage (the first was childless) and her first. They met at the Mormon church's ward at Arizona State University, where Shawnie was finishing nursing school. Kevin still works in electrical systems maintenance for Salt River Project. He was raised in metro Phoenix and she grew up in Prescott, but they figured out that when she was in fourth grade and he was in tenth, they'd been at the same Donny and Marie Osmond festival. It was meant to be.

Both are the middle kids in families with five children, so they figured they'd have four or five kids, too. Shawnie was only twenty-five when she got pregnant with Braxton, and there's no history of Down syndrome in either of their families, so they never thought about invasive genetic testing, which is usually not recommended for women under thirty-five. It is recommended for a woman who has already had one baby with Down syndrome, but Shawnie did not get an amniocentesis or the other tests that could have determined if her second and third children would have genetic disorders. Shawnie was already certain that she would not terminate the pregnancies.

They'd been through so much with Braxton, she explains, that she couldn't imagine risking a miscarriage by having an amnio just to satisfy her curiosity.

When Braxton was born, the fact that he had Down syndrome was the least of the Huffs' concerns. An ultrasound late in pregnancy had showed that his esophagus wasn't fully developed. As soon as he was born, the nurses took him to a baby warmer and someone tried to stick a tube down his throat. It stopped. It's a rare health problem associated with Down syndrome, and a serious one. Shawnie had not had an epidural, and she was exhausted. Then she started hemorrhaging. Kevin went to intensive care with Braxton. They gave the baby a taste of a lemon swab, used to clean out a newborn's mouth, and Braxton coded.

Shawnie was already in surgery. When she came to, Kevin had shot some video of Braxton, which they watched. Less than a day later, Braxton had his first operation, to put a feeding tube into his stomach. He looked healthy, and Kevin asked the doctors, "You can fix this, right?"

The doctors just stared at him.

When Braxton was a month and a half old, doctors performed a six-hour operation to connect his esophagus to his stomach. Halfway through the procedure, the surgeon came out and said it wasn't going to work. Ultimately, it did. Braxton had his first bottle ever when he was almost two months old and came home a week later. His first burp was very exciting. So was his first Cheerio, even if it was only a half.

His entire life, Braxton had such bad reflux that he had to sleep at a sharp incline, Kevin said, holding his arm at an uncomfortable-looking slant to demonstrate. When he left the hospital, the prognosis was good. The Huffs got Braxton signed up for therapy through the state and started living a relatively normal life.

But there was scarring where the connection was made between the stomach and esophagus. And Braxton was prone to congestion, which meant that he couldn't eat much, which made the small connection start to close up. Every three weeks, he needed his esophagus dilated.

A week after his one-year immunizations, Braxton started running a high fever of 102, 103. He was back and forth to the doctor, tested for meningitis, x-rayed. The pediatrician said it was the flu. They went to the doctor on a Tuesday; he sent them home.

"Wednesday morning when we went to go check on him, he was dead," Shawnie said. The autopsy report said pneumonia.

In between his bouts of being sick, Shawnie said, Braxton was a happy little boy. She stared at the carpet as she talked, dry-eyed.

"He always had issues," she said, "but he was happy, so happy."

Tia was born two years later.

"We said, yep, she looks Asian," Shawnie recalled. Both she and Kevin laughed. "She was pink, she was crying, she was beautiful."

Tia came home two days later. When she was walking, her parents started talking about having a third child. It never really occurred to Shawnie or Kevin that Tyler might have Down syndrome, too.

But they were okay with the possibility.

When I met the Huffs in 2004, both Tia and Tyler were doing well. Tyler was practically off the Down syndrome growth charts, weight-wise, and at eight months was sitting by himself and looked ready to crawl. Tia walked at eighteen months (very early for a child with DS), and during my visit she raced around the house, using the piano as a climbing wall. When we met she knew more than fifty signs, and was set to start preschool in January. She loved to "put your nose in" during the "Hokey Pokey." The whole family had just returned from Disneyland.

With Tia's heart fixed and Tyler so far having suffered nothing worse than a really bad case of croup, life in the Huff household was relatively normal.

Four mornings a week, state-paid therapists came to the house to work with both Tia and Tyler, and Shawnie was the ultra-efficient mom, balancing sleeping Tyler on her shoulder while helping to arrange an intricate obstacle course of musical toys and benches for Tia to use with the physical therapist.

Saturdays were just like anyone else's day off—a recent one had included a trip to the Phoenix Zoo, where the Huffs realized they'd left the stroller in the other car, rented one, but still wound up chasing Tia around the zoo. She insisted on spending most of her time petting the goats and then fell asleep in Kevin's arms.

On another Saturday, Tia watched Barney (her favorite) on the television in the playroom of her family's Gilbert home. The house was new and clean, and so was the neighborhood, which features a sparkling white Mormon church a few steps from the Huffs' front door. Tyler played on the floor, then napped. Tia bounced in and out of the room, jumping up onto her mom's lap to point out family members in a scrapbook filled with photos of Braxton.

"Daddy! Mommy! Baby!" Tia said, her speech hard to decipher if you didn't know her well.

"No," Shawnie corrected her gently, smiling. "Big brother!"

It's true that Braxton and Tyler look a lot alike. Sometimes Kevin still slipped and referred to Tyler as Braxton. On this particular day, Tyler was wearing a blue-and-green-striped onesie with Tigger on it. On a bookcase in the Huffs' living room, I noticed a photograph of Braxton wearing the same outfit.

Before I left the house after our final interview for the *New Times* story, Kevin wanted to show me something. He's the one who found Braxton that Wednesday morning, and he had the toughest time dealing with Braxton's death. As part of the healing process, he made a home movie of pictures and video of Braxton.

There are dozens of images of Braxton, from birth on. In most of them he's smiling, and I was glad to see the video, because when I heard about his life, it didn't sound like that year was much fun.

But it was. There was Braxton in the bathtub; dressed as a lion for Halloween; wearing a Santa hat; crying on Santa's lap. Laughing and smiling with his family. In all of the images, Braxton's got an ugly black string hanging out of his mouth, a reminder of all of his health problems. But the funny thing is that, looking at all of those images, I didn't notice at all that he had Down syndrome.

My favorite image was a video clip of Kevin and Braxton. Braxton's on the changing table, and Kevin's kissing his feet again and again, making his son laugh.

In the end, Ray and I never did have another child. But the Huffs did. Not long after I met them, they adopted a little boy from Serbia. And the kicker, as we say in journalism?

He has Down syndrome.

Over the years, I exchanged holiday cards with the Huffs and ran into Shawnie once or twice at Special Olympics, but we'd never really caught up. So I invited the family out on a hot Saturday afternoon in the summer of 2015. We met at a shopping mall halfway between our homes.

"You can't miss us!" Shawnie said, giggling, when she spotted me walking across the food court. She hadn't aged a bit, tall and friendly with shiny, long, dark hair and bangs. Kevin was a little grayer but had the same slow grin.

The kids were a different story. Tia was about to enter eighth grade, Tyler sixth. And Max, who made a beeline for some metal car rides in the middle of the food court, was going into second.

The two older kids sat at a table with their parents, and we caught up. Shawnie and Kevin were engaged in the conversation, but each kept an eye on Max, who was obsessed with the car ride.

"Bringing Max into our family rocked our world," Shawnie admitted.

"What happened?" I asked. "The last time I talked to you…."

She smiled, nodding. The Huffs had been prepared to adopt a typical kid. Then a friend decided to adopt a little girl with Down syndrome and mentioned that there was an eighteen-month-old boy in Serbia who also needed a home. The Huffs traveled abroad and met Max; they were hooked. The adoption process took ten months. Max's birth parents were in their early twenties; they hadn't known the baby had Down syndrome until he was born, and when they found out, his grandmother said, "Don't take him," so they left him at the hospital.

Max was "totally healthy," Shawnie recalled, except for a severe case of reflux that made him sound like Darth Vader. But he had no heart issues like Tia or esophagus problems like Braxton.

That particular orphanage won't give a baby with Down syndrome physical therapy until a family has agreed to an adoption, so when they brought Max home, he was behind—but crawling.

"I thought he was amazing," Tia said, sipping on the smoothie her dad bought her. "I named him Max-y Moo."

Kevin nodded toward Tia and Tyler. "These two especially are really getting predictable," he said, "mostly off on their own, at home at least."

Tia and Tyler are best friends, Shawnie told me. Hearing this, Tia leaned away from her smoothie for a moment to hug Tyler, who smiled, never pausing from the video game he was playing on his phone (unless it was to take a bite of the tiny Blizzard Kevin had brought him).

Shawnie admitted that Tia was getting "too cool to hold my hand" and had taken to saying "whatever" so much the word was banned. The other day, frustrated, Tia had disappeared into her bedroom, closing the door, and Shawnie heard her spell it—W-H-A-T-E-V-E-R—aloud.

The Huffs were happy to take some hormonal behavior in exchange for a clean bill of heart health; Tia had recently been cleared for four-year visits to the cardiologist.

Tia was a writer, her mom explained. She kept a notebook and wrote everything down. She was also really into spatulas; she turned them into everything from magic wands to drumsticks, Kevin said.

Tyler was into animals—books, television shows, movies about animals. He saw the Peter Pan live show on NBC that spring and began to tell people, "I don't want to grow up."

The adults around the table smiled, wincing a little, the Huffs recalled.

And Max's thing? Making messes, Shawnie said, shaking her head.

The last time the Huffs' state caseworker came to check in and make sure the kids were doing well, she asked each of them what they want out of life:

"I want to be a magician," Tia said. (That was the first either Shawnie or Kevin had heard of that.)

"I don't want to grow up," Tyler said.

"NO!" Max said.

Max had issues. He'd been diagnosed with ADHD, attachment disorder, and a sensory processing disorder. He only ate ten foods. He had trust issues, too.

It makes sense. At the orphanage, they had held the babies facing out and fed them through bottles with the nipples cut off, to make the process faster, Shawnie said. Max would gulp down his formula and then throw it right back up again.

"It's a three-ring circus," Kevin said. All of the kids are different, none defined by Down syndrome, he added.

Once a week Shawnie and Kevin have a date night, and every summer they get away together for a week alone. They are tired, they admitted. But not willing to trade it all in.

Not far from our table in the crowded food court, several older teenagers were sitting on a bench in full-out Cosplay gear: bright yellow wigs, crazy costumes, pale blue contact lenses. We'd been watching them and rolling our eyes during the conversation.

"I'll take this normal," Shawnie said, gesturing to her kids. Then she and Kevin cracked up.

lllll

Jerome Lejeune was reportedly heartbroken that his discovery led to abortions rather than to a cure for Down syndrome. "Like Albert Einstein before him, Jerome Lejeune had come to regret one of the technological uses to which his scientific discovery had been put," wrote Ruth Schwartz Cowan in her 2008 book, *Heredity and Hope.*

In the book, Cowan documents the history of the eugenics movement, which flourished not only in Nazi Germany but less famously in other places, including Scandinavia, England, and the United States. For decades, there was forced sterilization of "mentally retarded" women in many countries, including the United States, and while such laws are no longer in effect, some disability advocates argue that prenatal testing allows for similar results.

Cowan, now retired from her last position as professor of history and sociology of science at the University of Pennsylvania, argues in favor of prenatal testing. In 1979, when she was pregnant with her third child at thirty-eight, the doctor ordered an amniocentesis. It was there on the exam table that she decided to write a book about the history, science, and implications of prenatal testing.

I reached Cowan one summer evening by phone; she was out walking to avoid the heat of the day, and said that now that she's retired, she has time to talk to reporters.

We talked for an hour—about her career, her kids, my kids, life. "That child just had her first child six months ago!" she said of her third baby, the one she had the amnio with.

Cowan explained that for much of the twentieth century, scientists were close to figuring out chromosomes. But they just couldn't get the experiments right to prove their theories. And so when a baby was born and there was something wrong, all the doctors could do was tell the parents, "Don't try it."

Don't try to have more kids.

Abortion and even contraceptives were illegal, so the conversations got awkward. Even as late as the 1960s, she said, many people believed Down syndrome was inherited.

And now that prenatal testing is available, she said that 98 percent of the parents who find out their baby has Down syndrome choose to abort. (The 98 percent figure is widely reported, but often disputed. Most experts agree that there are no reliable figures for the rate of abortion of babies with Down syndrome in the U.S.—estimates range from 40 to 90 percent.)

"There's been a massive decline in the birth of Down syndrome children since the introduction of prenatal diagnosis in every country that's been studied. It's the easiest condition to diagnose," she said.

And the implications of that? I asked. Isolation, Cowan replied. Now, she guessed, my Sophie is in school, doing okay, right? Yes, I replied.

"It's another thing to think about what it's like when she's sixteen," she said. And after that, she maintained, it might get even worse.

I had to agree that I do worry about Sophie's future. But I don't wish I'd had an abortion, I told Cowan.

The ultimate implications of prenatal testing might be a continued decline in the number of babies born with Down syndrome. Or it might be something else. In the last several years, scientists have reported they are in the very early stages of being able to actually turn off the twenty-first chromosome. The implications of that if done in utero are pretty exciting. And Bianchi, the lab that's working on that early blood test with the 99 percent accuracy rate, reports that one of its goals is to develop medications that can be given to mothers carrying babies with Down syndrome that will improve cognitive function.

I wish Jerome Lejeune, who died in 1994, could be around to see that.

# 5

# TOMORROWLAND

When Sophie was a few months short of three, I broke my rule and we took her to Disneyland. It wasn't a Down syndrome rule; it was a three-year-old rule. I feel strongly that no child under three can fully appreciate Disneyland and that no parent should have to deal with handling a kid that young at a place like that.

But rules are meant to be broken. Ray and I had left Sophie at home once already to take Annabelle, and I couldn't bear to leave her again. Plus, Sophie was insurance that I wouldn't have to go on a roller coaster. Someone had to watch the baby. And I had a feeling she'd really love Disneyland.

So we went. And I learned a lot—mostly about how unprepared I was to have a kid with Down syndrome, let alone an adult with it.

I cracked at ToonTown, the portion of the park devoted to Mickey Mouse and friends, designed to appeal to the youngest kids, with Mickey and Minnie's houses, a tiny roller coaster, and lots of characters. We had only been at the park for two hours. This woman was staring at Sophie. Or maybe she was staring at my pale pink clogs and the way they clashed with my all-black outfit. Or she might have been staring at Annabelle, a tiny four-year-old with the demanding attitude of a tween and crazy curly blonde hair. The woman probably wasn't watching Ray, who emerged straight out of Central Casting with the word "normal" stamped on his forehead.

No, this woman was definitely staring at Sophie. People we knew tried to tell us that Sophie didn't look like she had Down syndrome, that she must have a "mild case" (whatever that meant), but trust me, you could tell. And more so every day. Sophie's occupational therapist, Connie, confirmed that.

Every once in a while, as though she was worried that I'd gotten complacent with my relatively easy baby and needed a kick in the head, during her weekly therapy session Connie would mention casually that I could expect Sophie's looks to change. She said that while some kids don't really appear to have Down syndrome when they're little, by the time they're three, the slanted eyes, smooshed nose, and flat back of the head are pronounced enough that you know what you're looking at.

Connie only ever worked with kids till they were three; the little ones were her specialty. I was beginning to think that kids with Down syndrome have an expiration date on their foreheads—adorable till they are three, a nightmare after that—or maybe not a nightmare, but definitely things would get a little messy.

And Connie was not the only therapist I'd met who talked about how much she *looooooves* little kids with Down syndrome. You always heard that, about how the therapists and the day care workers and the doctors and the nurses *looooooove* babies and little kids with Down syndrome. The only people I ever heard talk about how much they *loooooove* adults with Down syndrome were super-religious.

Sophie was in her stroller, while Ray, Annabelle, and I were resting on a bench designed to look like Goofy's car. We'd just been through Mickey Mouse's house and were contemplating the line into Minnie's. The mice lived next door to one another in brightly colored, prefab houses. Four months away from her third birthday, Sophie was nowhere near walking.

Now, you wouldn't necessarily have known that she couldn't walk or that she was almost three, because she was sitting in the stroller, and she was small, with spindly arms and legs and a big, round belly. Sophie had a voice on her—not exactly a squawk, but sort of. A very loud sound, usually accompanied by a lot of arm waving.

Sophie was extremely social. Most of the time, I thought it was adorable. We wheeled her through the mall, and she was like a mini–Miss America, waving, blowing kisses, and establishing eye contact and holding it. And holding it. And holding it, until I could tell it was getting creepy for some people, who didn't get what was up. Or did. I watched the smiles fade, the awkward looks develop as I quickly walked past. Sophie was oblivious, still blowing kisses, still hoping for a new friend.

On this particular day at Disneyland I was digging in the bottom of the stroller for goldfish crackers and juice boxes, so I'm not sure just what Sophie was doing to attract this woman's attention. But when I looked up, the woman was definitely staring. Hard. Sophie wasn't even looking at her.

"OK," I said to Ray through clenched teeth. "If that woman doesn't stop staring at Sophie I'm going to walk over and tell her,

"YES. SHE DOES. WHY DON'T YOU TAKE A PICTURE?"

Ray just looked at me, then at the woman, who had turned her attention to her own gaggle of tow-headed kids, who appeared to be around our daughters' ages. "It doesn't really seem to me that she's staring at Sophie. Anyhow, so what if she is? I always stare at people with Down syndrome."

It was true. He did. And so did I. Which is weird, because we were still avoiding the support groups. You'd think that would be the jackpot of staring opportunities, but for me, it was too much. I was more of a sideways starer. It's how I'd always approached Down syndrome. From the side, around the corner.

There was this kid named Paco, who worked as a bagger at our Safeway in Tempe. He went to Ray's high school (a couple decades after Ray) and, unlike Ray, was elected homecoming king. Someone showed us the story about it when Sophie was born.

I always stared at Paco.

It's so weird that you can have a genetic disorder that causes you to look like all these other (seemingly) random people out there. Paco and Sophie looked more alike than Annabelle and Sophie.

Over the course of the weekend, I had plenty of time to contemplate this. Because as it turns out, The Happiest Place on Earth attracts scores of The Happiest People on Earth. At least, it did on this particular weekend.

The people-watching on that trip was superb—from the teenage Japanese girls decked out in black-and-white striped knee socks with double ponytails and platform shoes to the fifty-something women wearing crowns and tiaras without irony. And the people with Down syndrome.

The truth is that Ray and I spent three days staring at people with Down syndrome. Each time, I'd immediately project into the future, and that person would become Sophie, and I'd imagine my life. It's sort of like how before I owned clogs, I used to stare at people wearing them, wondering how I'd look in them. Would I be able to carry it off?

"Red shirt, five o'clock!" Ray would announce, and I'd catch a glimpse of a teenage boy with his parents, disappearing into the crowd on Main Street. Often, there was nothing revelatory in the sighting. But Ray was in a funk for most of the trip after he spotted an extremely obese woman with Down syndrome near Playhouse Disney at California Adventure. I didn't see the woman, but I felt like I did, because Ray described her in minute detail, down to the huge rolls of fat around her middle, and her waddle. He claimed that she stopped the crowd—that people stood and gawked as she walked by.

After that, he wouldn't let Sophie have any French fries and started complaining about how big her stomach was. I think it ruined the whole vacation for him. I tried to explain that there are a lot of extremely heavy people in the world and that for the most part, Sophie ate really healthy and was barely on the charts in those days for height *or* weight. Ray just looked at me sadly, and I gave up. I knew there was a much greater chance Sophie would be overweight as an adult. People with Down syndrome tend to be chubby. (One reason for this is that people with DS tend to have slower metabolisms at rest, so they burn fewer calories.)

I tried to change the mood. I started looking as hard as I could for people with Down syndrome. And it was weird, because within just a few minutes, I spotted a really skinny boy. "There!" I said to Ray. "Look! That kid was practically a skeleton! Did you see him?"

Ray didn't look in time, and that was probably a good thing, because thinking back, I'm not 100 percent sure that kid actually did have Down syndrome. He might have just been a little odd looking.

I have to say that even if that kid hadn't had Down syndrome, I was really glad I told Ray about him, because his mood improved after that, and we had a great time watching the parade that evening.

By the end of the next day, we were all exhausted. Ray's good mood had faded; by now he'd seen several more examples that proved his point. Sophie was starving, and Annabelle was asking when we were going home.

As twilight approached, both girls fell asleep in strollers, so Ray and I killed some time playing skeeball on the "boardwalk" at California Adventure. It's my one sport, and I was beating Ray, something completely unheard of in our eight-year marriage. But I couldn't manage to get to 200 and win a prize, so twenty bucks later we moved on. Annabelle was still asleep. Sophie was up, and it was decided that I'd watch both girls while Ray rode California Screamin' one more time and then I'd take Sophie on the carousel.

The carousel at California Adventure was really cute, featuring sea creatures instead of horses, and they were brightly colored, not faded and worn like the horses at Fantasyland, over at Disneyland.

Sophie wasn't so sure. She was always afraid of the carousel. I had to remind myself that it was worth the effort to coax her, because by the time the music came on and the thing started to spin, she'd be laughing hysterically, waving her arms and leaning into me with glee. But she was fighting me hard this time as I struggled to strap her onto a sea creature, so I almost didn't notice the woman in the navy blue windbreaker whoosh past us.

I remember it in slow motion, even though the woman was running. She was older than the others I'd seen the past couple of days, scrawny, with a scrunched-up face, the features unmistakable under a tangle of dark hair. She was racing to get to her fish, and the look on her face was pure bliss. The kind of look I've probably never had on my own face.

The ride was filling up, and Sophie was squawking unhappily, not realizing that soon she'd be laughing. We were about to begin when another party approached the line. It was a boy in a wheelchair and an older woman; I think the boy was in his teens. The woman must have been his mom. He was wearing a long red jacket, sort of a cape, and he was breathing through a ventilator attached to the back of the wheelchair. This kid was not in good shape. His mother didn't look like she was holding up so well, either, but she stood her ground when the carousel operator tried to tell her she'd have to wait for the next go-round.

I'd never seen a Disney employee express the slightest bit of annoyance, but I could feel the vibe as the carousel woman stopped what she was doing to open the gate that allowed the wheelchair onto the carousel, near one of those benches reserved for people with disabilities. It happened to be just in front of Sophie's fish, so I watched the back of that boy's head for the entire ride. He didn't move. Neither did his mom.

When the ride ended, the gate went down again, and the boy and his mom left. I unbuckled Sophie from the fish, and we got off. As we left the carousel, the dark-haired woman in the navy windbreaker raced past us, her face still beaming.

Even from a distance, I noticed she had a runny nose. Watching her run, seeing that joy on her face—the kind of joy I could only imagine feeling myself—I knew in that moment that everything was going to be okay. Sophie was going to be okay, even if she did get chubby, even if she never remembered to wipe her nose. And I knew that even if everything wasn't going to be okay, I could live with that. I could live with Sophie.

I hugged Sophie hard, watching the boy and his mom slowly exit the ride and make their way down the boardwalk, and then walked back to Ray and Annabelle. I wanted to show Ray the woman in the navy windbreaker, but she was gone.

The woman in the navy blue windbreaker dragged me into the future, that spring. And then a man named Willard Abraham yanked me into the past. Looking back, I understand now that in both cases I was contemplating Sophie's future as an adult with Down syndrome, trying to figure out what it would look like, and desperately wondering how life would be for both of us, all of us. And despite my feelings about Abraham and what happened with his own daughter, really, he was doing the same.

Willard Abraham died many years ago. We never met. My introduction to him came by way of the death of someone else, a woman named Lorraine Frank.

Frank was a force. We were in the same book club. When I moved home to Phoenix in the early 1990s, a friend of my mom's called to invite me to join a "multigenerational" book club. It was a great idea—the chance to talk about literature with women from several generations offered perspective and stimulation, particularly at a time when I was reacquainting myself with the city of my youth, a city that at the time didn't have much of a cultural scene. The book club was more successful than most; we often actually did talk about the book. And when Sophie was born, many of these women were a source of advice, casseroles, spa trips, and other comforts.

But not Lorraine Frank. To be fair, she and I had never been close. She was a very active member of the local Democratic Party, which I'd written about, and not always in a positive light. (Though in my defense, Republican John McCain was my very favorite topic.) Lorraine didn't ever strike me as touchy-feely. Plus, she was in her eighties. So I didn't think anything of it when I didn't hear from her after Sophie was born.

Lorraine passed away in December 2005, around the time of our Disney trip. Not long after, her family invited the members of her book club to go through her large library (her husband, John, had died several years before) and take what we wanted. I didn't go, but another member, Raimie, did.

Raimie's a little older than me, with grown kids, and she's the kind of friend who knows what you need before you know you need it. She's the one who bundled me off to the spa when Sophie was three weeks old and I was refusing to leave the house. Once she saw me wearing cowboy boots at a holiday party, and the next day she dropped off a pair of her own vintage Fryes at my office, just because she knew I'd like them.

One day during the spring of 2006, she showed up at the newspaper with a pile of books from Lorraine Frank's collection. Raimie got a funny look on her face as she settled onto the worn Barcalounger in my office, a pile of dusty old hardbacks on her lap. The books were all written by a man named Willard Abraham. I'd later learn he was Lorraine's cousin; the Franks were the only relatives Abraham and his wife, Dale, had when they moved to Phoenix in the 1950s.

Abraham had been an education professor at what was then called Arizona State College. (Arizona State wouldn't earn its university status until the late '50s.) Specifically, his field was the "exceptional child," and the books were all about how to teach kids with special needs (referred to in the books as handicapped) as well as gifted kids.

Watching my face, Raimie handed over one more book, a slim hardback published in 1958 called *Barbara: A Prologue*.

Like me, Abraham's wife had given birth to a baby with Down syndrome. They didn't have a prenatal diagnosis, either; in 1954, no one did. Ironically, their doctors figured it out a lot sooner than ours did, and by the morning after the Abraham baby's birth, the infant had been diagnosed with mongolism, based solely on physical characteristics, since Jerome Lejeune's discovery of the twenty-first chromosome wouldn't come for four more years.

It would be decades before the technology existed to confirm a heart defect, although doctors knew that with mongolism came an increased risk; the doctor didn't hear a heart murmur when he listened to the baby's chest with a stethoscope.

The Abrahams named her Barbara, rejecting Ruth, the girl name they'd originally chosen. And Willard immediately began to contact colleagues in his field to figure out what to do.

The dedication of the book reads:

> *For the thousands of ill-finished children*
> *of generations to come,*
> *for their parents,*
> *and for the society which*
> *will be ready to welcome them*
> *with arms outstretched*
> *and doors open wide.*

Ultimately, the Abrahams were not ready to welcome their "ill-finished" daughter. In the book, Willard notes the odd coincidence (one of many) that on the very day Barbara was born, he was scheduled to take his students on a tour of the Arizona Children's Colony in Coolidge, a town about two hours south of metro Phoenix and home to what was then the state's largest institution for the mentally retarded.

"In talks I used to say the bell was tolling for all of us when it tolled for the neighbor with a retarded child—and now I was that neighbor," Abraham wrote.

In the book, which is written as a one-way conversation between father and daughter, he writes about sharing the news with family and friends during those first few days in the hospital. Those friends included the Franks—who, as it turned out, had a child with developmental disabilities living in an institution on the East Coast.

It wasn't just the Franks. Many friends shared stories about special-needs family members.

"Rabbi Fierman came and we found out his brother had had a mongoloid baby. A friend from Chicago, who now also lived in Arizona, called and during the conversation unburdened the story of her firstborn who at the age of nine was still a crib case, completely helpless; I had recalled seeing that beautiful baby years before, but upon renewing acquaintance out here, and knowing that they had only two little children, I hadn't brought up the subject of the first child. Another friend, a volunteer at the hospital, dropped in, and we found out that one of her children had lived only a day; diagnosis had been similar to yours. From every direction we kept hearing of these children. How often did the various kinds of mental retardation strike? Here, already, were four within our closest circle.

"When John [Frank]'s wife, Lorraine, came, she didn't talk very much; she just sat with us, and once in a while we talked a little bit.

"'I'm sure John's said it all, and much better than I can. There isn't very much to say anyway. Except maybe one of our partial solutions—to keep having children.'

"Your mother turned away, and shook her head silently.

"'It isn't an easy decision,' Lorraine continued softly. 'It takes nerve, a lot of it. But it's worth it.'

"Lorraine and John already had three beautiful, bright children, in addition to Petey, and were on their way with the fourth.

"'There's one trouble that can never be mended,' Lorraine admitted sadly. 'You always lag one child behind.'"

Barbara did not go home with the Abrahams. They sent her to live at a nursery for mentally retarded babies in Phoenix. They visited, ensuring she was kept clean and fed, and received updates about how she was doing, that she was gaining a little weight.

"There's something wonderful about your baby," Abraham recalled Barbara's caretaker telling him. "She's so much more alert than most mongoloid babies. And she's so sweet-looking with that half-smile playing around her cute little mouth. It's as though she's thinking some deep thoughts, and is thoroughly happy about them."

That quote is immediately followed by: "Some of the things we heard and saw gave us molecules of hope, but we were always careful not to build them up too much. We knew the terrible danger in that."

They visited her, but as best as I can tell from the book, Barbara's mother, Dale, only held the baby once, on the day she was born—and Willard never at all. Although it was not detected immediately, doctors ultimately noted a heart murmur, and when Barbara was four months old, her father received a phone call informing him she'd died of a heart attack.

I gasped when I read that. Odds are Barbara probably had the same heart defect Sophie did.

In concluding the slim volume, Willard writes, "If you had come fifty years from now, Barbara, your welcome would have been the happy, holding kind that parents now reserve for less-affected babies. But in that distant day you never would have been able to accomplish in many years what you've done now in just a few months. Your immeasurable contribution can spread until a half century from now a mongoloid baby will inspire the same warmth and love shown toward other babies. In the better day of that new century recognition of each baby's abilities may very well be the fruition of what you've done here and now as a prologue to a brighter future."

Sophie was born just a few months shy of fifty years to the day of Barbara's birth.

I've thought a lot about Willard Abraham in the years since I read *Barbara: A Prologue*. I want to say that it's okay that he did what he did, that it wasn't acceptable to take home babies with mongolism at the time. That he didn't know any better.

But that's the painful part. He knew better than most. Willard Abraham knew more about babies and people with what's now called Down syndrome than just about any other parent in that situation and still made the choice he did. In his book, he wrote of asking many experts for advice. Almost to a person, they told him that if one has to have a "mentally retarded child," a "mongoloid" was the best.

Not exactly a ringing endorsement. (And, frankly, not that different from what Ray and I were told when Sophie was a baby.) I was surprised that after years as an expert in this field of education, a man who made site visits and trained young educators on how to educate such people, he didn't take his daughter home and didn't really even seem to strongly consider it.

Or maybe he overthought it.

In many places, *Barbara: A Prologue* reads more like a text than a tell-all. Abraham cites a lot of research showing the tribulations of introducing a child with Down syndrome to a family, academic material that justified his decision.

That said, I do get that it was a different time, and he had a family to consider. (The Abrahams had a "bright-eyed, talkative, normal and wonderful little boy" at home already, as the book jacket describes.) And I understand firsthand the challenge of bringing a kid with special needs into such a scenario.

And really, one thing that struck me when I read the ending of Abraham's book was that his prediction that in fifty years families would embrace babies like Sophie and Barbara with no consideration of their differences did not come to pass. Not for me—I was filled with doubt and fear and the desire to run from the hospital even before the diagnosis was confirmed.

Not for any parent from the current generation with whom I've spoken.

The fact remains, however, that there were families who brought their babies with intellectual disabilities home in the early decades of the twentieth century. Few and far between, perhaps, but it happened. I've met some of them—or their relatives, at least. My friend Judy Nichols, a former daily newspaper reporter, has written eloquently about her Uncle Billy, born in 1925 in Kansas, who was brought home by Judy's grandmother and kept by her side for decades.

More famously, Roy Rogers and Dale Evans had a daughter with Down syndrome, Robin, born in 1950. They raised her at home until she died at two, of complications related to the mumps.

But more often, children with Down syndrome were kept in the shadows. The late playwright Arthur Miller was "outed" in a 2007 article in *Vanity Fair* magazine, which revealed that he had a son, Daniel, who has Down syndrome. Born in 1966, Daniel Miller was institutionalized pretty much at birth, and basically erased from his father's biography.

Those who did keep children with developmental disabilities at home often struggled.

Tim Shriver, who is now the chairman of the international Special Olympics, the son of its founder, Eunice Kennedy Shriver, writes in his 2014 book *Fully Alive* of his family's decision to keep his Aunt Rosemary at home—for a while.

As Shriver notes, some early pioneers tried to teach people with intellectual disabilities. One of these was Edouard Seguin, a nineteenth-century French physician who believed that people could learn and improve their minds through physical exercise.

But while Rosemary Kennedy's presence ultimately led to her family's decision to champion the cause of people with intellectual disabilities, her own story did not have a happy ending.

Rosemary was born in 1918, the third child and first daughter of Joe and Rose. She did not have Down syndrome; in fact they didn't know at first that anything was different about Rosemary.

Today they likely would have at least guessed, according to a 2015 biography, *Rosemary: The Hidden Kennedy Daughter*, by Kate

Clifford Larson. Larson had access to a lot of the Kennedys' papers and writes that Rosemary was delivered at home. It was the height of the influenza epidemic, and the doctor was delayed by several hours. According to Larson, the nurse on hand advised Mrs. Kennedy to keep her legs shut tight to avoid delivering the baby. Larson and others later surmised this led to oxygen deprivation.

As Rosemary grew up, his aunt "could not keep up," Shriver notes, and ultimately was diagnosed as mildly mentally retarded.

"Expert opinion at the time said that people such as my grandmother should give up the child with a disability in order not to compromise their other children's development," Shriver says. "Scholars agreed: mothers of children with disabilities spent too much time with their child with special needs and, as a result, neglected the needs of their other children and their husbands."

But the Kennedys ignored conventional wisdom. Rose had three more children, and when Rosemary was eleven, they did send her away to school for two years. The place sounds very advanced for 1929 (and in some ways, advanced for today): "not only reading, arithmetic, spelling and social studies but also arts and crafts, music and drama," Shriver writes. "She came home once or twice a year and struggled with this separation from her family."

That part is heartbreaking. Shriver quotes from a letter Rosemary wrote to her younger sister, his mother:

"I miss you very much. Didn't we have fun together when I was home? I was so sorry I had to leave all of you....I feel very upset when I don't hear from Mother. Tell her that. Write me a long long letter and make it as long as you can, darling."

(According to Larson, Rosemary likely had help composing such letters.)

By the fall of 1936, Rosemary was eighteen—and still functioning at a fourth-grade level. She was clearly frustrated. By that point she had been home schooled and sent away to several other schools. Two years later, her father was made ambassador to Great Britain, so the family "set sail," Shriver says.

In some ways, it was the best of times for Rosemary.

"She was allowed to make her debut in London society, was presented before the king and queen at Buckingham Palace, and attended the most fashionable parties. It was a dazzling life; she felt dazzling and adored rather than slow and lonely, and she loved every minute of it," Shriver writes.

Perhaps even more significant, Rosemary was employed as a teacher's aide at a Montessori school, where she was not shamed or pushed too hard, as she had been at previous schools, according to Larson.

But the war put a stop to life in Europe. Rosemary was sent back to the States in 1940 and put in a new school in Washington, DC. It was a bad fit; she had temper tantrums and acted out. Larson writes that Joe Kennedy was worried that Rosemary would get pregnant or kidnapped or somehow embarrass the family, at a time when the Kennedys were embarking on high profile political careers.

And so Joe took drastic measures. At her father's behest and likely without her mother's or siblings' knowledge, in 1941, Rosemary Kennedy underwent a frontal lobotomy at George Washington University Hospital, a relatively new procedure doctors claimed would make her more "docile." As was common practice, surgeons drilled small holes in her temples. (In later years they used short cuts, inserting an ice pick into a patient's eye socket.) Rosemary was given painkillers but was kept conscious.

In her book, Larson describes the procedure performed by surgeons Walter Freeman and James Watts:

"Watts inserted a specially made quarter-inch-wide flexible spatula into her cranium near the frontal lobes, turning and scraping as he moved deeper into her brain. Freeman asked Rosemary to sing a song, recite common verses, tell him stories about herself, count, and repeat the months of the year. At this point in the surgery, patients generally felt little pain, but their fear was palpable, their breathing rapid. Some tried to wrest their hands from the restraints or grab the nurse's hand with 'painful intensity.' "Watts claimed Rosemary complied with their requests to recite simple songs and stories. Encouraged, Watts boldly cut more of the nerve endings from her frontal lobes to the rest of her brain. With the fourth and final cut, however, she became incoherent. She slowly stopped talking.

"It would not take long—a few hours at the most—before the surgeons recognized that the surgery had gone horribly awry. Rosemary would emerge from the lobotomy almost completely disabled."

Tim Shriver writes, "Without warning or explanation, she disappeared from the lives of her brothers and sisters. She would never live at home again." She was sent to an institution in Wisconsin. For many years, she was a family secret, kept out of official photographs as Jack began his political career.

But Rosemary was not forgotten, and family members did see her. Tim Shriver recalls that his mother brought her out for visits to the Shrivers' home. And she inspired Eunice to start a summer camp on the family farm, Timberlawn, in Maryland in 1964.

Camp Shriver was open all summer long, welcoming dozens of people with intellectual disabilities from nearby institutions to play ball, learn obstacle courses, and bounce on a trampoline. In the morning, a flag went up, and everyone sang the national anthem; in the evening, buses came and picked up the campers.

"If you're four years old and your backyard turns into a camp, you're a pretty happy kid," Shriver said at a Special Olympics event in Phoenix in 2013, recalling that he didn't always understand what the campers said, why they were wearing helmets, or why they looked a little different. He was intrigued.

He wasn't alone. In 1968, hundreds gathered on Soldier Field in Chicago for the first official Special Olympics. These, Shriver says, were "the most forgotten people in the country," and his mother had the audacity to call them Olympians.

And today the term "Special Olympics" is a part of the world's vocabulary. Tim Shriver runs Special Olympics. His brother, Anthony, heads up Best Buddies, a school mentoring program with chapters across the world.

Rosemary Kennedy died in Wisconsin in 2005. She was eighty-six.

The Kennedy legacy has stretched far beyond Special Olympics and Best Buddies to make a significant impact on public policy as it affects people with developmental disabilities.

Although Larson writes that JFK avoided advocating for people with intellectual disabilities earlier in his career, the President's Panel on Mental Retardation was started in 1962.

In 1965, then–US Senator Robert F. Kennedy made a famous visit to Willowbrook, an institution for the mentally retarded—a facility in New York built to house four thousand; six thousand people lived there at the time, and RFK called it a "snake pit."

More attention was brought to the horrible treatment of people with intellectual disabilities in 1966, with the publication of *Christmas in Purgatory,* in which an undercover photographer named Fred Kaplan documented conditions in several institutions in the United States.

"The infant dormitories depressed us the most," wrote Burton Blatt, whose prose accompanied Kaplan's grainy images.

"In one dormitory, that had over 100 infants and was connected to 9 other dormitories that totaled 1000 infants, we experienced a heartbreaking encounter. As we entered, we heard a muffled sound emanating from the 'blind' side of a doorway. A young child seemed to be calling, 'Come. Come play with me. Touch me.' We walked to the door. On the other side were forty or more unkempt infants crawling around a bare floor in a bare room. One of the children had managed to squeeze his hand under the doorway and push his face through the side of the latched door. His moan was the clearest representation we have ever heard of the lonely, hopeless man."

In many of these places, excrement was ground into the floors and smeared on the ceilings. Residents were regularly kept naked.

Living quarters for adults were "gloomy and sterile." Blatt wrote, "We observed adult residents during recreation, playing 'ring-around the-rosy.' Others, in the vocational training center, were playing 'jacks.' These were not always severely retarded patients. However, we got the feeling very quickly that this is the way they were being forced to behave."

ℓℓℓℓℓℓ

By the time Sophie was born, infants with intellectual disabilities were no longer institutionalized. Almost never, anyway. But a few such places still existed, including the Arizona Children's Colony, the facility that Willard Abraham had been scheduled to tour the day his daughter Barbara was born.

I got the chance to tour the facility myself in 2008. It had been renamed the Arizona Training Program years before and no longer housed children, but it was still home to some of its original residents, who had moved in when the facility was built in 1952.

I had never heard of this place, unless you count the story my mom used to tell about David Silverman, the mentally retarded baby she received the call about when she was pregnant with me. But once I'd heard of it, I couldn't stop imagining what it might be like.

The Arizona Training Program made the news in 2008 because the state legislature was considering a proposal to close it. In many states, such information might be welcomed as something positive, but I'd learned a long time before that the Arizona Legislature was not to be trusted. So when advocates for the developmentally disabled community began to protest about the proposal to close the facility, I got interested and assigned a reporter to write a story about the controversy. And when one of my writers, Megan Irwin, scheduled a tour of the ATP, I invited myself along.

"It'll be fun!" I told her. "We can have lunch in Coolidge and find some thrift stores."

Megan eyed me warily. She knew how sensitive I was to the subject; in fact, I surprised myself by wanting to go on the tour. But Sophie was already five, and I was starting to toughen up. And I had to see this place for myself if we were going to actually publish a story saying it was an okay place.

It hadn't always been—that much we knew for sure.

In 1962, the Arizona Legislature had changed the law and allowed residents to remain there once they were adults, which led to horrible overcrowding and a class action lawsuit.

"For a long time, ATP was not a place you'd want a family member to live," Megan later wrote. "At one time, about 1200 people were crammed into a facility built for around 300. People slept on cots and sometimes went hours without attention…. Even the assistant superintendent admits that the only windows that existed were slits placed so high on the wall that residents couldn't possibly see out of them. If the facility were like this today, there would be no question about the need to shut it down."

But in 2008, the Arizona Training Program was not a bad place to live. Turns out, it was a very expensive place to live—that's why legislators wanted to shut it down. But for some residents, it was literally the only home they'd ever had. And the proposal to move them to Phoenix to be closer to their families and put them in group homes was not welcomed by advocates. In many cases, the residents' families were dead and gone. There was no one to visit them, no matter where they lived. Their family was the staff at ATP.

"So here's the challenge: In America, the ethic is integration, and I certainly support that. But for these clients, that's all they know," a psychologist told Megan.

The grounds were beautiful and expansive, with plenty of room and small cottages for the few remaining residents. (The facility had stopped taking any new residents years before.) ATP employed a highly trained chef, who customized meals, and caregivers who'd worked there for decades in some cases. We visited the metal shop, where wheelchairs and other devices were customized for residents, and I met a woman who'd worked there for thirty years. I asked if she recalled a resident named David Silverman. She wasn't sure.

In the end, the legislature didn't close ATP. By the spring of 2015, the population count was down to seventy.

There is no doubt that deinstitutionalization in general was a good thing.

But visiting that facility in Coolidge was good for me, a lesson in not rushing to judgment. At first I was horrified to hear that people with developmental disabilities still lived in such places, but seeing firsthand the lovely facilities and care provided was an important reminder that generalizations can be dangerous. These elderly people who had never known another home were in the right place.

And on the flip side, the newer convention—the group home—is not necessarily a better scenario. In theory, it's a wise concept—that smaller quarters with more specialized care work better. It's naïve to believe that all people with developmental disabilities can always live with loved ones. I think back to that visit to Disneyland and wonder how many of those adults we saw that weekend were on field trips with group homes. I wondered then where Sophie would live as an adult, and I've wondered it pretty much every day since.

I am glad that Sophie will most likely never live in an institution. Ray and I have already taken measures to ensure she will be safe financially, and we plan to be with her or nearby (I suppose she might not want to live with us!) for the rest of our lives. But that does not mean I'm not terrified for her future. I know she will likely outlive us. And I know too much.

In 2012, a journalist I know did some amazing work uncovering terrifying conditions in group homes in northern California. Ryan Gabrielson, who was working for the Center for Investigative Reporting, uncovered a series of cases in which police had failed to protect victims from sexual abuse in group homes for adults with developmental disabilities.

From the description of the project: "In August 2006, caregivers at the Sonoma Developmental Center found dark blue bruises shaped like handprints covering the breasts of a patient named Jennifer. She accused a staff member of molestation, court records show. Jennifer's injuries appeared to be evidence of sexual abuse, indicating that someone had violently grabbed her.

"The Office of Protective Services opened an investigation but detectives took no action because the case relied heavily on the word of a woman with severe intellectual disabilities. A few months later, court records show, officials at the center had indisputable evidence that a crime had occurred."

These are the kinds of stories that keep parents up at night. I e-mailed Ryan a quote I found in a 1974 update to *Christmas in Purgatory*, from a Yale psychologist named Seymour Sarason who wrote of his time visiting institutions.

"As the years went on, it became increasingly clear to me that the conditions I saw—and which are documented in this book—were not due to evil, incompetent or cruel people but rather to a concept of human potential and an attitude toward innovation which when applied to the mentally defective, result in a self-fulfilling prophecy....

"I would not deny that increased appropriations will make for better physical care. But spending more money is easy compared to the problem of how one gets people to change their concepts and to view innovation and experimentation as necessities rather than as subversive suggestions or the terminal points of the meandering of the academic mind."

Ryan responded almost immediately:

"That Sarason quote is spot on. In my experience and opinion, the murder/rape/assaults are a symptom of institutions' staff viewing the residents as a kind of pointless burden, as people who are hopelessly limited if not subhuman. Caregivers seem to, largely, view themselves as managing degradation. Never about building something within their residents, aiding human growth.... Some of the caregivers are bad people. But the solution requires more than background checks and more than increased funding. The solution is to view the disabled, regardless of diagnosis, as capable of meaningful achievement. Because they absolutely are."

# 6

## CRISPIN GLOVER HAS A COLD

Pretty much from the time Sophie was born, I began to see Down syndrome everywhere—and nowhere.

When she was about a month old, I was out running errands and drove by a sign near my house that I must have driven by hundreds, maybe thousands of times, before I had Sophie. "DOWNS Wholesale Florist" the sign exclaimed in green and white. I had a physical reaction, like an electric shock. I didn't have to pull the car over, but I remember sitting at the next stoplight, breathing hard, my eyes stinging—irrationally pissed at the person who'd put that sign up, who'd dared to have the name Downs and throw it in my face.

As time went on, and I began to adjust, the word *down* became just another word again. And then I began to search for signs of Down syndrome in the universe, for clues in pop culture about what Sophie's life might be like. I began to report, and I began to shop, staying up late at night, the laptop glowing as I searched eBay and Amazon for old books, obscure movies, ephemera that depicted life for people with DS.

There wasn't much. But I bought a Rubbermaid container and filled it with what I found—a documentary about a young man with Down syndrome who loved wrestling and sex; an old medical text that linked Alzheimer's and Down syndrome; the first season of the hit TV series *Life Goes On*; a copy of *Life* magazine with the series' star, Chris Burke, on the cover. There were so few children's books written about Down syndrome; every one I could find went into the box.

But what I really wanted—what I thought I wanted, anyway—was something more sophisticated. I couldn't figure out why people with Down syndrome never just sort of popped up in pop culture. Like Jews in a Woody Allen movie or blacks in a Spike Lee picture—where the film is clearly about ethnic and racial issues (or at least steeps the viewer in the culture) but doesn't necessarily mention them. The only references I could find were so overtly about Down syndrome in a "Hey, look at us, we're making a TV show that stars a kid with Down syndrome!" kind of way.

It reminded me of a story I loved to tell when Annabelle was little. One morning, before Sophie was born, Annabelle was perched in her high chair, eating Cheerios and watching *Sesame Street*. Ray walked through the kitchen and stopped to observe the kid on the screen. The child was talking to one of the characters—maybe Grover or Elmo, but could've been Big Bird; I don't recall—but I do remember that the kid happened to be in a wheelchair.

"Why are there so many kids in wheelchairs on *Sesame Street*?" Ray asked.

I groaned, wanting to whack him upside the head but refraining in front of the toddler.

"So that when Annabelle grows up she doesn't ask questions like that!" I said, exasperated.

*Sesame Street* really has offered a wonderful template for how the media can integrate people with differences without making a big deal out of it. A lot of the credit goes to Emily Kingsley, whose son, Jason, has Down syndrome.

Emily joined *Sesame Street* as a writer in 1970, the year after the show premiered. Jason was born in 1974. She is credited with the show's efforts to sensitively showcase people with disabilities; Jason himself appeared on the show and was later the topic of a documentary and book.

Of course, Ray and I were both raised on *Sesame Street*. We were three when it first aired, the perfect target audience for lessons in diversity along with ABCs. That clearly hadn't been enough for either of us.

And now, what I was getting felt like a smack on the face, rather than a constructive lesson. When Sophie was three, the movie *The Ringer* premiered, and I gasped when I read the description of Johnny Knoxville (best known as the star of an MTV series called *Jackass,* featuring crude behavior and dangerous stunts) pretending to have an intellectual disability so he could crash the Special Olympics and win a bet. "*Not funny,*" I grumbled to myself, vowing to never see the movie, even though people like Tim Shriver backed it.

Another example: one of *New Times'* sister papers ran a cover story all about how people with intellectual disabilities love Huey Lewis and the News and flock to their concerts. I'm not the biggest music snob in the world, but I found myself playing Elvis Costello and Arcade Fire in the car for Sophie, determined that she wouldn't fall in love with cheese ball music, worried she'd already been pigeonholed.

My world, her world, felt like it was shrinking by the day. I wanted to encounter Down syndrome in a *Sesame Street* kind of way—in a side glance, a crowd scene. I needed to know that people with Down syndrome were out there living their lives, not being made fun of, not limited in their musical tastes.

Late one night, I got a dose of what I thought I wanted. I was up reading Augusten Burroughs's latest collection of essays—the author of the bestseller *Running with Scissors* takes no prisoners, himself included—and I came to one that delved into one of his favorite topics, cruising at bars. Burroughs recounted a tale a friend told him about going out drunk and picking up a guy, waking up the next morning and realizing, to his horror, that his conquest had Down syndrome.

I thought I was going to vomit. I put the book down, climbed into bed, and lay there and thought, "Well, at least that guy with Down syndrome was high functioning enough to go out to a bar by himself. And to know he was gay. That's something."

But, as you might imagine, that was not enough.

So I was pretty excited when I heard that Crispin Glover had made a movie with a cast of people with Down syndrome—that never mentioned that they had it, that wasn't about intellectual disabilities at all.

I don't recall how I first heard that Crispin Glover had made a film with a cast comprised almost entirely of people with Down syndrome, but as soon as I did I knew I had to see it. Accomplishing that was not so easy.

To this day, Glover has not released *What Is It?* publicly, but instead has toured with it to small art cinemas. If you've seen it, you likely understand why. The film does, in fact, include people with Down syndrome, with no mention that they have it. After that, explaining it becomes murky.

*What Is It?* debuted at Sundance in 2005; my friend Kathleen and I saw it in 2007 at the Egyptian Theater on Hollywood Boulevard.

Kathleen Vanesian is a phenomenal critic. Trained as both a lawyer and a photographer (and several other things; she can remodel a bathroom if need be, or hang just about any piece of art, no matter the size), she'd worked as *New Times'* visual art critic for years, and knows a lot about just about everything. Years later, I asked for her assessment of the movie.

"I'm still trying to figure it out—I'm rarely left speechless, but in this case, it's warranted."

The Egyptian Theater is absolutely gorgeous. Built in 1922, it was rehabbed in 1998, with ornate ceilings, columns, and red velvet chairs and was definitely the highlight of a road trip that included drinks at Musso and Frank on Hollywood Boulevard before the show, a side trip to Little India, and a mad dash from Kathleen's condo in Huntington Beach after we got locked out shortly before the movie started.

The event was clearly a big deal for Glover, with a packed house and a special guest, his father, actor Bruce Glover. Crispin himself has been in several feature films, including *Back to the Future* and *Charlie's Angels.* He explained to the crowd that he made the latter film (not really in keeping with his hipper-than-thou persona) in order to fund *What Is It?*—his directorial debut, ten years in the making.

I settled into my seat, so excited to be on a grown-up vacation, to be seeing an art film—my mainstay in college and after, since replaced by Ray's sci-fi blockbusters and the kids' cartoons.

And—I was left giggling and shaking my head, but not in a good way. All I could do was imagine Ray, who does not suffer fools, particularly those with high IQs, watching this parade (*movie* is too advanced a term for the scenes strung together) of images.

Glover made a movie that features—along with naked women wearing monkey masks and smashing watermelons, a man with cerebral palsy naked in a conch shell, and a lot of Nazi and Shirley Temple references—a large number of people with Down syndrome. (And if you're confused, join the club. That's about how haphazardly those elements are introduced.)

The people with Down syndrome do not appear naked, though one couple does appear to have sexual intercourse once during the movie. One of them crushes snails a lot, and they generally cause some trouble.

The most notable thing about the actors with Down syndrome in *What Is It?* is that they are not playing people with Down syndrome. They're just playing regular people. Well, regular if you consider murderers (of both snails and people) to be regular people.

If none of that makes sense, try watching the movie yourself and be even more confused.

When the lights came on, Kathleen and I looked at each other and then around at the packed house, wondering what would happen next. Boos? Silence? I felt terrible for Bruce Glover.

And then, after what felt like minutes but must have been seconds, the crowd erupted in applause, either loving Crispin Glover and his movie or thinking they should.

I sat quietly, wondering what to think myself. I mean, I had asked for this, right? For an avant-garde take on Down syndrome?

Later, I stood in line to say hi to the moviemaker. I told him I had a daughter with Down syndrome, and he was surprisingly engaging—kind and inquisitive, told me he'd wanted to make a movie with people with DS because when he was a kid he'd attended a school next door to a school for kids with developmental disabilities. He also mentioned that people who saw the movie tended to get much more upset about the snails that were harmed than about the use of people with Down syndrome as cast members.

The line behind me was growing longer, so I asked Glover if I could get in touch to interview him sometime. Of course, he said, inviting me to contact him through his website.

I walked away still scratching my head but figuring I'd get to talk in depth sometime with the moviemaker; maybe then it would make sense. Or maybe I just needed to see the movie again.

I got busy and maybe a little shy and didn't try to contact Glover online. Then I heard he was coming to Phoenix with *What Is It?*

I bought tickets and reached out to him on his website. Nothing. I got in touch with the organizers (Phoenix is such a small arts town, I knew them personally) to let them know I really wanted to talk to Glover when he was in town. Nothing. I got in touch again. Nothing. I became a stalker. I was reminded of the famous magazine article, "Frank Sinatra Has a Cold," in which the star simply refused to make himself available.

I went to the event, tried to talk to Glover, sat with my hand in the air during the Q&A. Nothing.

I felt eyes in the crowd on me, and not in a good way. Like I said, Phoenix is a small town—lots of people in the audience knew about Sophie, and I felt like my mere presence made them uncomfortable. I know it made me feel uncomfortable.

In the end, here's what I've got from Glover—the description of the movie and its relationship to Down syndrome, from his website:

"*What Is It?* is not a film about Down's Syndrome but my psychological reaction to the corporate restraints that have happened in the last 20 to 30 years in film making. Specifically anything that can possibly make an audience uncomfortable is necessarily excised or the film will not be corporately funded or distributed. This is damaging to the culture because it is the very moment when an audience member sits back in their chair looks up at the screen and thinks to their self 'Is this right what I am watching? Is this wrong what I am watching? Should I be here? Should the filmmaker have made this? What is it?… What is it that is taboo in the culture? What does it mean that taboo has been ubiquitously excised in this culture's media? What does it mean to the culture when it does not properly process taboo in its media?' It is a bad thing because when questions are not being asked because these kinds of questions are when people are having a truly educational experience. For the culture to not be able to ask questions leads towards a non educational experience and that is what is happening in this culture. This stupefies this culture and that is of course a bad thing. So *What Is It?* is a direct reaction to the contents of this culture's media. I would like people to think for themselves."

Okay. I don't think it's a good movie. I watched the movie again and realized that I just didn't like it. I was not alone.

Amber Wilkinson, who reviewed *What Is It?* at Sundance for a British website called eyeforfilm.co.uk, asks:

"It is different, it is surreal, but is it good?

"On balance I would say, not really…although it can be clever—and, boy, does it know it!

"Whether [Glover] likes it or not, the end result feels faintly exploitative. Just because you operate a policy of equal opportunities, offending everyone does not let you off the hook. It isn't the blatant affronts—the aspects aimed to shock—that upset me, but the fact that the film lacks heart.

"If the emperor looks like he's naked, the chances are that he really is wearing no clothes."

She's right. Simply stacking up taboos doesn't mean you're knocking them down. And putting people with Down syndrome in a film doesn't necessarily mean you're doing them any favors.

Years later, I got up the nerve to ask why Glover never wanted to talk to me. Amy Young, one of the organizers of the Phoenix event, remembered his Arizona visit well, in an e-mail exchange she was more than happy to have published.

"He probably just didn't talk to you because he doesn't have anything to say," she told me when I asked.

Young continued:

"I hope you didn't take it personally that he didn't talk with you. He is unable to think about anything else other than himself—to a degree that he cannot see at all. Like, not normal behavior or any sense that there is self-reflection or introspection of ANY sort. He's paranoid. Steph (one of the other organizers) took him to Whole Foods, not the one he mapped out and he thought she was trying to do something shady, like kidnap him. He rambled on to audiences about nonsense like how he's moving to a castle in Prague because their bills (money) are very crisp and clean. Finding a dialogue with him is nearly impossible. You initially think it's a show …but soon realize and become VERY annoyed with the fact that it's not a show. You WISH it was pretense, it's so incomplete of any sort of self-connection.

"Steph and I STILL love to tell people the story of the three days he was here because it was so unreal and exhausting."

Young included Glover's explanation of why he used people with DS in his movie, then continued, "Other people have speculated, very unfortunately, that it isn't anything so intellectual but more that he'd be working with people he could have more direction of. I don't know if I agree with that, though, maybe just because I certainly don't want to think that to be the reason. He's a weird case, Amy. He's simultaneously complex and uninteresting!!"

Afterward, she talked to other art house cinema people in other cities who'd had similar experiences with Glover.

"First night, he demands all of his money up front, to quote him 'in the Vaudevillian style' before he would go on," Young wrote, adding that he wore a money belt under his shirt.

I asked her what she thought of *What Is It?*

"I love weirdo cinema and surreal films....Crispin's fit the low budget and surreal qualities and it had a level of intrigue but overall it just didn't have a real sense of depth, which is what I ended up thinking about him in the end."

She admitted she might not be the best person to ask for an assessment of Glover's work: "He was so draining that I couldn't watch anything with him in it again until he was in *Hot Tub Time Machine*."

So the art house crowd didn't think much of Crispin Glover or his film. Neither did the critics. I wondered what people from the Down syndrome community thought.

I e-mailed Gail Williamson. She runs an agency called Down Syndrome in Arts & Media in California; I follow the agency on Facebook. I had a hunch that Williamson would know of Glover's film, and in fact, she did.

Her response: "I know it pretty well. I have never seen the full-length film, Crispin usually only shows the film in art houses when he is present to follow with a Q and A. I spent a little time with him when he started the project. Back then it was about my son being involved in the film, but since he was under 18 we decided not to include him since he would have required a studio teacher on set. Also, I wasn't sure I wanted him in it. But Crispin was a nice enough man and was very gracious whenever we were with him."

I nudged her a little harder, trying to get some sort of criticism, but only got: "It's very unique. Crispin has an interesting voice to share."

"But, but, but—" I sputtered at the computer screen and stopped. To be fair, Williamson hasn't seen the entire movie—and she has a business to run.

She does a good job. A decade after the release of Glover's film, people with Down syndrome were finally finding places in pop culture, thanks in part to Williamson. She represented Lauren Potter long before the young actress was cast as Becky Jackson on *Glee,* a role that might have ended after one episode but instead continued for several years.

I learned a lot from watching Potter's character on *Glee.* The show is uneven, obnoxious at times. Some hated that Becky was mean and foul mouthed; I loved that part. I really loved the episode where Arnie, the boy in the wheelchair (*Glee* seems to subscribe to the *Sesame Street* philosophy of showing one of each), takes Becky to tour a college program. Others thought it was condescending that it was Arnie who took her, that the kids with disabilities on the show were ghettoized. That didn't bother me, either. But I was uncomfortable during the final season when Becky suddenly began to date a typical young man. I have a feeling I wasn't the only one; that plotline disappeared as quickly as it had appeared, with no explanation.

*Glee* wasn't perfect but it was a wildly popular, prime-time show—and it was constantly prying up the edges of the collective comfort zone. I loved it for trying.

So did Sophie, although I think for her it was more about the singing and dancing. Still, I was thrilled when she decided she wanted to be Lauren Potter for the fifth-grade Wax Museum, which was pretty much the last event held at her elementary school before graduation. I ordered her a McKinley High School "cheerios" costume and big cheer bows for her hair, and Sophie memorized a speech about Potter and her life both on and off stage, so that she could take her spot in the cafeteria among the Amelia Earharts and the Jackie Kennedys.

While Sophie was preparing her role, I mentioned on Facebook that she'd chosen to be Lauren Potter in her school's wax museum. A friend of a friend knew Lauren's mom, as it turned out, and in a few days a package arrived addressed to Sophie, with Glee stickers, bracelets, and a note from Lauren. Sophie's eyes got big when she saw it; she was speechless, almost shaking as she opened the envelope. In that moment I realized that a good role model will trump a lousy art house film any day.

And when Johnny Knoxville's movie *The Ringer* came on cable late one night, I didn't flinch and change the channel. I watched the whole thing. It was excellent—funny, sensitive, and purposeful.

*lllll*

After I struck out with Crispin Glover, I felt like something was missing from my research. I wanted to talk to a serious artist about what it was like to depict people with disabilities—and why he or she did it.

I found that conversation in Chris Rush. Rush is a painter who lives in Tucson, a couple hours south of Phoenix. I first learned of his work when he had a show at a Phoenix-area gallery, the Mesa Arts Center, in 2010. The show was called STARE, and it was a retrospective that featured paintings Rush made during the three years that he volunteered with a group in Tucson called Arts for All.

The work is stunning, straightforward, and unapologetic. I sent Kathleen Vanesian to review it, and she agreed.

She began her review with some background:

"In the past few years, the culture of disability has become increasingly popular, not to mention vocal. Books like *Disability, Art and Culture*, by Susan Crutchfield and Marcy Epstein, have become required reading. Depictions of Franklin D. Roosevelt without his wheelchair or crutches have come under attack by the disabled community. Mr. Magoo, the loony, nearsighted cartoon character, has been demonized as being stereotypical, and Barbie has a new plastic playmate, Share a Smile Becky, who comes with her very own wheelchair.

"Gone are the days of disability portrayed only as a medical model or object of morbid voyeurism and exploitation—like those captured by photographers Diane Arbus and Weegee or those in the film *Freaks*, a Depression-era drama about a traveling circus starring people with strange bodily and mental disabilities. Now, there's even a British sitcom called *Cast Offs*, an edgy mockumentary starring actors with disabilities playing characters with the same disabilities. The show pokes fun at reality TV and the way disabilities are generally portrayed.

"Chris Rush has somehow managed to entirely escape issues of political correctness and disability activism in his beautifully intimate work."

Kathleen is right—in his work, it's just Rush and his subject. His paintings are so realistic they appear at first to be photographs.

I found Rush to be equally open when I reached him. It was easy. I found his website, e-mailed him, and within minutes we had a phone date. Rush grew up on the Jersey Shore, privileged. His mother thought she was Jackie O.; his dad was convinced he was John Wayne. Rush didn't know anyone with a disability.

As a young artist he became a jewelry designer in New York City (that along with the "street artist phase, the public artist phase, the rock and roll band phase," he laughed. But he abandoned that for life in Tucson, a place where he'd spent time as a kid. There, he began to paint, and he happened to paint a boy with "brittle bone disease." His partner urged him to apply for a grant from the Arizona Commission for the Arts; he got it and signed up to volunteer at Art for All, with the director's blessing to paint the people in the program, who had intellectual and physical disabilities.

By his own account, Rush had lived "a sheltered life." "I had no sense of what I was doing…completely overwhelmed and freaked out by what I saw," he said.

The people who participated in the program were age five to early twenties, from "comatose to ecstatic," and included brothers, sisters, and friends. "It was pretty fucking great."

Rush came in with his sketchbook and camera and tried to get to know his subjects, "their joys, their pleasures." He made twenty portraits in three years, and the Tucson Museum of Art gave him a show. He also got a show at the Phoenix Art Museum.

The acclaim was nice, but other rewards were greater, Rush said. Through Art for All, "I suddenly joined the human race," he told me, and realized that not everyone is perfect.

"These are the faces without guile."

Rush had e-mailed me an image of his latest version of my favorite of his paintings, this one painted on copper, of a young girl, probably a teenager, in profile. Her chin is tilted up, there's a beach towel wrapped around her head the way I always wrap my own head after a shower (my girls called that a "Mommy hat"), and she has a simple tattoo of a heart on her arm. She happens to have Down syndrome.

He encountered many kids and young adults with DS when he volunteered, he said. He was fascinated by them.

"The Down syndrome tribe is needed among us. If they were to go away it would be tragic," he said. He'd read about studies in England showing high rates of abortion after prenatal diagnoses.

"They are more like each other than they are like their parents," he said.

"Mmm-hmmm," I replied, noncommittal.

And they aren't at all competitive, he continued. I didn't say anything.

Rush paused and asked, "Is Sophie competitive?"

Well, yeah, I said, she is. Very competitive, particularly with her sister. She wants to do everything Annabelle does.

He thanked me and said he still has a lot to learn. I really loved him for that.

We left Down syndrome aside, and went back to disability in general, to the portraits and why he made and continues to make them now.

"What this all comes down to is do people want to be smart or kind?" Rush asked. "I'm pretty smart, but I had to question my kindness when I ended up in this community."

Rush giggled, explaining that his paintings sell for a lot of money and hang in many private collections. He considers this "subversive," his way of quietly educating others about people with disabilities. He doesn't like the hang-ups we have here in the United States. He's traveled in India, he said, and it's "hard" seeing everything on the streets. But at least you see it. "At least it's not dishonest like we are."

He told me about a show he had coming up at Tucson's most prestigious gallery—portraits of a mix of people, including some with disabilities, convicts, cartoon characters.

"All of it is what makes my world a great life," he said. The lesson he takes away from doing portraits? "All the ugly people disappear. They're just stories."

# 7

# ONE PILL MAKES YOU LARGER AND ONE PILL MAKES YOU SMALL

We all read stories in childhood that have stuck with us to this day. "The Lottery" by Shirley Jackson, of course, and for me, growing up in the hot desert, that Ray Bradbury short story "All Summer in a Day"—the one set on the planet Venus, where it rains all year except for one day and a bunch of mean kids lock one little girl in a closet so she misses the sun. I read that and imagined losing a rare, rainy day in Phoenix.

And then there's *Flowers for Algernon,* about Charlie Gordon, a man with developmental disabilities who undergoes experimental surgery and becomes very intelligent—only to realize that his genius is short-lived when a mouse (that's Algernon) operated on before him begins to deteriorate.

I definitely pictured that happening to me; I'm pretty sure anyone who read it did. And a lot of people read it. "Algernon" practically became a cottage industry. Daniel Keyes turned his 1959 short story (originally conceived as a storyline for a comic book) into a 1966 novel. It was a made-for-TV drama, then an Academy Award–winning feature film remade many times in different languages. Everyone from rock musicians to contemporary dance choreographers have taken a dip in the well; Keyes even wrote a memoir, *Algernon, Charlie, and I,* that recounts the impact of the story's success on the author's life.

Keyes's story was just that, of course—a story. Science fiction. No way could you ever open up a brain and turn a guy's IQ from 68 to 185, right? In any case, although Keyes did spend some time teaching English to special-needs students, the story is said to have been mostly inspired by a quarrel with his parents, who wanted him to go to medical school while he preferred a career as a writer. And that's what made the story such a good, universal one. It didn't really strike me, at the time I read it, as a story just about intellectual disabilities. It was about everyone. It was a good read.

That was before Sophie was born.

When Sophie was two, my dad clipped a piece from the *Wall Street Journal* with the headline "New Hope for Treating Down syndrome."

The story was about clinical trials being conducted with drugs meant to increase intelligence in people with Down syndrome. Nothing like what happened to Charlie Gordon. But, as scientists explained, a ten- or twenty-point boost to an IQ could still make a tremendous difference.

The drugs mentioned in the article, Aricept, Exelon, and Reminyl, were first developed to treat Alzheimer's disease. Somewhere along the way, I believe even before the genetic connection was made, someone noticed that people with Down syndrome tend to develop Alzheimer's relatively early in life, and decided to try the drugs on them. Turns out, the medications had improved cognition in some people with DS. So small trials had been underway—for years in some cases—at Duke University and other research spots around the country. Both children and adults were being tested.

To be honest, the results reported in this *Wall Street Journal* article weren't so remarkable. Some families said that their child seemed a bit sharper, spoke a little more clearly. One parent said her son, an actor, was better able to remember his lines. But no one was even sure it was because of the drugs. Perhaps the most impressive results came in the last paragraph of the story, which made my eyes well up:

*Mary Ann Dawedeit, whose 14-year-old son, Eli Lewis, participated in the Exelon trial last year, noticed improvements in his language. He described water as "Caribbean blue," and when he got angry at his older brother, called him a "lummox," words he had never used before. Their insurer refused to pay the estimated $300 a month to continue the drug after the trial, and his parents couldn't pay for it. Eli stopped taking the drug in September, and his mother has noticed that "he has retreated into his contented, less-aware self," she said. The language gains she noted haven't remained.*

*Flowers for Algernon*, I thought suddenly. That story. I'd never made any sort of connection between Charlie and Sophie. It had never occurred to me that someday there might be a pill that would make her smart. I panicked. Did I need to get Sophie into one of these trials right now? Was it already too late? Could there be a magic pill that would make her smart, make her more like us?

Calm down, I told myself. It was too soon to worry about IQs and vocabulary. Sophie was only two, still a year away from walking. The scar on her chest from heart surgery was still too fresh. I didn't even know where she was going to preschool; it wasn't time to start thinking about college. Like that would ever happen!

I forgot all about the magic pill. But one day when Sophie was about three, I was going through a big pile of old mail, and I found a flyer advertising a local visit by Dr. William Mobley, a scientist at Stanford University whose work focused on finding drugs that increase the intelligence of people with Down syndrome.

Algernon again. In fact, Mobley and his team were actually conducting experiments on mice that had been "given" Down syndrome in the lab.

I'm not a big fan of rodents, but since Sophie's birth I'd wondered whether animals can get Down syndrome. (Turns out, it does not naturally occur in animals, beyond our closest primate relatives, because Down syndrome is the result of an impact on human chromosomes—and animals aren't human. Animals can be born with chromosomal abnormalities, but typically they don't survive a disruption as significant as the equivalent of an extra twenty-first chromosome.) I wanted to see mice with Down syndrome. Would they be smaller? Slanty-eyed and small-nosed? Would they be alternately stubborn and extra-loving, just like Sophie?

Beyond that, I found myself wondering if there would be a pill for Sophie any time soon. The idea made my heart race. Suddenly, instead of feeling panicky, trying not to think about Sophie's future, I began daydreaming. Maybe she could go to community college. Live on her own. Raise kids? *Flowers for Algernon* was fiction, but this was real! Right? The paragraph about Dr. Mobley in the newsletter made it sound like the drugs were already available or about to be—and why not, I reasoned; it had been a year since that *Wall Street Journal* article. I'd missed his talk in Arizona, but I was already planning a trip to Northern California in the fall. Maybe I could stop by the lab, meet Dr. Mobley, and learn about these drugs that were going to change Sophie's life. And mine.

It only took one e-mail. Dr. Mobley would be delighted to meet me, to explain his research and prospects for the future. When would I be in town? I booked my ticket.

I'm guessing there's not really a bad time to visit Palo Alto, California, but I highly recommend October. The leaves were just starting to turn; the sun was bright but not hot; a breeze chilled my wimpy Arizona skin as I opened the door to Stanford's shiny, chrome-trimmed Center for Research and Treatment of Down Syndrome.

I was coming here as a mother, but I was wearing my journalist armor, figuring I'd report on Sophie—and these drugs—as if I was writing a story. Maybe that would clear the fog in my head that seemed to appear every time someone wanted to explain something about my kid's medical condition. As a journalist, I'd researched stories about science—about Freon, water policy, organ donation. If I pretended this was for a story, instead of for real life, maybe I'd understand better.

Plus, I felt more legit with my all-black outfit, narrow reporter notepad, micro-tape recorder—everything but the fedora with the "Press" sign on it.

Dr. Mobley was a kind, grandfatherly type who looked like Orville Redenbacher without the glasses. He had an MD and a PhD and a big team of researchers under him. Things were looking good in the field; two months earlier, Mobley and some of his colleagues had published a study called "Using Mouse Models to Explore Genotype-Phenotype Relationship in Down Syndrome." We sat in his cubbyhole of an office, and he showed me a PowerPoint presentation meant to explain, in simple terms, what this all meant.

The charts and numbers and graphs and big words swam in front of my eyes, and I felt like Charlie Gordon—before the surgery. The hippo-what-part of the brain? The cholinergic neurons do what? And the mice have Trisomy 16, not Trisomy 21? In segments? I was totally lost.

"So. What does this mean for Sophie?" I asked, still optimistic, after he'd finished talking like the teacher in the Peanuts television specials and handed me a printout of the PowerPoint.

Dr. Mobley didn't meet my eye. Well, he said, it means that someday, when she gets Alzheimer's, there might be a pill to help with that. Almost without exception, he explained, every person with Down syndrome will develop Alzheimer's by the age of forty. Those are the ones that make it to forty.

I'd known there was a link to Alzheimer's, but this was the first I'd heard that it was almost a certainty for Sophie. (I'd later learn that while the chances are very high that she'll get it, they aren't quite that high.)

I felt my face get hot. I began adding years in my head while trying to make it look like I was still paying attention to the PowerPoint. My own kid had an expiration date. Suddenly Dr. Mobley's small office was feeling like a prison cell.

I didn't want him to think I was upset, or—even worse—ignorant, that I hadn't known the statistics that would doom Sophie. So I smiled and nodded, and it obviously worked, because Dr. Mobley kept chatting about his research.

And then he had a question: Did I have any family members who might be interested in donating money to help with his research? I looked at my lap and told him I'd get back to him. Then I asked for a tour of the lab. I'd come this far; I really wanted to see those mice. And maybe the researchers would have better news.

Dr. Mobley took me down several snaking hallways to a big bright-white room and dropped me off with several young research assistants with thick accents

"Where are the mice?" I asked.

Wrong question. I guess the Stanford people worry about PETA infiltrators, or at least government regulations, because the mice were kept in a locked lab on another floor, far from where we were. The closest I got was a photo in the PowerPoint and more pictures in the lab of slices of the brains of dead mice.

I was out of questions. The researchers were really nice but didn't seem to know what to do with me. I dug in my purse for a couple snapshots of Sophie and held them out. In one Sophie was sitting up on the bed, in a blue flowered bikini, laughing, her hair shiny and her eyes bright. One woman took them gingerly and smiled, but looked really uncomfortable. Finally, another assistant—a man from Ukraine—walked me over to the door, which opened onto a bank of windows overlooking the Stanford campus, silver-gray and red-brick buildings and green grass sparkling in the fall sunlight.

"See those trees?" the researcher asked, pointing to a row right next to the lab. "Those are ginko biloba. There's fruit on them right now. It's supposed to stimulate brain development and help memory. The parents who bring their kids to our center, they pick the fruit and give it to them."

Pick it and give it to your daughter, he said, making it clear that's all there was and that's all there was going to be—for a really long time, anyway.

I stared down at my notepad. I hadn't written anything down. The reporter in me appreciated the moment. The mom in me wanted to run. I felt so stupid for believing in a miracle, for thinking there was such a simple solution to Sophie's problems, to my problems. I tried to think of something to say, of a question to ask. But there wasn't anything left to say. Not to these people, anyway. At least they were honest.

The researchers stood around some more, waiting politely for me to leave.

Outside, I picked a piece of the ginko biloba fruit, wrapped it in a Kleenex and tucked it in my purse. I snuck it back to Phoenix and put it on my office windowsill.

After Stanford, I gave up on the idea of a magic pill for Sophie.

We never did give Sophie ginko biloba. Years earlier, Ray and I had considered the nutritional supplements pushed hard on the Internet—along with therapies that include swimming with dolphins—and decided against them all.

I'm not saying that all of these treatments are bogus or that the parents who use them are naïve. (Although that dolphin thing is another story.) I do think that having a baby who needed heart surgery at four months and again at four years left us with little patience for anything beyond traditional medicine's offerings.

Plus, I felt depressed and a little cheated every time I thought of that trip to see Dr. Mobley. The piece of ginko biloba fruit stayed where I'd left it, a shriveled and dusty reminder.

When Sophie was five, she took her first IQ test. Just agreeing to have her tested was controversial. Some parents choose to never test their kid with Down syndrome, refusing to label their child with a number that's likely without much meaning.

Because many people with Down syndrome have so much trouble communicating on a basic level—particularly as young children—standard IQ tests like the Wechsler and the Stanford-Binet are widely considered all but useless. And yet until recently there hasn't been any sort of alternative for measuring intelligence in a person with DS.

In fact, a lot of people consider IQ tests to be bullshit in general. You don't have to know much about education or psychology or testing or even intelligence to know that IQ tests are widely viewed as bogus, or at least not super-accurate. And yet, they are ubiquitous.

We have been trying to measure one another's intelligence for a long time. Experts estimate that the earliest such tests came about in 605 in China, where games were used to test would-be soldiers. In the nineteenth century, the French were the first to use modern methods that helped distinguish between the mentally ill and the cognitively disabled.

And in all the time that's passed, methods haven't advanced enough to make results anywhere close to definitive. But much is still made of them—for all of us.

I do not know what my own IQ is. When we were young, my parents had my sister and me tested, but my mother has always refused to tell us the results. She says she doesn't want us to know whose score was better.

I've always assumed my sister has the higher IQ and that my mom told her and swore her to secrecy long ago. When it comes to my own daughters, there's no question, obviously, even though we've never had Annabelle tested.

Sophie's been tested enough for all of us. But to be honest, I have a better idea of what my IQ is than what hers might be.

When Sophie was born, the doctors and nurses kept pointing out how "mild" her features were. I had never seen a baby with Down syndrome, so I really didn't know what that meant—only that it was obvious they were trying to make us feel better. "Mild features mean a mild case," more than one medical professional told us. Apparently that is not true, though it is true that if Sophie had mosaicism —a form of Down syndrome in which only some cells in the body are affected by the third twenty-first chromosome—we probably would have seen less of an impact.

But genetic testing confirmed it: Sophie has garden-variety Down syndrome. Every cell is affected. You can see it on paper—literally. We have images of her chromosomes. If only there was a test that definitive for things like intelligence, I thought more than once.

For a long time, it didn't occur to me that anyone would want to test Sophie's IQ, at least not if they weren't measuring to see if miracle drugs had worked. Down syndrome means intellectual disabilities, right? It's included in all the medical definitions. What else needs to be said? Not necessarily, the psychologist at Sophie's preschool explained one day a few months after my visit to Stanford. Turns out, Down syndrome isn't the deciding factor in determining where you'll go to school and what sorts of services you'll get, in Arizona anyway. That's all based on your IQ. In many cases, it's not the DS diagnosis that counts; it's whether you qualify as intellectually disabled, or as, they said back then, "mentally retarded."

I need to add here that I've only had experience dealing with this in Arizona; it differs from state to state, and in many places the threshold is lower, and sometimes can have nothing to do with IQ at all.

In February 2008, we began the long process of figuring out where Sophie would go to kindergarten. She was a few months short of five, and wouldn't start kindergarten until the following August. But it was already time. I perched my butt on a tiny navy-blue plastic chair in

Sophie's preschool classroom one morning before school, and faced her team: the preschool teacher, speech-language pathologist, occupational therapist, physical therapist, principal, and school psychologist.

Team Sophie. I trusted these people. Sophie had been in preschool for a year and a half with them and had made great strides—recognizing letters, learning classroom procedures, riding the bus to and from school. She was so small I had to lift her onto the bus; by the end of the first week, she had the bus driver and aide wrapped around her finger, singing her songs, bringing gifts. I wished she could stay here forever—or at least for another year. But that was not possible. In the fall, she'd be someplace else.

The psychologist was the first to talk—a gentle man with a good reputation (I'd checked him out).

"We've called you here today to ask you to sign some paperwork, so we can test Sophie. We don't think she qualifies as mentally retarded." (That was the term still used in federal education law at the time.)

"You don't think she *what?*" I asked. I stared at him.

"We don't think Sophie qualifies as mentally retarded," the psychologist repeated. "We want to test her to find out." He shuffled a pile of paperwork.

Immediately, I had a feeling that this had to do with money. Almost all of Sophie's services were paid for by the government. In fact, she got them from two sources: the state's Division of Developmental Disabilities, as well as the public education system.

"Why?" I asked. "Why wouldn't Sophie be retarded? Isn't mental retardation included in the formal medical definition of Down syndrome?"

"Early intervention services boosted her IQ," he replied.

"And what if she doesn't qualify anymore as mentally retarded?"

"Then," he said, "she'll lose the services she gets from the state."

So here I was, sitting in front of Sophie's team of therapists and educators, while they were saying to me: We intervened in your retarded child's life so early and so well that she may no longer be "retarded."

The whole thing was absurd. And frustrating. But also kind of cool.

Could I actually have a kid with Down syndrome who didn't have an intellectual disability?

A few weeks after our first meeting, Sophie's teacher e-mailed me to say the test results were in. Could we meet again?

I e-mailed back. Yes, I could meet. But I couldn't wait. I had to ask. "She still qualifies as mentally retarded, doesn't she?" I wrote. "I know you can't say, that's just my prediction—services aside, of course, that will still make me a little sad. This whole thing has been a little like *Flowers for Algernon*—did you ever read that story in school?"

Yes, she'd read the book. It made her really sad. And no, she told me, Sophie does not qualify as retarded.

I was stunned. I'd spent four years, nine months, and a few days getting used to the fact that my kid was mentally retarded. And now it turned out she wasn't? And it was because of what we'd done, getting her therapies? I felt pretty kick ass. Mom of the Century!

But there had to be a catch, right?

We scheduled the meeting and the teacher sent the test results home. Sophie's IQ measured at 81. The cut-off for intellectual disability is 70. Sophie, the test said, was able to correctly identify the color of her shoes (pink) and her pants (black). When asked her age, she said, "Four, almost five." The test said a lot more, and concluded she had "below average intelligence." That startled me. I was so used to seeing the word *retarded* it had lost meaning. But how dare someone say Sophie was below average?!

I sat at the table facing Team Sophie and looked at the psychologist.

Instead, the principal spoke first. "We all know what will happen if Sophie isn't labeled as MR," she said. "She'll lose her services, services we all believe got her where she is today."

Then she floored me.

"And so you have a decision to make," she said. "You tell us what to do. You have to decide today. You can label Sophie as mildly mentally retarded, and she can keep her services. Otherwise, she'll lose them."

My jaw dropped, and then I clenched it, pushing back the tears. I'd barely had a moment to digest the fact that Sophie did not test as mentally retarded. Since the moment we got the news she had Down syndrome, I'd worried that she wouldn't be able to function in society at all, that she'd never read a good book or carry on a real conversation. I'd gotten so stuck in the rut of that, in trying to accept it, that it had never once occurred to me that she'd somehow be deemed *too smart*. It was like someone finally opened a door and there was sunlight, but it was way too bright. Blinding.

"Yes, she looks and acts like a normal baby now," the doctor had told us that first week, "but soon she'll begin to miss milestones." And she did, and I kept worrying. We exposed her to books and educational videos and other kids, but in my heart, I figured none of it was of any use. In casual conversation, I began referring to my "mentally retarded" kid, bracing myself for life with Sophie.

And now this?

I knew the answer to my next question, but I had to ask.

"What if I don't label her mentally retarded? What will that get her, other than bragging rights for her mother?"

"Nothing," she replied.

And so I signed the paperwork acknowledging that Sophie was mildly mentally retarded. The principal was nice enough to write on the forms that the team, including the mother, "agonized" over the decision. The psychologist left the room and edited the test results. The numbers stayed the same, but he added a part about how it was believed the results were inflated, due to early intervention services.

I'm really not sure what was said after that. I walked out of that school like a zombie, my eyes barely focused. I unlocked the car door and sat inside, wondering if it had all been a cruel dream. After almost five years, I'd thought I had the whole thing figured out. But the truth was that I had no idea what I was doing, or what was to come. I felt totally unequipped to parent this little girl, this little girl I now needed to begin to think of as smart. But not too smart.

llllll

That was far from the end of it. That little edit on those test results was a gateway drug to the much harder stuff I'd soon be doing. A few months later, preschool was over, but we still hadn't decided where Sophie would attend kindergarten. The team gathered again, and this time the message from the principal was much different.

I wanted Sophie to attend kindergarten with typical kids at our neighborhood school. Annabelle would be in second grade the next year, and Sophie was already familiar with the school grounds and many of the kids and teachers, including Annabelle's beloved kindergarten teacher, who had made it clear she really wanted Sophie in her class.

"Oh no," the preschool principal said. "We think Sophie would be much better off at another school in the district, a school designed to include kids with special needs. At least promise me you'll take a tour."

I did. And I did my homework, learning that the other school had lower test scores than the one I wanted Sophie to attend. The big selling point on my tour: the segregated room for the "MR" (mentally retarded) kids. I held my breath and pushed hard for Broadmor, Annabelle's school. Sophie's team grudgingly agreed. (Her preschool teacher privately applauded the decision.)

Still, I worried someone from the district would see Sophie's records and try to pull her, arguing that she didn't test well enough to be mainstreamed. That's how we came to spend a good part of that summer in a private psychologist's office, getting Sophie's IQ tested—again. This time it was 83, with no caveats. "*Nice!*" I thought, tucking the results away in case I ever needed them.

Sophie had a terrific year in kindergarten, and her teacher recommended that she be placed in a first-grade class at Broadmor the following year. She was keeping up. But as Sophie approached her sixth birthday, another problem arose.

As it turns out, the public education system and the social service system operate totally separately. The tests that Sophie takes in school apply to *school,* and the services she receives there. But there's a whole other world that we dwell in, involving the governmental programs that provide assistance to people with developmental disabilities.

Federal law mandates how much of these services—both through the state Department of Education and Department of Economic Security—are doled out. But some things are up to the discretion of the state. And the Arizona legislature is not a particularly friendly place for people with any sort of challenges or need. This is Barry Goldwater country, a place where libertarians rule and the rest are largely left to fend for themselves. Arizona ranks at the bottom nationally for spending on education, our child protective services department is constantly under fire, and we don't take good care of people with mental illnesses.

So while it should come as no surprise that it's not easy to qualify for services for the developmentally disabled in Arizona, it really amazed me to learn that just because a person has a medical diagnosis of Down syndrome does not mean he or she is qualified for help. (And by help, I mean everything from therapy and medical care for children and adults from age six up, to housing for adults.)

In fact, in the state of Arizona, to qualify for assistance, a person age six or over must have one of the following four diagnoses: epilepsy, cerebral palsy, autism, or mental retardation (since renamed intellectual disability, but still defined by an IQ below 70).

When Sophie was born, Ray drove over to the nearest Department of Economic Security office and signed her up for services, which included weekly visits from physical, speech, music, and occupational therapists as well as respite care.

But now, as she approached her sixth birthday, we got a letter from DES. Sophie needed to be screened again to see if she qualified to keep the services she received out of school. According to the paperwork, Sophie needed an IQ of 69.

I had paperwork that listed her IQ at 81 and 83. That wasn't going to work. But the good news was that the state didn't have to be the one measuring it, and that is how Sophie and I came to meet Dr. Death.

That's not her real name, of course. I wondered, shaking the hand of this demure, grandmotherly type, if she knew that's what people called her. I'd been hearing about her for years. As the story went, this psychologist disagreed with the rigor with which the state applied its qualification standards, so she'd give pretty much any kid who came to see her the low test scores necessary to get services.

I totally understood why people called her Dr. Death. No one wants to hear their kid has a really low IQ or autism. She was the queen of the doomsday ball, the fortune teller with nothing but dire predictions. She was also someone who understood the value of hard-to-get state services.

I was dying to ask her about this, but that seemed inappropriate and unwise, considering this whole arrangement was obviously a "Don't Ask, Don't Tell" setup. On the hottest day of the year (and that's saying something in Phoenix—it was 115 degrees that July day), I strapped Sophie into her car seat—because at six she was still small enough to need one. Then we drove across town to Dr. Death's office, a tacky setup in a strip mall.

A small, red-headed woman came out to greet us. Turns out, I liked her, even though she was about to tell me my kid was retarded. I sat down in her small office and figured she'd give me a schedule. The previous times Sophie had been tested, it had taken place over several visits to ensure that she didn't get tired, and I had taken home multiple questionnaires to fill out; Ray had to fill some out too, and so did teachers and caregivers.

Not this time. Dr. Death asked me questions for a few minutes and then I left Sophie alone with her for an hour. I came back and perched on the edge of her couch while Sophie played on the floor with some books. The doctor didn't mince words. She didn't apologize or explain why she was giving Sophie this score. She simply delivered her news.

"Sophie's IQ is 55," she said.

I felt like someone had hit me over the head with a baseball bat. I shouldn't have been surprised—after all, that was what we were here for—but somehow I still was. Sophie and I said good-bye to the doctor and headed off in search of the chocolate ice cream I'd promised as a treat if she answered all the lady's questions. I strapped her into the car seat and looked into her eyes.

"I love you, Sophie!" I told her. "You know you're a smart girl, don't you?"

And then my daughter did something I've never seen her do. She looked at me wordlessly, opened her mouth, and let some drool spill out onto her chin.

Really. Maybe it was the heat.

I wiped it off, kissed her, and got in the car. We never did get chocolate ice cream, only because Sophie fell asleep immediately, obviously exhausted from several days' worth of testing crammed into sixty minutes. I drove around for hours, making calls to Ray, my mom, Sophie's kindergarten teacher—anyone who would answer.

They all listened patiently and then said, "Well, this is what you wanted, right?"

Yes. No. Not exactly. It was great news, right? Sophie would continue to get the help she needed. But, oh my God, 55? That's not just sort of retarded; it's really retarded. And while I knew Sophie was smarter than that, my psyche was so precarious at this point that I had to fight from believing it.

I sent the results to the state, and they let Sophie keep her services. They even added some on. Mission accomplished, I suppose. By this point I'd had time to contemplate the whole thing, but I still didn't know what to think. Sophie's IQ was in the mid-50s or the mid-80s, depending on the day and the test and the person giving it.

By now, I knew the numbers should be meaningless; they had become a tool to get what I wanted and what Sophie needed. And while it would be years before she would emerge to me as her own person—terrible at handwriting but better with an iPad than I am, horrible at counting money but able to read (and at least sort of understand) Judy Blume books—I was starting to get glimmers of Sophie's unique intelligence.

In the fall of 2012, when Sophie was nine years old and in fourth grade at Broadmor Elementary School, she'd established herself as a smart kid—regardless of test scores. I'd learned to ignore the results on the forms that came home, tests that showed Sophie slipping further and further behind her classmates. Math had all but eluded her, but she was still reading close to grade level. She had certainly developed a set of opinions, announcing to anyone who would listen that she planned to vote for Barack Obama and that she didn't particularly care to wear underwear to school.

I didn't have much time to read, but one day another article about Down syndrome research popped up in my e-mail inbox, this time about research going on at the University of Arizona in Tucson. My parents' alma mater, practically my backyard. Scientists there had developed a test called the Arizona Cognitive Test Battery for Down syndrome.

Apparently I was not the only one who'd noticed that traditional testing methods don't work so well on kids with DS. In the years since I'd stopped paying attention, Lynn Nadel and Jamie Edgin, professors in UA's psychology department, had actually created a research consortium in Tucson devoted to understanding cognitive impairment in people with Down syndrome.

I called Dr. Edgin and arranged a meeting, explaining that I was a journalist interested in her research and a mom of a nine-year-old with Down syndrome.

It was easy enough to make a trip two hours south during Sophie's fall break from school, which is how I found myself on the mall at UA on a still-warm autumn day, looking for the Space Sciences building—an odd place to locate a Down syndrome research lab, I thought. Turns out it's next door to the psychology department, where I met with Edgin in her office.

Edgin was warm and personable, with a busy schedule and a Neale Donald Walsch quote on the wall: "Life begins at the end of your comfort zone." I forgot to ask much about the assessment once she began talking about the general philosophy behind her work. In any case, it was obvious I was wrong—that test wasn't for use in academics or run-of-the-mill measurements, it was for hardcore research. Edgin believes that there are a number of physical conditions that can contribute to cognitive performance in people with Down syndrome. It's not just about the brain itself, she said.

The best example she had was sleep, which she was currently studying. Edgin said that the difference between a kid with DS who has sleep apnea and one who does not can mean an eight-point difference in IQ. I thought about Sophie, who spent much of a typical night falling asleep on the couch in her school clothes, wedged up against me, then wandering from her bed to my bed and back to the couch, snorting herself awake, sleeping sitting up. When she did make her way into my bed, she was a whirling dervish of arms and legs, and when I'd sneak out of bed—at any hour—she'd appear just behind me, my tiny, sleepless shadow.

Improving sleep: What a reasonable, rationale approach to making a real difference in the life of a person with DS, I thought, instead of that hooey with the magic pills.

Edgin explained that she had begun her career as a scientist studying autism, but switched to Down syndrome when she noticed it got so little attention. Now, Edgin said, there was more research going on into how to improve the cognitive abilities of people with Down syndrome than there ever had been.

I told her about my trip to Stanford and made a face.

Hers lit up.

That was several years ago, she said. Call Dr. Mobley now. He'd have much different things to say today about the hope for that medication. Turns out Edgin was working on the drug research, too, and explained that clinical trials for the drug Stanford developed are going really well.

The side effects aren't great, she admitted. When the drugs stimulated the brain to increase cognitive performance, it did sometimes result in seizures.

No thanks, I thought, smiling politely. But I did sign Sophie up for the sleep study.

*lllll*

I took Dr. Edgin up on her suggestion that I contact Dr. Mobley. And I have to admit that I got a little excited again, thinking there might soon be a pill for Sophie. Not one that caused seizures, but one that would help her get through middle school and high school, maybe even community college.

I heard back from Dr. Craig Garner, the co-director of Stanford's Down syndrome center. Dr. Mobley had left Stanford, Dr. Garner said, but he'd be happy to talk about the research going on at Stanford any time.

We made a phone date.

This time I asked Dr. Garner to go really slowly and explain what Down syndrome looks like in the brain.

That, he said, is a great question that doesn't have very good answers. It seems that it's the subtleties that make this stuff so hard.

For the most part, he told me, the brain of a person with DS is fundamentally no different than any other. All the brain regions are there, unlike in some other genetic conditions. The issues with how the DS brain uses and processes information are nuanced. The parts that share and store information are different, and it's difficult to figure out what that means.

So researchers leap over anatomy to focus on function. Dr. Garner told me to think of it as a "break" in the system that contributes to learning issues. The brain has three neurotransmitter systems. One is "inhibitory" and prevents information loss. The second is "excitatory" and stores pictures and other information. These two work like a car. The brake is the inhibitor and the gas is the excitor. When you step on the brake and the gas at the same time, you spin your wheels and go nowhere. To move, you need balance between the two, but research shows that the fundamental problem in the brain of the person with DS is that the brake is on too high.

This manifests itself in some but not all regions of the brain, namely in the areas that affect learning, memory, and the storage of memory. Using the brain a lot can help, he said. That means pushing the person harder, providing enriching environments—but it's not enough.

That's where the third neurotransmitter system—"modulatory"—comes in. This system involves the modulation of behavior through the body's natural creation of serotonin, dopamine, and other chemicals that help strike that balance between the brake and the gas pedal.

The drugs are meant to help with the modulation, he said, and it's a very subtle process, getting the right level of change.

And that's where Alzheimer's and Down syndrome intersect. According to Garner, the areas of the brain that cause Alzheimer's are the same areas where the memory and learning problems for people with Down syndrome occur.

"What I really don't like about this discussion is that it involves drugs," Dr. Garner said, which I thought was a really weird thing for a neurobiologist doing drug studies to say. He avoids drugs himself, he said, joking about those television commercials with the long lists of warnings about pharmaceuticals.

I decided not to ask him about the risk of seizures. Instead, I changed the subject to the mice. The mice, Dr. Garner said, are why advances in this area are happening relatively quickly. A scientist named Muriel Davisson at the Jackson Laboratory in Bar Harbor, Maine, developed the mice in the late 1990s. They are unromantically called Ts65DN, and according to the laboratory's biography of Davisson, the mice have "three copies of about 60 percent of the related human chromosome 21 genes, survive into adulthood, and exhibit many of the behavioral, learning, muscular, and neuronal defects associated with the syndrome in humans."

What this all means is that they haven't been able to replicate human Down syndrome in a mouse exactly, Dr. Garner said, but they are close enough to be able to study the effects of drugs on the mice. Others have now bred mice with some Down syndrome characteristics, but Davisson's are widely considered the best.

I wanted to know more about the mice. Yes, Dr. Garner said, they have learning disabilities and a lack of long-term recall. They also have sleep apnea.

And what about their personalities, I asked. Were they really loving? Stubborn?

Well, he said, the mice are bad mothers.

There was a long, awkward pause, during which I imagine he was saying to himself, "Now why the fuck did I say that?!" and then Dr. Garner changed the subject.

He asked about Sophie's sister. Has Annabelle changed as she's grown? What about me? ("Just wait till menopause," he said, laughing.)

Our hormonal levels change, as does the wiring in our brains, he said.

But when it comes to the brain's wiring, not so much with the mice. Or Sophie. And suddenly, I understood Sophie's childlike behavior a little better. Her tastes have changed over the years, but much more slowly than Annabelle's. I still caught Sophie watching cartoons meant for toddlers or clutching the Junie B. Jones books she loved in kindergarten. She'd have an Elmo-themed birthday party if I let her.

Then I told Dr. Garner the story about my visit to the lab and the uncomfortable researchers and the ginko biloba tree. I waited for him to laugh, to contradict them. He didn't.

"One of the major ingredients is ginko," he said of the drug he's currently testing.

"What we're doing is going to still take time," he added gently, explaining that while they were now testing the drugs on people, it was just the Stage 2 clinical trials. It would be five years at least before they'd even have an idea of whether there would be a pill for Sophie, and longer still until something was actually on the market.

"We'll know more in twenty years," he said.

I thanked him for the call and hung up feeling stupid, again.

After I talked to Dr. Garner, I reread *Flowers for Algernon*.

In the book, thirty-three-year-old Charlie Gordon lives on his own in New York City and works at a bakery owned by a friend of his late uncle's, who promised his pal that Charlie would have a job as long as he wanted one.

Charlie's parents had turned him out early, the reader learns through a series of flashbacks that Charlie undergoes after the surgery. He was destined for a state institution before his uncle rescued him. The scientists found him because he took a night class for adults with developmental disabilities, and his teacher was impressed enough with him that when researchers came looking for a promising student, she recommended him.

Ultimately, Charlie and the teacher, Alice, fall in love, though the relationship is complicated. He loses his job at the bakery after his personality changes confuse his coworkers and boss, and he finds comfort in the arms of a flamboyant woman who lives across the hall.

And then he notices that Algernon, the mouse whose own surgery was so successful that it led to the first operation on a human being, is beginning to fail. Charlie knows his own regression isn't far behind.

Funny, before I reread the book, I was certain that the part I wouldn't be able to bear would come at the end, when Charlie's journal begins once again to include misspellings and misused words—when the news comes that he's going to be sent to live in that institution he'd thus far resisted. When he knows the decline has begun and that there's nothing he can do about it.

But the end came as a relief. The tough part was watching Charlie get smart—not even 185 IQ smart. Just 100 IQ smart was enough to make me wince. Because then he was smart enough to realize that his buddies from the bakery had been laughing at him, not with him; to realize in sharp relief what he'd looked like to the world.

No thank you, I thought, putting the book down, resolving to quit thinking about magic pills and *Flowers for Algernon*. It was time to live in the moment, to face who Sophie was—and who that made me, as her mother. There would never be a pill. And oddly, I was suddenly totally and completely okay with that.

# 8

## NICE TO NOT MEET YOU

Years ago, I interviewed a pediatric neurologist in Phoenix for a story I was writing about autism. He was a gentle older man confounded by the fact that the rate of diagnosis was rising; in contrast, my story was about parents who resist a diagnosis, who are in denial.

Before we dug into science and statistics, I explained to the doctor that I was intrigued by the way autism was diagnosed because I had a young daughter with Down syndrome—a question answered with a blood test at birth (or a diagnosis before that, even) as opposed to the never-ending questions surrounding an autism label. Autism can't be diagnosed with a blood test, and not prenatally at all, and symptoms typically don't appear or aren't noted until the child is two or older.

And then actually testing for autism is a tricky proposition. In many ways, it's like pornography—the medical profession knows it when it sees it. That's not good enough for some parents, understandably.

It's a tricky, complicated subject, and, at the time I was writing the story, it was frankly a welcome relief from thinking about Down syndrome 24/7. I didn't mean to make Sophie more than a passing reference in my conversation with this busy physician. But as soon as he heard "Down syndrome," the doctor was up and out of his chair, rushing out of the room and returning with a grin and a typed sheet that had obviously been Xeroxed many times. The words were hard to read, tilted and worn.

No matter, I'd already read "Welcome to Holland." I smiled and thanked him and tucked the paper inside my notebook, trying not to cringe visibly. The short passage was written by *Sesame Street's* Emily Kingsley in 1987 about her son Jason, who was then thirteen.

"I am often asked to describe the experience of raising a child with a disability – to try to help people who have not shared that unique experience to understand it, to imagine how it would feel. It's like this," she begins.

Then Kingsley shares a metaphor that will later be used in the title of books, published all over the place, Xeroxed repeatedly, and handed to parents like me.

It's like you've planned a trip to Italy, Kingsley writes—but instead wind up in Holland. It's still beautiful, it's still amazing, but it's different, disconcerting at first.

"The important thing is they haven't taken you to a horrible, disgusting, filthy place full of pestilence, famine and disease. It's just a different place.

"So you must go out and buy new guidebooks. And you must learn a whole new language. And you will meet a whole new group of people you never would have met. It's just a different place. It's slower-paced than Italy, less flashy than Italy."

Kingsley concludes:

"If you spend your life mourning the fact that you didn't get to go to Italy, you may never be free to enjoy the very special, the very lovely things…about Holland."

I love *Sesame Street,* and I have nothing against Emily Kingsley. But I was never a fan of "Welcome to Holland."

I'm sure many parents have found solace in what they see to be great insight. Not me. I'm not alone; in fact, there are entire online forums devoted to the hatred of this piece.

It's sappy. It's simplistic in a way that having a kid with disabilities is not and never will be, not for me, anyway. And for a long time, I was still too hurt and angry for platitudes. Looking back now, I realize that part of what upset me was that it felt like this was all anyone was handing me: this comparison between these two places. I needed more.

Ray and I had been to both Italy and Holland before Sophie was born, and I didn't need to be reminded of carefree trips to Europe at a time when I was quite sure my life had ended.

"You know, I've been to Amsterdam, and *this is not like Amsterdam,*" I said to Ray, waving the paper, gritting my teeth. "I don't see hash bars or tulip fields or awesome flea markets in this scenario, do you?!"

He just made a face.

I knew I was supposed to fit into this new role as parent to a kid with a disability, but I didn't know how to do that. Those moms were harried but tender, stoic, and knowledgeable. They kept their hair short, drove light-colored mini vans, and always had a Wet Wipe ready. They were selfless, kind, and accepting. They did not wear makeup. I had the last one covered; other than that, I was fucked.

"You know, I'm not your typical special-needs mom," I told a nanny candidate when Sophie was very young.

"Yeah, well, who is?" the confident young woman shot back— snarky but correct. I hired her, warily, and added my faux pas to a quickly growing list of things I was ashamed I'd said.

The truth is that I was watching my friends go somewhere while I was stuck someplace else, a place with medical scares, staring strangers, preschools that wouldn't take my kid, sleepless nights worrying about her future—and mine.

I was drowning and I needed help. But I'm stubborn, determined to do it on my own. I am not a joiner, haven't been since high school, when, in an attempt to stave off what I now know was clinical depression and to avoid having to do actual homework, I signed up for every club I could find. As an adult I have resisted joining everything from a gym to a synagogue to the PTA. At our wedding, my vows paraphrased Groucho Marx: I'd never wanted to join a club that would want me as a member—until Ray.

My aversion to joining held true, more than ever, when it came to Down syndrome. I never did go to a meeting of Sharing Down Syndrome, the group run by Gina Johnson, the woman who'd wanted to "smooch on my angel baby." Too touchy-feely.

Nor was I drawn to Down Syndrome Network, a local support group that had been created as an alternative to Sharing Down Syndrome. I'd heard for years that the members of the two groups did not get along, which I found pretty ironic considering the stereotype of people with Down syndrome being kind and loving. Clearly, no one's ever said that about the parents of people with Down syndrome.

As the story went, Sharing Down Syndrome was sponsoring a fundraising auction, and someone donated a case of wine and was turned away because no alcohol was allowed at Sharing Down Syndrome events. That was apparently the latest in a series of disagreements that had taken place over the years, and a reason to start another support group, Down Syndrome Network.

Those people drank, which was a plus in my book, but they were so serious, so laden with information—always flying in an expert or offering a seminar. I could barely get my little family showered and out the door every day. It was too much. The newsletters for both groups continued to gather dust on my mail table.

I was like Goldilocks, never finding the right bowl of porridge, wandering through the forest alone—destination unknown. Not Italy or Holland, I knew that much.

Then I met Maya.

♋♋♋♋♋♋

I met Maya online. I'm pretty sure she's the first person I ever met online. I came of age before Internet dating (before the Internet, for that matter) and the only way I knew of to meet people other than in person was through the ads in the back pages of newspapers like the one I eventually worked for, *New Times*.

I met my husband at work. The funny thing is that he used to sell those personal ads in the back of the paper. He was even required to attend happy hour parties sponsored by the paper, at which *New Times* employees helped customers write their ads. That actually led to a couple of dates for Ray (smart guy—that was clearly a good lake in which to fish), but luckily they were all disasters, and he was still single by the time I came to work at *New Times*.

When Sophie was born, we picked up the phone and called people to tell them. We mailed out birth announcements with stamps and paper. We sent a few e-mails, but it was nothing like it is today, when you can document every moment of your pregnancy, birth, and child's life online. I am grateful that these options did not exist when I started having children. I actually have a friend who posted a photo of her baby vomiting. The yellow puke was quite literally flying from her mouth as the image was snapped. It was gross, yes. And hilarious. If I'd given birth in the summer of 2015, I'm not sure I could have resisted doing the same.

Thankfully, Facebook was not much more than a spark in Mark Zuckerberg's eye in 2003, so I avoided the overshare. But I would have benefited from some connection, I know that now. There were online forums, and looking back I'm sure I could have found other parents of babies with DS that way. But I wasn't about to try. The only people I knew of who used chat rooms were religious freaks and sex addicts. And so my isolation continued.

Even once Facebook was up and running and all my friends had discovered it, it took me years to sign up. My chosen profession had taken a swift kick in the ass, and I was reeling from the double whammy of a bad economy and the Internet revolution.

My bosses kept talking about this thing they wanted us to do called blogging. I had no idea what that meant, but I had a feeling that it would involve a lot more work, so I resisted for a long time. Plus I hated the idea of news delivered online. It felt like sudden death. Where was the smell of newsprint, the joy of ink rubbing off on your fingers as you relaxed with the paper and a cup of coffee? No one cared what I thought. Eventually, the little weekly newspaper that produced a cover story, a few reviews, and some listings every seven days was starting up blogs about news, music, food, and art and expecting us to post stories on them every day.

Sick of my resistance, a tech savvy colleague in the editorial department came up with a creative way to show me the power of online journalism.

"I know you like to write about Sophie," she said. "How about I help you start your very own blog?"

"No way," I said, more than once. I had no interest in writing something that would not be edited and for which I would not be paid. What a waste of time.

And then I—like the rest of the world—read the book *Julie and Julia,* the account of a young woman named Julie Powell who spent a year cooking her way through *Mastering the Art of French Cooking* by Julia Child. I got it. I wanted to blog.

We did it in off hours on WordPress, using a very simple template that allowed me to see firsthand how satisfying it was to write something and hit "publish"—sharing it immediately. Girl in a Party Hat was born.

I wasn't sure if the girl was Sophie or me—the name was more inspired by a piece of art I'd bought on etsy—but it didn't really matter. In the end, the girl was both of us, and the blog was devoted to documenting Sophie's kindergarten year because in 2008, everyone was starting a blog designed to document a year of something, thanks to Julie Powell. My first post was published on Sophie's fifth birthday.

"This thing is going to totally take off!" Ray said.

I was grateful for the confidence but shook my head. "No, it isn't, but that's okay."

This was no *Julie and Julia*. There was no grand plan beyond raising Sophie. I was pretty much just documenting what it meant to have this kid with Down syndrome, to be putting her out there in the world. In the end, I'm pretty sure not even Ray read the blog. But seven years in, I was still posting. I never had a post go viral and never did much more to promote it than post a link on Facebook, which I did eventually join.

I began with a very small following comprised of family and friends. Occasionally someone knew someone who'd had a baby with Down syndrome and they told the new parents about Girl in a Party Hat. Once in a while someone would find it during a Google search.

It didn't matter; I was hooked. I really surprised myself. Going back to the earliest days of childhood, I'd never wanted to keep a diary or journal. I always felt self-conscious jotting down notes about my life, for no one to read. Now I found myself really looking forward to blogging, and if too many days went by without a post, I'd begin to feel like a mosquito filling up with blood, ready to pop.

And then there was Maya. I'm not sure exactly how we first interacted; I think she found my blog and left a comment, along with the address for her own blog. As it turns out, I was not the only mother of a young child with Down syndrome who had started a blog. There were dozens of us out there, all over the country and world.

It was like *Horton Hears a Who*. "We are here! We are here! We are here!" my soulmates called. And it began with Maya.

She lived outside New York City. Her son, Leo, was a year younger than Sophie, and she had another child, a younger daughter. We were both Jewish and had gone to the same graduate school, both in the same field. Over the years we'd crack up over other similarities, as well—our love of musicals, the same bad TV. Candy corn–inspired Halloween decorations. I wrote about it in a post on Girl in a Party Hat in 2009, on a morning Sophie had barfed on her favorite stuffed animal and I was stuck at home.

*"I threw up on Piglet."*

*And the couch. And—well, we'll leave it at that. I got her settled in the bathtub, entered negotiations with Ray about who would stay home (I either won or lost, depending on your perspective), and sat down on the toilet (seat closed) to check e-mail on the iPhone.*

*There was one from Maya. "Seasons of Love? Really? Amy, are we the SAME person?"*

*She loves the song as much as I do. I had a feeling. Maya and I have a lot in common, and not just the fact that we each have kids with Down syndrome (Leo is 4 and a half). Same grad school, same religion, same tastes in pop culture. She works in Manhattan, which, damnit, I always meant to do. Most important: We have the same fears and hopes and love, as the mothers of Leo and Ellie, Sophie and Annabelle.*

*I've met other moms of kids with Down syndrome, moms who seem like truly great people, moms I'd like to be friends with, but none I have more in common with—and if you don't think a mutual love of a cheesy Broadway musical song is an important component for lasting friendship, you've never had one—than Maya.*

*Technically, Maya and I have never met. Only through our blogs.*

*"Mama, why are you laughing?" Sophie asked, looking up at me from the tub, as I cracked up over Maya's e-mail. "My friend likes the same song I do!" I told her. "I'll play it for you."*

*So I did. Sophie loved "Seasons of Love," too. We watched the video four times and she didn't even puke on my laptop.*

When I wrote about how depressing it was to watch the baggers at Safeway, adults with Down syndrome afraid to catch your eye, obviously trained to avoid strangers, Maya totally got it. Her comment on my post:

*Your description of the kids at Safeway? Heartbreaking. As much as I don't want Leo shaking his butt at 21, it kills me a little to think of someone sucking all the joie de vivre out of him. I know he has to "behave," and all, but I hope that joy sucking out thing never happens. It's part of what makes them who they are. But not so cute on the grown-ups I guess.*

*OK, forgive me if this is too corny but do you know what song runs through my head constantly, about Leo? Often when he does something that drives me bonkers (and we KNOW that happens daily, multiple times)—the one from Sound of Music—"How do you solve a problem like Maria"—How do you solve a problem like Leo? How do you catch a cloud and pin it down? Not to say that Leo is a problem, of course, but certainly a challenge. The things he does are so perplexing, endearing, aggravating, fill-in-the-blank. But they are also what make him who he is and we all know I wouldn't have it any other way.*

We called those crazy-long comments "blogging on your blog." I did it too, on hers.

Without realizing it, I'd joined a support group. Maya was funny and down to earth—and way more adjusted than I was. She went to Buddy Walks (held mostly in the fall in cities all over the country, community gatherings that raise money for the National Down Syndrome Society through pledges) and other organized events. And she was handy online. She introduced me to other moms around the country who had blogs. I put them in my "blogroll" and friended them on Facebook. It was pretty awesome.

In 2010, Ray and I took the girls to New York City, and one morning I grabbed Sophie and met Maya and her family for brunch.

*Our trip to New York City was full of high points, but I have to say that the best moment came when Sophie met Leo.*

*I walked into a busy restaurant, looked around, and suddenly, this little boy I've been reading about almost every day for months leapt off the computer screen and into real life, before my eyes.*

*Sophie ran right up to him for a hug. (Contrary to popular misconceptions about people with Down syndrome, she doesn't do that with everyone.)*

*I felt the tears well up even before I could take my coat off.*

*I need to back up. This will sound horrible, but there's no way of saying it without just saying it (and somehow, reader, I bet you'll relate).*

*I'm not a Support Group Kinda Girl. Not that there's anything wrong with support groups. In fact, there's a lot of good—and I know I'm missing out by avoiding the two (I might add warring—I do love that part—at least they were warring at one point not long ago)—Down syndrome support groups in Phoenix.*

*I know. I know I know I know I know. But that whole thing's just not for me. Maybe it's because I live where I was born. I am incredibly blessed with family and friends and all sorts of resources (like a kindergarten teacher who continues to look out for Sophie even now that she's in first grade, and plays a mean game of poker in her off time) to help us navigate all sorts of situations.*

*Even so, I didn't realize something was missing—til I found it. The thing is, just because you have something in common with someone (say you're both journalists, or both Jewish, or both obsessed with rickrack and vintage toys and certain kid books/movies/music, or both think way too much about things like where you live, or both have kids with Down syndrome), that doesn't mean you'll wind up friends.*

*Now, if you have all of those things in common and more, yeah, then it might happen.*

*That's Maya. . . .*

*And I've said this before, but in honor of meeting Leo (and the fact that his parents schlepped him and his two-and-a-half-year-old sister from New Jersey on a truly horrible day to meet us) I need to say again that starting a blog was a Really Important Thing for me not only because it gave me the ability to go on (and on and on—and on) about Sophie, but because it led me to some pretty terrific people. My (frankly) arm's length support group, including Robert Polk (who lives in Texas and has an adult son, Ryan, with DS, and goes by Bobby but will forever be RobertPolk to me) and Joyce and Sarah, and Cate and Starrlife.*

*And Maya.*

*Technically, Sophie's an older woman (she's got almost a year on Leo) but he towers over her, and we all thought they made a lovely couple. They ate scrambled eggs, French fries and ice cream, colored, and played with Leo's sister, Ellie. Sophie showed off her new life-like "FurReal" guinea pig, which I think is really gross but Leo and Ellie appreciated. (Ray and Annabelle were at The Met with his aunt....)*

*We had a wonderful brunch and hung out at a bookstore and when Sophie and I said goodbye and settled into a cab, the song "Goodbye Girl" was playing and I had another cry—an I Heart New York But I Don't Live Here cry, thinking about that movie, which is one of the movies that made me fall in love with New York when I was a kid—and I thought, I bet this song makes Maya cry, too.*

Over the years, we all slowed down on the blogging, and some of the moms stopped entirely. Mostly, we all kept up with each other on Facebook. Maya got pregnant with twins, and we didn't talk as much. But when it came time to figure out where to send Leo to middle school, she texted me, and I teared up when she posted that he got to take part in the school spelling bee. She was always the best with a quip—like "I've decided that kid fashion is not a hill I want to die on" when I posted a photo of one of Sophie's more unfortunate outfit choices.

We've both shown our kids *Charlotte's Web* in its various forms—book, movie, remake, stage play—and I always think of Maya when I hear that last line:

"It's not often that someone comes along who is a true friend and a good writer. Charlotte was both."

She rescued me, Charlotte to my Wilbur. And on top of that, she's a kick-ass writer:

And then there's Elaine.

We also met online, but not because we both had kids with Down syndrome—her child does not. Instead, it was because we both had daughters named Sophie. WordPress hooked us up.

Elaine's Sophie is a few years younger than mine, and she started blogging about her little girl and motherhood. One day WordPress offered a "you might like this blog" plug and a link to my blog. Mom of Sophie, meet mom of Sophie!

Never mind that Sophie tops the charts for popular girl names in the last decade or so. It was a long shot that worked. Turns out, Elaine and I had a lot in common—both American Studies majors, both married to rock climbers, and eventually both parents to two kids. When Elaine and I first "met," Sophie was an only child. A year or so in, in 2011, Elaine posted a comment on one of my posts.

*…I have been meaning to write you a note myself. Because I'm 37 (nearly 38) and pregnant, my midwife has been encouraging me to get the non-invasive tests to check if my baby has the likelihood of chromosomal abnormalities. When she first asked if I wanted this, I said, "What would I possibly do with that information?" And then I realized the obvious answer: "I would phone up Amy Silverman and get even more tips than I've already gotten from her about how to parent a kid with Down syndrome, and I'd get myself as prepared as I could be for the adventure to come."*

*The tests came back negative, so my chances are down to 1 in 11,000 or so. But the nice thing was, it didn't really matter. Because reading your blog has made me think that parenting a kid with Down syndrome IS an adventure ("the best thing that ever happened to you," I think your profile used to say), not an easy adventure, but certainly one that I could embark on, knowing already to expect heart problems and social-service-negotiations and IEPs and struggles around friendships and finding fashionable eyeglasses and everything else you write about. It's an enormous demystification you're doing for all of us.*

*What could have been terrifying suspense in all those visits to various doctors' offices (drawing blood, measuring the fat-folds in the back of the fetus's neck, drawing more blood later…) became far less terrifying, because your blog has made Down syndrome seem so much less foreign to me.*

*I know I'm not quite your intended audience, if such a creature even exists. I don't live in Arizona, don't have a child with Down syndrome or any reason to care particularly about it—before this pregnancy at what I'm now learning is apparently old age. I just happened on your blog and loved your writing and your attitude.*

*And it turns out I've been learning a whole lot all along, from you, without realizing it.*

*Thanks.*

I was the one who needed to say thank you. Elaine gave me a great gift in that comment, validation that what I was writing mattered, and not just to another mom of a kid with Down syndrome. It was a wonderful moment.

A few months later, just before she gave birth to Everett, Elaine brought Sophie to meet us at the beach in San Diego. Coincidentally, we vacation near where she lives. This time my whole family was in on the meeting, and I wrote about it afterward on Girl in a Party Hat:

*"So this is like a blind date?" my sister asked, not entirely kindly, smoothing on another layer of sunscreen.*

*"No," I said, adjusting my sun hat a little nervously. "Of course not. That's ridiculous. Okay, sort of."*

*This was embarrassing. One of the completely unexpected things about writing this blog is the friends I've made through it. I'm not one for virtual friendship, really; I don't have enough time to see the brick-and-mortar friends I've got here in Phoenix. But Girl in a Party Hat has been a terrific way to create my own little Down syndrome support group at arm's length—right where I'm comfortable keeping it.*

*Elaine's different. The only thing we have in common is that we both have daughters named Sophie. And blogs about those daughters, which is how she stumbled on mine.*

*Her Sophie is exactly half the age of my Sophie. I've written about Elaine before, about what a gift her insights are to me, since I'd always hoped with this blog to reach people who don't have kids with Down syndrome. People like me, before I had my Sophie.*

*Elaine is an American Studies professor in Southern California and she's wicked smart and for years now we've sworn that we'll get together when my extended fam makes our annual trek to the beach.*

*This year it happened; Elaine and Sophie schlepped over and I was honored, particularly since Elaine's Sophie will soon have a little brother.*

*After five minutes, my entire family was enchanted by Elaine (including my sister), and the Sophies were fast friends—though my Sophie was, perhaps, a bit quick on the draw (and a little huggy) for her new young friend.*

*Right away we noticed that the two girls are exactly the same height.*

*It was a sweet visit, and too soon, it was time to go. Elaine packed up her beach gear, stuck Sophie's shoes on her feet, and they were off, amidst promises that we'd meet next time at Elaine's favorite taco shop.*

*I wasn't surprised that my Sophie spent the rest of the week begging for her new friend, but I wasn't sure how Elaine's Sophie felt about the encounter. Apparently, my Sophie made an impression, as well. The day after the visit, I got this note on Facebook from Elaine:*

*"My Sophie is pretending that two of her Lego people have Down syndrome. At least, I think that's what she is pretending.*

*"She told me, 'They are like Sophie, the Other Sophie from the beach. When they were in their mommy's tummy, they missed something, and now, even though they're eight-year-olds, they're not as big as an eight-year-old. And they really love to hug. And they're very happy.'*

*"These two Lego people also happen to be astronauts."*

I'm not going to say that all is pleasant online. I'm in some pretty scary Facebook groups. And as I've long known, having a child with Down syndrome is not enough to ensure we'll be fast friends, even if you do have a blog, too.

But for the most part I've learned to ignore the comments, and my tiny readership has made for friendly readers. I did have to end one online friendship after another mom of a kid with DS chose to comment on an Instagram photo of Sophie and her beloved elementary school principal that he looked like a pedophile and I better report him to the authorities. The man had been kind enough to show up for Sophie's pajama birthday party in one-piece, fuzzy purple PJs in 100-plus-degree heat. The man's a saint, not a sex offender. I blocked her.

My arm's-length relationships have given me a comfortably distant view of what it's like to be an adult with Down syndrome. I've long followed a wonderful blog called My Name Is Sarah, started by a mom and her adult daughter, Joyce and Sarah Ely. Sarah has DS and works in her mom's quilting shop; she has her own sewing lounge. Joyce (and sometimes Sarah) writes honestly about everything from Sarah's health scares to what it's like to be a member of the sandwich generation.

I messaged Joyce in the spring of 2015 to ask if she and Sarah were coming to Phoenix for the National Down Syndrome Congress's annual convention. For years, I'd been watching others post about attending the convention, but I'd never gotten the guts to even register, let alone book a flight. This time the convention was literally coming to my backyard. It had to be a sign.

Joyce and Sarah couldn't come. Neither could Maya. But several of my Facebook friends were coming, including Lisa.

Lisa and I had met before. She lived in Northern California and had come to Phoenix on business. We had lunch and compared notes and kids. Older daughters both named Annabelle Rose, two years apart; younger kids with Down syndrome, also separated by two years. Sophie was barely twelve; Cooper, almost fourteen, when they met.

We'd joked for months about planning a wedding and how much we'd love to be in-laws. But by the end of the weekend, it was clear that Sophie still had a crush on Niall from One Direction, and Cooper and I had had a lengthy conversation about supermodels. A connection was made, nonetheless. Lisa and I sat by the edge of the hotel swimming pool on a hot June night and watched the boy and girl, similar expressions framed by the pool light, as they played a clapping game.

It felt like a Ray Bradbury story, watching these two young people interact, so similar not just in the stereotypical Down syndrome ways but in other ways, too. It felt like they were from the same tribe.

The rest of the conference was overwhelming. I got that Goldilocks feeling, navigating the schedule and listening to speakers. Everything was either too inspirational or too scientific.

I sat in the lobby of a fancy Marriott with several of my Facebook friends and watched people come and go. It was surreal, like watching a movie of what my family must look like—groups of three or four people, parents and kids, and one of the kids looks a little or a lot like Sophie. We ordered cocktails and told stories, and that was good.

But I was happy to retreat to my safe place online after that.

# 9

## FLOATING UP THE (MAIN)STREAM

The night before Sophie's fifth birthday, I put her to bed and snuck a few more minutes with Annabelle—the privilege of being the older, almost seven-year-old sister.

"Sophie's turning five tomorrow," Annabelle said as we settled in on the big red couch in the living room.

"Yes."

"Is she really going to kindergarten? She doesn't talk very well."

"You know why that is, right?"

"No."

"Well, Sophie has Down syndrome. That makes her a little different from us, from other kids her age."

"Yeah."

Luckily, Ray had just come in from a bike ride. He was summoned to the couch, where he explained that every person starts with one cell, and that in Sophie's case, that cell was different, and, therefore, every part of Sophie is just a little bit different. Sometimes more than a little.

"Does that make you sad, that she's different?" I asked.

"No," Annabelle replied, matter of factly. "If that's her, that's her."

I hugged her and wished the rest of the world was as sensible. I also had to silently agree that I, too, wasn't so sure about this whole kindergarten thing. It was the end of May; the school year was a wrap. Preschool was over. Elementary school loomed large.

As I've already mentioned, the preschool administrators had been so encouraging about Sophie, telling me she was one of the smartest kids with Down syndrome they'd ever seen, that testing showed she didn't technically qualify as having an intellectual disability. Yet they had no intention of mainstreaming her at our home school with her sister. Instead, they wanted her in a self-contained classroom at another school.

*Mainstream her in kindergarten*, my new Facebook friends said in unison, a Greek chorus.

> *If it's ever going to work, it will work now.*
> *This might be your only chance.*
> *You don't know what will happen unless you try.*
> *Do it for Sophie.*
> *Try! Try! Try!*

I held my breath and insisted on the home school, hiding my panic when the principal warned, "Fine. But if Sophie wants to go to a typical school, she'll have to act like a typical kid."

"Of course," I said, nodding. I tried to smile. Instead, I should have walked out and hired a lawyer.

*lllll*

Special education laws in this country—when enforced—really are pretty awesome.

Technically speaking, the public school system is supposed to collaborate with parents and other members of a child's team (often including a principal, teachers, therapists, a school psychologist, parents, and sometimes the child herself) to ensure success by creating a custom-designed plan—an Individualized Education Program—a living, legal document that can be changed at any time to reflect new needs, knowledge, and skills.

And it's all supposed to happen without concern for cost. Really.

Yeah, you're thinking, and unicorns exist. But it's true. That's pretty much what the law requires. Of course, making it happen can be tricky. But it's true that special education law (in theory, anyway) has come a long way in a short time. So far, that reality often can't keep up.

In 1954, the U.S. Supreme Court took the first fundamental step in ending segregation based on race and ethnic background with its decision in Brown v. Board of Education. That ushered in the civil rights era and, years later, the notion that kids with special needs should—and could—be integrated into regular education settings. The simple idea that these kids should attend regular public schools did way more than simply put special-needs kids in the classroom; it helped to get them out of institutions and introduced them to their peers.

The Kennedy family's influence on quality of life for people with special needs extends beyond the Special Olympics playing field. John F. Kennedy deserves credit for advocating for special education during his presidency. At the end of the Eisenhower administration, a federal law was passed that funded training for teachers who were instructing students with mental retardation. Kennedy championed the increase of public awareness and expansion of federal laws to govern special education. Kennedy's administration created the

Division of Handicapped Children and Youth under the U.S. Department of Education.

In the '60s, it was a numbers game—namely, increasing the number of special-needs kids served in public schools. In an eight-year span, the number of school districts with special education programs increased from 3,641 to 6,711. In a three-year period, the number of teachers in special-needs schools and institutions went from 71,000 to 82,000.

That didn't mean the services provided were so hot. Far from it. For pretty much the first time, the idea occurred to more than a few do-gooders that children with developmental disabilities had a right to an education. It was an obvious, important first step, as states passed laws creating special education policies and communities began to recognize the contributions of people with developmental disabilities and other special needs.

In a 1964 textbook for teachers titled *A Time for Teaching*, Willard Abraham, the education professor at Arizona State University who had written that memoir about his daughter Barbara a few years earlier, reported that "trends in the education of mentally retarded children are encouraging."

"We have come a long way since the Middle Ages, when children and adults like these were the court fools and were denounced as 'evil spirits,' and since the days when persecutions were the rule," he wrote. "But our public and our teachers have…to accept the fact that children limited in mentality can be educated or trained."

By 1970, according to the U.S. Department of Education, only one in five children with disabilities (both physical and mental) was enrolled in public schools. Indeed, it took more than the legacy of an empathetic president and a sideways glance from the civil rights movement to cause much change. It took two landmark class-action lawsuits.

The first, Pennsylvania Association of Retarded Children v. the Commonwealth of Pennsylvania, was filed in 1971 by the Public Interest Law Center of Philadelphia over a state law that said

Pennsylvania didn't have to educate any child who hadn't reached the "mental age" of five by first grade. That lawsuit quickly ended in a consent decree in which the state agreed to provide a free public education to children with mental retardation.

The second lawsuit, Mills v. the Board of Education of the District of Columbia, ended in favor of the plaintiffs, as well, and specifically declared that money is no object in the education of children with mental retardation (as it was then called) or mental illness. Both cases provided impetus for Congress to pass the Education for All Handicapped Children Act in 1975. The law mimicked language in the court cases and was the first sweeping legislation passed to ensure appropriate education of these children. It serves as the framework for the current law, the Individuals with Disabilities Education Act, passed in 1997 and amended in 2004 (note the change from *Handicapped* to *Disabilities*).

The basic message: Figure out how to educate these kids alongside their peers, without regard for how much it costs. Of course, it's way more complicated than that—hundreds-of-pages-complicated— including several reauthorizations by Congress to tweak the law.

My challenge to educate Sophie began even before she was old enough to attend public school.

When she was two, I began looking for a preschool/childcare option that would be both safe and enriching. In 2003, the year she was born, no one told you to institutionalize your baby with DS. To the contrary, the advice from most quarters was to put her alongside her typical peers as much as possible.

But making that a reality was more difficult than I anticipated.

Frustrated with a lack of quality among some of the childcare centers I'd visited, I figured I'd go for broke. I called Awakening Seed, a prestigious, expensive private school well known in Phoenix as the place where progressive, well-educated parents sent their children from an early age.

I was shocked when the owner informed me, "We don't take children with Down syndrome" and then told me to call the state, which she assured me offered the services I was looking for. (The state didn't, by the way.)

From then on, I learned not to take any placement for granted. But that's not to say we didn't have tremendous luck. An early childhood program run out of Arizona State University had never had a child with Down syndrome, as far as I knew, but Sophie was accepted with open arms and thrived there. Yes, it was a challenge as other kids learned to walk, potty train, and replace sign language with spoken words while my child lagged in those areas. But her language and other comprehension skills developed quickly, and eventually, Sophie did walk, talk, and learn.

And then Sophie transitioned into a formal program run by our local public school district, a preschool that mixed kids with special needs with typical peers. She rode the bus every day, carrying a tiny backpack embroidered with her name, and learned how to unpack the backpack, keep still during circle time, and recite letters and numbers.

In many ways, she finished preschool better prepared for kindergarten than most of her typical peers. But the transition to kindergarten wasn't perfect. Unlike those who had not attended preschool, she knew classroom etiquette and was comfortable with teachers and peers. But while she was potty trained, she was way too small to climb onto the toilet in the kindergarten bathroom. The school agreed that she would be walked by another student to the nurse's office when she needed to use the bathroom. But that was the only accommodation they'd make. No aide, no extra help, unless it came from a five-year-old.

It might have all been okay if it hadn't been for lunch recess.

The first day of kindergarten, I helped Sophie get dressed in a polka-dotted top and skirt and matching tennis shoes with Velcro straps that I'd scored on the sale rack at the Gap, and convinced her to let me pull half her hair up off her face. At school, I felt other parents watching me, convinced, I was sure, that Sophie was someone's younger sister, not someone who belonged at this school. She was so much smaller than the other kindergarteners. I lurked in the corner of the classroom as the kids took their spots on the bright blue carpet.

The bell rang and the rest of the parents left, but I stayed. The principal's voice announced the pledge of allegiance over the loudspeaker, and to my surprise, of the two dozen students just one kid popped up, put her teeny tiny hand over her heart and began to recite along with the principal and teacher.

Sophie.

Well, at least preschool had taught her something, I thought, grinning through my tears as I slipped out the door to join some of my mom friends on the grass outside the classroom.

I worried a lot about the student-teacher ratio, but I wasn't worried about the teacher.

I had first spotted Jennifer Zamenski two and a half years earlier at Annabelle's kindergarten orientation night. The woman scared the crap out of me. Pretty and tall, with smooth blonde hair and long French manicured nails, Ms. Zamenski was loud and brash, announcing to a group of cowering parents that she didn't intend to take any flack from their kids. In contrast, the other kindergarten teacher at the event was older, demure and sweet, almost trilling her words. I expected birds to fly out from behind her, Disney-style.

I knew which teacher Annabelle had to have. But a few weeks later, I ran into an old acquaintance at Trader Joe's, a reporter for the local daily newspaper. Her son Sawyer was already at Broadmor, going into second grade.

"Hey, is she ready for kindergarten?" Karina asked, pointing at Annabelle. "You *must* request Jen Zamenski."

"Oh no, not her," I said. "Are you kidding? I heard her at orientation night. She's terrifying."

"Really? She's my best friend."

Awkward. Turns out, Karina's son Sawyer had been assigned to Ms. Zamenski's class, where he'd thrived. The two women now traveled together to Disneyland and Ms. Zamenski nannied for Sawyer in the summers. I took Karina's advice, and it was one of the single best decisions I ever made on my kids' behalf. Ms. Zamenski, as it turns out, is a strict but compassionate, dedicated teacher who adores her kids. I saw that with Annabelle, and even before Annabelle was done with her own kindergarten year, I saw it with Sophie.

In more than a decade of teaching, she'd only had one other student with Down syndrome, but Ms. Zamenski and Sophie had chemistry. From the day she met her, Sophie would pretty much do anything Jen said. Never before or since has anyone had that kind of sway with the kid. Jen couldn't wait to get Sophie in her kindergarten classroom, which was all I needed to know. Sophie was wanted.

When it was Sophie's turn at kindergarten, Ms. Zamenski invited her to come to her classroom before school started—even before Meet the Teacher Night—so she could get comfortable. She knew Sophie had trouble with scissors, so she got assignments ready ahead of time, modifying them so Sophie wouldn't have to struggle.

Late on the afternoon of the first day of school, my cell phone rang. She must have been exhausted, but Ms. Zamenski was calling to fill me in on Sophie's day, which had gone really well.

"Where are you?" I asked, hearing noise in the background.

Jen was at Wal-Mart, buying a stepstool.

"Some of the kids can't reach the sink in my classroom," she said. Later I realized it was probably Sophie who couldn't reach; I bet the rest did just fine.

As Sophie's future kindergarten teacher, Jen had been at a meeting the previous spring at Sophie's preschool where the occupational therapist had announced that Sophie would never write her name. "She'll have to make an X," she said.

I didn't forget that and apparently neither did Jen.

At the end of that first week, the phone rang.

"Guess what Sophie did today?" Ms. Zamenski asked. She sent home the proof, the letters large and crooked, faint in pencil, but discernible. I cried.

It was all good—except for thirty minutes a day: lunch and the recess that followed. The kids were expected to unpack and eat their lunches, pack up and throw trash away, and head out to the playground—all without assistance. I couldn't stop thinking about lunch. One wrong turn and Sophie would be on the street. I was worried, and I know Ms. Zamenski was, too. Any other time, she was around and she'd find Sophie—eventually. But lunch was her only break all day, a half hour mandated by the teachers association (Arizona is a right to work state; there are no unions).

A month into school, Sophie's IEP team met to see how things were going. (IEP stands for Individualized Education Program, the plan each qualifying special ed student must have in place.)

We began by reviewing Sophie's progress in therapy. I brought reports from her outside physical therapist and occupational therapist, and we went over her daily schedule and achievements in class. Everything was going well, I was assured.

Not long after the meeting began, the principal stepped outside. I knew she was busy; her job was obviously a demanding one and she had checked her phone several times already.

She never returned.

The principal hadn't said she needed to leave early. I wish she had, because I wouldn't have saved my most significant concerns for the end. But I was nervous. My main goal with this principal, with this school, had been to avoid rocking the boat. I was worried about sharing my concern about Sophie's safety at lunch.

We scheduled another meeting.

By that point, I was steaming. I'd spent time in the cafeteria, and what a mess. The lunch situation wasn't just unsafe for Sophie. I didn't see one kid finish his or her lunch. Probably a good thing, considering what they were serving—something that passed for a BBQ rib sandwich. I had to ask a kid what it was.

Sophie brought her lunch, mostly so I could put stuff in that she could eat easily and quickly. The day I visited, she ate half a mini-quiche. Raisins, cheese, and crackers were untouched.

I was practically thrown back against the wall when someone blew a whistle and most of the kids cleared out to the playground. Before the half hour was over, I'd clapped my hands over my eyes at least twice.

And then there was the playground. The day my mom visited, a little girl wet her pants. The day I was there, a kid fell and skinned her hand; the staff member on duty looked at me, unsure of what to do. I didn't know, either.

When we had the second IEP team meeting a week later, I explained all this to the principal. The ratio at the aftercare program at the school was 12 to 1, I said. What was the ratio at lunch? I guessed about 100 to 1.

The principal told me that legally, there was no ratio at lunch. And she told me that no, she could not assign someone to walk Sophie from the cafeteria to the playground each day.

"Are you sure?" I begged. "It would be half an hour a day to keep her safe at school."

No, she said. If Sophie couldn't act like a typical kid, we'd need to explore options elsewhere in the district.

I left the meeting and called the state department of education and confirmed that there was no student/adult ratio requirement at lunch at public schools in Arizona. I stayed up nights, trying to figure out what to do.

I couldn't bear the thought of sending Sophie to lunch alone another day. I couldn't leave work and drive across town each day to be there. I didn't want to pull her out of the school.

So I did the only thing I could think to do. I went rogue.

If the school wouldn't provide an aide for Sophie, I'd do it myself. I hired three college students to take turns "volunteering" in Sophie's classroom, deciding that as much as she loved and wanted Sophie, Ms. Zamenski did not have the time to keep an eye on her. She needed help.

No one ever asked why these sweet, energetic girls were so interested in helping out in Jennifer Zamenski's kindergarten class, or why they took such a specific interest in Sophie, particularly at lunch. They simply showed up for the shift I'd assigned them, signed in at the front desk and put on a big "volunteer" sticker. I'm sure there wasn't much legal about it, but it quickly became clear that we had a "don't ask, don't tell" policy—and no one ever asked, not as far as I knew.

The young women were instructed to hold back, not to hover over Sophie. To make sure she was safe, to help the teacher if she needed it. To keep an eye on Sophie—and to be my eyes and ears, too.

It wasn't cheap but it was worth every penny.

*eeeell*

I worried a lot about Sophie. I worried about Annabelle, too. This was the first time the two were attending school together. How would the other kids react?

I asked Annabelle about it every so often, trying not to make a big deal out of it. She was proud to be Sophie's "reading buddy," in the second-grade/kindergarten match-up, and aside from the occasional query about whether Sophie was a midget, there wasn't much to report.

When the science fair rolled around in late winter, the topic came up. Annabelle had originally decided to do a display on her fossil collection. I couldn't resist suggesting that she change her topic to Down syndrome and was surprised when she jumped at the idea.

It was fascinating, watching Annabelle process something I hadn't fully digested yet myself. One night she worked on a drawing—a family portrait—entitled, "Ahh…the life of…Down Syndrum Sister."

It depicts the four of us, lined up on a ski slope (Annabelle and Ray had gone recently for the first time). In the drawing, Annabelle's saying, "Wow! Steep!" I'm giving her advice: "Keep it steady," and Ray's warning, "Be careful." Sophie's at the end, clearly about to fall, yelling, "Mom! Dad! Help! Help!"

Ray wasn't so sure about the idea of a science fair project on Down syndrome and asked, "Will Sophie have to sit in the cafeteria for a week?"

Very funny.

But he played along, and even explained chromosomes to Annabelle. She titled her project "Up Down syndrome."

For the model accompanying the project, Annabelle created a karyotype—a design of the twenty-two chromosomes of a person with Down syndrome (minus the twenty-third, which determines sex).

She made the chromosomes out of wax-covered string. Then came the report:

*What is Down syndrome? You may ask. Well I will tell you. You see, if you have Down syndrome, you have one extra chromosome (which is a thread like looking thing that tells your body what you look like and other things) in your body. Which causes problems. See, I can't really tell you why it causes problems. Because scientists have not figured it out yet. But I know that I can tell you lots of other things about Down syndrome! When you have Down syndrome you look a little different from every body else. And it takes a little longer to learn as well as you and me do. But even though they look different, it doesn't mean that you can't like the same things and be friends. I even know someone that has Down syndrome! And I know her really well because she is my sister! Her name is Sophie. I hardly notice Sophie even has Down syndrome. She knows lots of cool and elegant words like "I think not!" She really cracks me up! And Sophie has lots of friends in kindergarden! And all of her friends like her alot! Sophie has special therapies to help her up! She has a great life! the end*

Sophie was talking more, taking pictures with my iPhone. One day she sat at the kitchen table with paper and pen and wrote "Gaga" (the girls' name for their grandmother). She turned to my mom and said, "G A, G A, that's a pattern!" My mom told the story for days.

Then there was the day that Sophie punctuated for the first time. Ms. Zamenski called to report that Sophie wrote, "I am at Gaga's" and then paused and turned to the teacher.

"I'm excited!" she announced and then drew an exclamation point at the end of the sentence.

"I put on an exciting mark!" she announced.

That's what all the kindergarteners call it, Ms. Zamenski explained before I could protest.

And for a split second, Sophie was just like all the other kids.

The school year had rounded the halfway bend, which meant the end was well in sight. Funny how it works that way. In February it's time to sign up for summer camp.

And it was time to think about the next school year.

I was hopeful that Sophie was on track to stay at this school, to advance to a typical first-grade classroom, but I was constantly worried, too. Maybe she should stay in kindergarten forever? Or at least another year?

So I was already nervous when Ms. Zamenski asked me to meet her for coffee one morning before school. She was uncharacteristically vague and formal. All she said was that we'd be discussing Sophie's progress, which had been great, and that I was not to worry.

I was petrified.

There was definitely an argument to be made for holding Sophie back for another year.

Or what if Ms. Zamenski was going to suggest that Sophie go someplace else entirely the next year? I didn't want her at a strange school, warehoused in a self-contained program. I wanted the girls to stay at the same school as long as possible. Just days earlier, we'd been going through the valentines they each had collected at school, and stuck in Annabelle's folder was one for Sophie.

It didn't say much, just "To Annabelle's Sister Sophie," signed by a kid I've never really spoken to (not the mom, either).

But for me, it said it all.

When I arrived at Starbucks, Ms. Zamenski was already stirring her oatmeal and complaining bitterly about how they were out of Venti cups. We chatted about random stuff until I couldn't stand it anymore; then finally I said, "OK, what about Sophie?"

She took a deep breath. She admitted that she'd been avoiding me, some, the last few weeks, because she was really thinking hard and doing research and observing Sophie. Also holding back from Sophie herself, to see if Sophie was able to do tasks on her own.

And her conclusion, she said, was that Sophie would be ready for first grade the next fall.

"Don't decide anything today," Ms. Zamenski said as I sat there, stunned. She explained her thought processes on the whole thing—that Sophie had mastered her kindergarten academics (knew her letters, numbers, sounds) and needed extra help in writing, but was already able to compose simple sentences.

Perhaps even more important, the teacher added, was the social element. When Sophie began kindergarten, Jen expected that if the kids interacted with her, it would be in strictly a caregiver role. That had happened some, but increasingly, she said, Sophie was relating to this group as peers.

As friends.

"She leads the kids in 'duck, duck, goose' and they play on the playground together," Ms. Zamenski said. "They aren't just taking care of her."

"So you don't think she needs to go to the school for the retarded kids?" I asked.

"No," she said, shaking her head. "I don't."

What do you say to the person who gives you that gift? I couldn't think of a thing, so I gave Ms. Zamenski a hug as we got up to leave. And when she noticed they'd finally gotten some Venti cups in, I bought her another iced coffee—to go. It was time for school.

Sophie's sixth birthday fell on the last day of school. I knew what was going to happen—Ms. Zamenski had the same tradition every year—but I still wasn't prepared. I snuck into the classroom, which was a disaster, with empty bulletin boards and half-filled boxes ready to pack up for the summer.

First the class sang happy birthday to Sophie and to all the kids with summer birthdays. Then Ms. Zamenski settled into her rocking chair and read A. A. Milne's poem "The End."

> *When I was One,*
> *I had just begun.*
> *When I was Two,*
> *I was nearly new.*
> *When I was Three,*
> *I was hardly me.*
> *When I was Four,*
> *I was not much more.*
> *When I was Five,*
> *I was just alive.*
> *But now I am Six,*
> *I'm as clever as clever,*
> *So I think I'll be six now for ever and ever.*

I really didn't get too upset during the final good-byes. Each child was called to the front of the room, wearing his or her backpack, and asked to turn around, so Ms. Zamenski could place a folder with Important Papers like report cards and a summer reading list in the backpack.

Then the child turned back around and could choose a handshake, high five, or hug from Ms. Zamenski.

Almost every kid chose a hug.

By the middle of first grade, I ditched my makeshift "volunteer" system. It was getting expensive, and I wasn't so sure Sophie needed it anymore. She was spending time each day in the resource room with the special education teacher, getting extra instruction in math and reading, and it seemed to work to have her peers help her at lunch.

But second grade was tough. The teacher who had seemed so sweet and unflappable when Annabelle had had her two years earlier clearly struggled to get Sophie to follow classroom rules and sit still for lessons.

It was time to change things up, to call in reinforcements. This was a potential war, and I figured I had only one strike; I had better be strategic. I decided to go nuclear. I did my homework and hired the best special education lawyer in town.

Over the next several years, Lori Bird would be incredibly helpful, less with regard to big legal issues and more with regard to the nuances of special education law and writing IEP goals. But at that first meeting, it was her mere presence I was paying for.

Word that a lawyer was coming to Sophie's IEP meeting freaked out the powers that be at the school and above more than I anticipated. The school district sent over its own lawyer, along with the district's director of special education. And a tape recorder, placed in the middle of the table. I put my own next to it.

But I knew it was a big deal to ask for an aide.

Of all the issues that confound school professionals and parents and that lead to debate over interpretations of the laws that govern special education services, the most difficult is the classroom aide. And that's what I wanted.

I got it. I was shocked. For all the pomp and circumstance of that particular IEP meeting—on both sides—the discussion about whether Sophie needed an aide was congenial and quick. *Yes,* they said. *She needs an aide in order to continue to succeed at this school, and this school is the best place for her.*

One thing you always hear is that an aide isn't enough—it has to be the right aide. In order to put the child in the least restrictive setting, the aide needs to be sensitive to pulling back and only jumping in when necessary. We lucked out. I had no influence in the hiring of the aide, but someone chose right. Lynn Wright was quiet and wise, a mom with grown children of her own. Years later, I learned that her son had learning disabilities and she hadn't known how to fight for him when he was in school. She saw Sophie as a "do over," and the two developed an amazing bond, even though Mrs. Wright was so subtle that Sophie didn't realize for years that she was there specifically for her.

Looking back, I am convinced that getting an aide is the thing that allowed Sophie to finish school at Broadmor, to learn and grow and feel so comfortable.

The aide—plus pretty much every other person at the school.

One day toward the end of fifth grade, Sophie asked Ray to print the lyrics to the song "Counting Stars," explaining that she and her choir teacher were working on a private arrangement. She was that comfortable with everyone at the school—but most particularly, Jen Zamenski. Each year, Ms. Zamenski would invite Sophie in at the beginning of school to introduce her to her students, explaining that they were great friends and that Sophie would be stopping by often. She was a regular visitor, looking for a cuddle and lotion on her chapped skin.

The daily visit to Ms. Zamenski was not Sophie's only ritual. She had special games, secret handshakes, and shared jokes all over campus. "Como estas?" she called to Amparo, the crossing guard, each morning, then replied, "Bien!" just as Amparo had taught her.

Sophie's rituals were bittersweet—in some ways immature, in others loving. "They are her way of refusing to be invisible," my friend Trish commented once, after telling me that every time Sophie comes to her house, she asks Trish to explain the ingredients in the homemade barbeque sauce she made for Sophie years ago. I cringe when I hear of things like that, but Trish said she didn't mind, it made her know that Sophie loves her.

"It's a really important way that she's staking out her identity," Trish said. We want that for our kids, we both agreed, but we also want them to grow out of it.

As Sophie's days at Broadmor waned, I silently counted down her final visits to Ms. Zamenski's room and wondered how she'd ever be able to leave all those rituals. And whether she'd be able to find new ones in middle school.

# 10

## THAT'S SO RETARDED

By third grade, Sophie had become a bit of a tattletale.

"Someone used a really bad word at school today," she told me one evening after dinner.

"What word?"

"The S word!"

"Really?" I said. I was sort of surprised my eight-year-old knew the word *shit*. Then again, I had taken her to work at the newspaper with me on occasion. I had to ask to be sure.

"What's the S word, Sophie?"

"Oh, I can't say."

"C'mon. It's okay. It's just us."

"Okay," she said, looking around to make sure no one else heard, before stage-whispering her answer. "Stupid."

Before I could think, I blurted out, "Did someone call you stupid?"

"No," she said, looking surprised. It had nothing to do with her. She'd just overheard the word *stupid*.

"That's not a nice word," she told me.

"You're right," I replied. "It's not."

I hugged her tight, feeling proud of my sweet, sensitive kid—and also a little horrified.

Are we raising humanitarians or wusses? I asked myself silently, kissing the top of her head. Pretty soon, there won't be any words left.

I was still mourning the loss of the word *retarded*. I don't remember ever using the word as a pejorative in my life, but I know I must have, because years after I stopped (upon the occasion of Sophie's diagnosis), I would still find it on the tip of my tongue, feel myself craving it like a cigarette. *Retarded* is rich, satisfying in its cruelty. It's a word that gets its point across, perfect when you're describing a particularly devastating move by an Arizona politician or that guy who just cut you off in traffic. Sometimes there's no good substitute— and yet it's gone.

Like a former cigarette user offended by second-hand smoke, I became the first with a dirty look or an admonition when I heard someone else use it. Hey, if I can't say "retarded," then neither can you.

And neither should you. As Sophie's mom, there's so much I can't do to make the world more accepting—but I can make damn sure you quit using that fucking word.

I get it. I get that words hurt.

But *stupid?* That's a tough one. Really, I can't use it anymore? After that conversation with Sophie, I thought about it for days, caught myself every time I used the word, took note when others did. I started thinking about all the other euphemisms for *stupid*—*dumb, idiot, moron, imbecile*—and the more creative ones like *mouth breather* and *drooler*.

And then I felt sick. It's commonly assumed that people with Down syndrome have above-average-sized tongues, because they often protrude from their mouths. The truth is that there's nothing different about their tongues; but people with Down syndrome do tend to have smaller mouths, making it appear as though they have super-long tongues. They also can have breathing problems because all of their openings—including nasal passages—tend to be smaller than average. And because they have weaker immune systems, they tend to get more colds. That's why you'll often see a person with Down syndrome mouth breathing. Or drooling.

I ran across a list on Wikipedia of "disability-related terms with negative connotations":

Blind, crazy, cretin, cripple, daft, deaf and dumb, deaf-mute, deformed, derp, differently abled, the disabled, disabled people, dumb, epileptic, feeble-minded, fit, freak, gimp, gimpy, handicapped, hare lip, hysterical, imbecile, incapacitated, idiot, invalid, lame, lunatic, looney, mad, maniac, mental, mentally deficient, mentally defective, mentally disabled, mentally deranged, mentally ill, midget, mongol, mongoloid, mongolism, moron, nuts, patient, psycho, psychotic, retarded, schizo, schizoid, schizophrenic, simpleton, slow, spastic, spaz, special, stupid, sperg, sufferer, tard, victim, whacko, wheelchair bound, Yuppie flu, zip.

That's when I started using the word *ridiculous* a lot. I couldn't think of anything else to say.

Of all the words used to describe people who are differently abled, *retarded* currently tops society's list as most offensive.

That was not always the case. The word *retarded* has a slang-free history. For a long time it simply meant slow.

According to the Oxford English Dictionary, it's derived from the Italian word *ritardato,* and the first definition of the adjective version is "held back or in check; hindered, impeded; delayed, deferred."

It's traced to religion in 1636 ("he to his long retarded Wrath gives wings"); to medicine in 1785 ("Polypus, sometimes obstructs the vagina, and gives retarded labour"); and later to politics ("Arguably, the legacy of communism manifests itself most acutely in the retarded economic development of the east").

It also means "characterized by deceleration or reduction in velocity," as in a 1674 reference: "When it hath passed ye vertex ye motion changeth its nature, & turneth from an equably accelerated into an equably retarded motion."

Actual references to retarded intelligence did not come until the turn of the twentieth century.

Tim Shriver, head of the Special Olympics, ties that to the development of IQ tests, which he discussed in his 2013 speech in Phoenix.

IQ tests first became popular at the turn of the twentieth century. And that led to a whole new toolbox full of terminology.

"The words we use in common language—imbecile, idiot, retard—these are medical terms developed around the turn of the last century to classify people with intellectual differences according to their IQ," Shriver said.

"All of a sudden we get classifications, we get labels. They are quite horrible. And the labels lead to this idea that people are somehow lower and lower in the value chain...and become more and more desirable to get rid of."

As noted above, the terms *idiot* and *imbecile* are no longer formally used. But *mental retardation* remained an acceptable medical term until very recently. While I immediately struck the terms *retard* and *retarded* as slurs from my vocabulary, in my earlier work about Sophie I routinely used *mentally retarded* to describe her medical condition (which, as noted in Chapter 7, got awkward when for a time Sophie actually didn't qualify as such).

When I first heard noise about officially switching the accepted term from *mentally retarded* to *intellectually disabled* or *cognitively disabled,* I balked. I thought the Arizona Legislature's time and money could be better spent creating and funding programs for these often-neglected people, rather than debating what to call them. And I actually liked (and continue to like) the term *mentally retarded.* I think it does a better job than the others of describing what the situation is. In some ways, Sophie is slower than the rest of us in our house. I can live with that more easily than *intellectually disabled*—I don't like either of those words.

Plus, I wondered, how long was it going to be before kids were calling each other "cog" on the playground? A friend pointed out that "cog" would actually be a compliment, so probably never. But you know what I mean.

As a parent of a kid with Down syndrome, I have naming issues aside from how Sophie's IQ is addressed. How should we refer to a person with her genetic condition? J. Langdon Down came up with the term *mongolism,* because he believed the condition he'd identified was marked by features similar to those of the Mongol people, and because these people he was working with were slower mentally, he believed this to be sign of racial regression. Gross, huh? And then the syndrome was officially named after him. This makes little sense to me. Why not name it after Jerome Lejeune, the man who put that theory to rest once and for all by discovering the third twenty-first chromosome? Or just call it trisomy 21?

And then there's the whole "people first" thing.

In any case, the R-word train left the station without me. Before I could decide how I really felt about it, there were campaigns everywhere to get rid of it completely. It also departed without a man named Christopher Fairman.

Fairman, a professor at Ohio State's law school, literally wrote the book on the word *fuck.* I was kind of in awe after I learned that. His book, *Fuck,* is a historical, political, and legal account of how the word became taboo—and why, in his view, it shouldn't be.

He felt the same about the word *retarded.* His article on the topic was published in *The Washington Post* in February 2010, the month before Tim Shriver's Special Olympics launched a special awareness day for its "Spread the Word to End the Word" campaign, and months before President Obama signed legislation officially removing the word from federal legalese. (Arizona followed suit in 2011, and by then many states had as well, although as of this writing, a few had not.)

Fairman asked if the word *retard* had only weeks to live, referring to the most recent controversy over the word.

Just a couple weeks before Fairman's piece was published, Rahm Emanuel, then the White House chief of staff, had apologized to Tim Shriver and people with disabilities everywhere after the *Wall Street Journal* reported that Emanuel had called a group of liberals "fucking retards" at a private meeting held the previous summer.

The conservatives—usually the politically incorrect name callers—had a field day with this one. A democrat at the highest level of government dissing members of his own party with such language? Classic.

Things escalated, as Fairman explained, when former GOP vice presidential candidate Sarah Palin, who has a son with Down syndrome, "quickly took to Facebook to demand Emanuel's firing, likening the offensiveness of the R-word to that of the N-word. [Rush] Limbaugh seized the low ground, saying he found nothing wrong with 'calling a bunch of people who are retards, retards,' and Palin rushed to his defense, saying Limbaugh had used the word satirically. Comedy Central's Stephen Colbert took her up on it, calling Palin an '[expletive] retard' and adding, with a smile: 'You see? It's satire!'"

Can you see how the word *ridiculous* just doesn't begin to cover it?

"I sympathize with the effort," Fairman continued, "but I won't be making that pledge. It's not that I've come to praise the word 'retard'; I just don't think we should bury it. If the history of offensive terms in America shows anything, it is that words themselves are not the culprit; the meaning we attach to them is, and such meanings change dramatically over time and across communities."

He made a good case, mentioning how *mental retardation* was actually meant to supplant *imbecile, moron,* and *idiot*—in a good way. And he took issue with Palin's comparison of *retard* to the word *nigger*.

"In some respects, the comparison seems overblown. The N-word invokes some of the foulest chapters in our nation's history; 'retard,' however harsh, pales in comparison."

And then he recounted a story in which a political staffer was forced to resign after using the term *niggardly*—an unfortunate choice of words, perhaps, but not technically an offensive choice. *Niggardly* means stingy or cheap and is supposedly derived from the Norse verb *nigla*. (The staffer was ultimately reinstated.)

Ultimately, Fairman argued, getting rid of the word *retard* won't get rid of the sentiment behind it.

"If interest groups want to pour resources into cleaning up unintentional insults, more power to them; we surely would benefit from greater kindness to one another," Fairman concluded. "But we must not let 'retard' go without a requiem. If the goal is to protect intellectually disabled individuals from put-downs and prejudice, it won't succeed. New words of insult will replace old ones."

Christopher Fairman also talked about efforts to reclaim words like *nigger* and *gay*. Could the same be done with *retard?* Good question.

I wanted to ask him about it, but he passed away in the summer of 2015.

I found an expert close to home. Amy Shinabarger is a lecturer in the English department at Arizona State University and a socio-linguist. We met at a coffee shop in Tempe near ASU, and by the time I arrived, a little late, Shinabarger was settled into a worn leather couch. She has wavy, blonde hair and several striking tattoos, including a large purple looking-glass and several words I couldn't quite make out; I tried not to stare.

The words seemed fitting for a socio-linguist and I knew she was the real deal when Shinabarger raised her eyebrows when I told her Sophie's name. She obviously knew that Sophie is the French version of *Sophia,* "wisdom" in Greek.

"Yeah, I know," I said. "I actually asked my husband if he thought we should change it."

Shinabarger majored in journalism as an undergraduate at ASU, but fell in love with an introductory linguistics class. She explained that a socio-linguist looks at how people use words. "It is humanities but also social science and biological science," she said, adding that she surprises her dentist on a regular basis. "I know anatomy really well."

She explained that hers is a qualitative field, not quantitative, because if you ask people about their word usage, they tend to self-edit. It's hard to study. Shinabarger is particularly interested in how people use words at home.

So, I asked, do words come back from the grave?

Yes, she said, they definitely have within the gay community.

"They'll call each other faggots and 'mos and dykes," she said. Shinabarger is not gay herself, but she has what she calls "protected ally status"—her friends say it's okay for her to use the word *queer*. She did so sparingly, she said.

Then there's the whole movement to reclaim the word *cunt,* she said.

I cringed visibly at that one. I think of myself as pretty open to language and have the potty mouth to prove it, but there are a few words that have always stopped me short. Like *cunt.*

And I found, to my embarrassment, that as we moved into a discussion about the word *retard,* I have developed the habit of referring to it as the R-word.

"So uncool!" I taunted myself silently. "Not in front of the socio-linguist!"

New habits die hard.

Shinabarger echoed Fairman's philosophy. She said that *mentally retarded* is a medical term, whereas *nigger* is not. That's the word where she draws the line, she said, although she does have African American friends who use it.

*Retard* doesn't bother her as much, she said, but admitted she's not a big fan of it as a noun, or of its increasingly common abbreviation, *tard.*

"We don't even need the 're'—that's how powerful the word has become," she said.

We also discussed *fucktard,* a particularly nasty one, and a play on the word that some of her gluten-intolerant friends had adopted, *glutard.* Those friends asked her to call them *glutards,* Shinabarger said, shaking her head. She couldn't.

We did pause for a moment to agree that it was a pretty accurate, descriptive word. Gluten does slow those people down.

Shinabarger wasn't about to start calling people glutards and fucktards, but she didn't want to ban the R-word, either.

"Any time a word is banned, something else steps in to take its place," she said, adding that she often asked her students, "Do you want to have the power or do you want the word to have the power over you?"

Shinabarger made reference to a Lewis Carroll exchange between Humpty Dumpty and Alice:

"'When I use a word,' Humpty Dumpty said in rather a scornful tone, 'it means just what I choose it to mean—neither more nor less.'

"'The question is,' said Alice, 'whether you can make words mean so many different things.'

"'The question is,' said Humpty Dumpty, 'which is to be master—that's all.'"

I get that, I said. But what about Sophie? Could Sophie reclaim the word *retard?*

"I think it could be done."

I sat for a minute, staring at my iced tea and then asked, "Why would you want to be called a retard?"

"But then why," Shinabarger asked, "would somebody want to be called a bitch?"

*lllll*

So here's the thing. I don't want to be called a bitch. I'm not about to use the words *nigger* or *cunt,* and I'm happy to use the most acceptable current terminology for homosexual. If you're gay, call yourself whatever you want.

Which raises what to me is the fundamental question. If you have an intellectual disability, do you have the ability to choose what you are called? The answer is complicated. Using words is hard enough. Reclaiming them is a real mindfuck. Will Sophie ultimately be capable of such nuanced reasoning? Maybe. I don't know.

But I do know for sure that I've met plenty of people with intellectual disabilities—and so have you—who are most definitely not able to make that kind of choice. Some people can't speak at all. What are we going to do, reclaim the word *retard* and paste it on their foreheads?

No, we are not. We—and not just we as their families but we as a society—are charged with protecting them, with making decisions for them. And the truth is that while convincing people to stop using the R-word is not, in and of itself, going to create acceptance, Tim Shriver and the Special Olympics and a lot of other interest groups focused on people with intellectual disabilities have, at the same time, launched programs designed to educate the public about these people, to bring them out of the shadows and on to television, the runway, and the playing field, and that is what will have a lasting impact.

And these people who see these people with special needs, who want to do something to honor them, have an easy choice in one respect: they can choose to not use the word *retarded.*

Has this ended prejudice? No. But I can tell you (from a qualitative, not quantitative analysis) that in the months leading up to the writing of this chapter, I heard the word *retard* less and less. In fact, in eight months, the only time I can recall hearing it was out of the mouth of a new employee at the newspaper.

She was almost thirty, a dancer, tall, elegant, and soft spoken, with a degree from the same fancy journalism school I attended. Rumor (which turned out to be true) had it that she was quite religious. It was her very first day on the job, and I'd taken her out to lunch, where we talked about time she'd spent recently as a journalist in Egypt.

After lunch I got her a keycard so she could enter the building on her own. I left her in the lobby to use the bathroom and joked that we'd see if she could find her way in alone, using the keycard to access the security system.

She couldn't; there was something wrong with the keycard.

"I'm so retarded!" she called down the hallway when we finally found each other.

"Yes, you are!" I wanted to respond, but instead I just shrugged and looked away. It was her first day, after all.

No matter how hard we try, we won't get rid of the word. And I'm not so sure we should. It is a part of our history and to deny it, to erase it, would be dangerous. I learned that lesson when Sophie's fourth-grade class read the book *Because of Winn-Dixie,* a story about a young girl who moves to a new town and learns to adjust, published in 2000. The book is a classic, an award winner, and the word *retarded* appears in Chapter 13.

I absolutely adored Sophie's fourth-grade teacher. Annabelle had Amy Wisehart first, and we found her to be strict but kind, a mom of boys who wrote thank-you notes on Olivia the Pig stationery and loved both my girls; she made sure Sophie was in her homeroom. I knew the kids were in good hands, but still, I was taken aback when I saw "the word." I opened my laptop and wrote an e-mail:

*Tonight Sophie and I read Chapter 13 together—actually, I began by reading it aloud. I was glad I did because I noticed the word "retarded" is used a couple times. I have real issues with that word, as you might imagine, but as a journalist by training I am also not at all in favor of censorship—particularly of books! (Although to be totally honest, I do ask people to consider not using the word "retarded" when I hear it in public or see it on Facebook—which happens a lot) but I'm curious: How do you handle it when the word comes up in class, if it does, in the context of discussing the book? I don't know if Sophie knows the word or if she'd ask about it; probably not. But I'm guessing some kids in 4th grade do.*

*I hope that question isn't too much—curious to hear what you think!*

She wrote back immediately, and for me, it will always be the best thing I've read about the R-word:

*As you know, now that we are entering the realm of big kid books and all of their glory, we will come across a few words that we would never utter and definitely find offensive. There will be many a discussion this year about words that authors feel they need to include, how the characters react, how we feel about them, and how they are treated in our society. Each year we encounter the "r-word" and I am kind of bummed that it is in Winn-Dixie right off the bat….I am totally open to your suggestions…but here is how I have traditionally handled it. I talk about how words can change meaning throughout time based on how it's used. I tell them about my parents' friend Gay [that's her first name] and my former coworker Linda Gay [it's her last name] and how the word gay has gone from being a word that meant happy and was acceptable in names, literature, and daily use. In more recent years, some people use the word as a derogatory name and to pick on others. Then I talk about the r-word…in the book. I talk about flame retardant pajamas and how retardant means to slow down to give them a round-about definition. Typically I avoid saying that it was a word used to describe people with a cognitive disability. I share that some people, kids and grownups, without seeming to find offense with it, call friends and others the R-word or say they are so r-ded. I talk about how this truly is a hateful word and is just as bad a word as they can imagine and that we need to tell people when we hear them say it that it's not OK to say. I also tell them that if they hear anyone use it at school, it is a super bad word and they need to tell a teacher. (Side Note: Usually I don't give a consequence the first time if they were not part of this conversation but use it as an opportunity to have this talk.)*

*That's pretty much how I've discussed it in the past. Not too much opportunity for them to share because I don't want them to tell me where they've heard it, that's too sad.*

# 11

## THERE WILL BE
## BLOOD

"It's not a graduation, Mom, it's a celebration!" Sophie corrected me in her best annoyed tween voice as we approached the school gym on a hot Thursday in May, days before the end of fifth grade, and days before the end of Sophie's time at Broadmor Elementary School.

Technically, she was right. There were no diplomas or mortar boards. But as my eyes welled with tears, I knew there was nothing celebratory about this. Not for me, anyway. This was a rite of passage for which I was not prepared.

Sophie was excited enough for both of us. She'd actually brushed her hair and put on a dress with a flippy blue chiffon skirt and a purple flower on the chest, like a corsage. She ran ahead and, with considerable effort, opened the heavy door to the gym, skidding across the linoleum to take her spot among her classmates. After six years, Sophie knew every inch of this school, navigated the hallways and stairwells with ease. And every inch of the school knew her.

Ray, Annabelle, and I took our places in the audience, saying hi to other parents, waving to teachers. Knowing we'd be late, because we're always late, our friends Gilda and Jeremy had saved us seats; we've been close since Annabelle and their daughter, Teadora, struck up a friendship in first grade. Their younger daughter, Gracie, and Sophie are tight, too. Gilda had brought Sophie a bouquet of purple flowers, her favorite color.

I was sobbing even before I sat down, fully aware of what a jackass I was making of myself. But I couldn't stop. A friend sitting in front of me ran to the bathroom for toilet paper. The principal appeared, purposely staring in the other direction, holding out a box of Kleenex. He couldn't look at me, he said in a small voice, or he'd start crying, too.

The original principal at Broadmor was a dud, not welcoming at all—she's the one who told me Sophie would have to act like a typical kid or go elsewhere. Barry Fritch was a different story; he'd arrived when Sophie was in fourth grade, and it was love at first sight. Sophie and Mr. Fritch share a birthday. He's the one who'd come to her birthday pajama party in a pair of fuzzy purple onesie pajamas. As far as Sophie was concerned, the guy hung the moon, and I was inclined to agree. Sophie's kindergarten teacher, Ms. Zamenski, was there, too—I saw her, and the tears started up again.

It was a simple event, with cardboard stars taped to the walls and folding chairs, bouquets of red, silver, and black balloons flanking each side of the stage. The sound system didn't work very well, but I could still hear each kid's name as he or she was called: a hundred or so fifth graders in all, most of them kids Sophie had known since kindergarten.

One by one, the students crossed the stage, solemnly shaking hands with each of the three fifth-grade teachers and then the principal, before taking their seats again. As they walked up to accept their accolades, I noticed how tall some of the boys were, how a few of the girls were just starting to develop. But for the most part, at age eleven, they were all still little kids.

Not like Sophie. Sophie was still the size of a kindergartener, the smallest by several inches. When it was her turn, she walked across the stage just like every other kid, marching proudly in her tiny, Guatemalan-print Toms espadrilles, her chiffon skirt swishing. But when the first teacher held out a hand to shake, Sophie ignored that, hugging the woman instead. She hugged the other two teachers, too, then threw her arms around Mr. Fritch and refused to let go until he gently peeled her arms from around his waist and sent her back to her seat.

Although the audience had been asked not to clap till the end, Sophie got a big round of applause. I smiled through my tears. Onstage, she settled back onto her folding chair, and I thought for the millionth time about how comfortable she was at this place, with these people. I couldn't bear the thought of leaving, of ever having to drop her off in front of another school. My heart beat so hard that I wondered if I was on the verge of a full-blown panic attack.

There were speeches about how much the kids had learned, how much they'd grown, how ready they were for middle school. All around me, other parents dabbed their eyes and nodded. I continued to sob, struggling to catch my breath.

I tried to take Ray's hand, but it was stiff; he was staring straight ahead, face hard, expressing his angst in his own way. I wanted to focus on the speeches, but I could feel the walls closing in around me. How could this be happening? There's been a mistake, I wanted to scream. Sophie wasn't ready to leave elementary school. She still sucked her thumb. She could barely write a paragraph. She didn't know math. She came up to the other kids' armpits (or belly buttons). How could anyone think she was ready to go to middle school?

Logically, I knew she was ready—as ready as she was going to be, anyway. Although she'd trailed her peers in academics every year since kindergarten, Sophie was never asked to repeat a year of school. As I had been told so many years ago, that's how it works with a kid with an intellectual disability; she simply falls behind, never to quite catch up.

Everything was in place for the next step in Sophie's education, whether I liked it or not. The previous day, I'd sat through a transition meeting in the library of the middle school Sophie would attend. All the plans were made for a personal aide, for extra help in math. There was talk of starting a special program to introduce Sophie and other kids with disabilities to their typical classmates. The people at that meeting were very nice, but they didn't know Sophie the way the people at Broadmor did. I wasn't sure they ever would.

Broadmor was our world. My eyes darted around the room, blinking through tears at the fluorescent lights, knowing the celebration was coming to an end and willing it not to, desperately wondering how I could make time slow down.

It was like that recurring nightmare I still have about high school, the one where someone has realized years later that I really shouldn't have passed Algebra 2, and I've been hauled back to the classroom to finish my work. Or a similar one where I'm back in college—eating in the dining hall, sleeping in the dorm—because someone has just noticed I should have failed Italian. Only this was the opposite. Sophie was being drop-kicked from the nest, and I was racing around underneath it, trying to catch her, terrified she'd crash to the ground.

This was no dream. This was real life.

No more picture books or monkey bars. It was time for Sophie to grow up, whether I was ready or not.

I still remember the very moment I began to worry about Sophie growing up—and realized just how ill-equipped I was to deal with it.

When Sophie was about three weeks old, I was driving fast on the freeway, headed to the office or my mom's or Target—I don't recall where. Some place, any place. The destination didn't matter as much as the fact that I'd escaped from the house alone. On the freeway, I had time to think about what it meant that I'd had this baby who wasn't perfect, who had this thing, Down syndrome, that I knew absolutely nothing about.

It was during one of those thinking-and-driving sessions that it suddenly hit me. I *did* know someone with Down syndrome. Well, I didn't know her personally, but I'd certainly spent time observing her.

Her name was Jill, and she was the subject of a 1960s instructional video called *Pink Slip*—the kind they show in grade school during Sex Ed, specifically the "what's happening to me" session.

Only this one was designed specifically for girls with intellectual disabilities. I didn't even know at the time I first saw the video that Jill had Down syndrome—only that she was slow. And that the film was hilarious.

The whole family gets in on the act: Jill, her older sister, Susie, and both of their parents. The video is only a few minutes long, and the repetition is what makes it so funny. All three of them (Susie and the parents) keep telling Jill that once a month she will bleed. They show her a giant calendar. Then Susie takes Jill into the bathroom and pulls down her pants to reveal that she, Susie, is menstruating—and wearing a giant pad—and shows her how to use feminine products.

Like I said, hilarious.

Watching instructional videos about how to teach girls with Down syndrome about menstruation was what passed as entertainment in my world when I was in my twenties.

My friends and I didn't just watch that video once (and I do mean video; the friend who ordered a copy out of a catalog somewhere got it on VHS). We showed it at parties.

Remembering this, I felt like I was going to throw up. Was I going to have to find a copy of *Pink Slip* to show Sophie when she was ready to get her period? Suddenly, none of it was funny anymore.

I vowed that when the time came, I was going to find something better than *Pink Slip*. There had to be. Already, Ray and I had been bombarded with books about development in babies with Down syndrome, with phone numbers for therapists and specialists who would help with early intervention.

It's weird. The information, the help—even the interest—gradually expires as your kid with Down syndrome gets older. Babies and kids with Down syndrome are adorable, angelic, loads of fun. Teenagers and adults? Not so much. I realized it a long time ago. Ray did too, and began to warn me that Sophie's elementary school years were her salad days, her pinnacle, her time to shine.

After that, he said, things would go downhill. No one would want to be around a teenager who collects paintbrushes and sucks her thumb or an adult who throws temper tantrums and wants to watch *Wonder Pets*. As he said it, I got a queasy feeling in my stomach. He was right.

And although Sophie had greatly surpassed both Ray's and my expectations as she grew into a little person—reading fluently, holding sophisticated conversations, swimming and dancing alongside typical kids—he was right about the salad days. I could see them waning, and coming to a close in a pretty big way the night of the fifth-grade celebration. Sophie might be okay in middle school, but she'd never really shine again. Her days of being a little girl were over.

Ray and I both cringed at the thought of puberty, and not in the way other parents cringe.

It's one thing to have a daughter who has the impulse to hug strangers and invite people she's just met over for playdates. But what would happen when Sophie wanted to have sex? And what if she didn't, but someone wanted to have it with her—and she wasn't able to say no? Could she ever have a real relationship? Her heart is so big; would she ever find true love?

In my darkest hours, I cursed the universe. If I have to have a child with developmental disabilities, that's fine. But why does her body have to develop normally? Years ago, lots of people were outraged over a story in the news about a family with a child who had a severe genetic disorder (far more involved than Down syndrome) that left the child unable to walk or talk or care for herself in any way.

The parents chose to give the child hormones to keep her small, so she was easier to lift.

I felt guilty siding with the parents, but I saw their point. And to be honest, I've always been grateful that Sophie is so tiny. At first glance, people often think she is in first or second grade and are slower to realize there's "something wrong."

But like a typical child, Sophie would go through puberty. She would get breasts and hair, have mood swings and crushes. And yes, she'd get her period.

She just wouldn't understand any of it as well as her peers would. This filled me with terror. At random times—in the shower, in the car, when I was trying to fall asleep at night—I'd flash forward to scenes from Sophie's life and imagine the worst. Rejection. Loneliness. Abuse. Rape.

Slow down! I told myself, but that is easier said than done. No one prepares you for this. And no one tells you how to prepare your kid.

There is no good instruction manual for how to teach your kid with Down syndrome about middle school, but when Sophie entered fifth grade, approaching her eleventh birthday, I began to wonder if there might be a better way than *Pink Slip* to teach her about the facts of life.

And then an e-mail popped up in my inbox, advertising a puberty seminar for parents of children with Down syndrome. How fortuitous—I pounced. Ray and I signed up for the parent meeting, and Sophie and I were set to attend the mother/daughter session. I hadn't been to many Down syndrome-centric events, and I was nervous, wondering what the other kids would be like and if I could handle the information. But anything, I figured, would be better than *Pink Slip*.

The timing was perfect. Sophie was showing no signs of puberty, but it wasn't for lack of trying on her part. She'd been desperate for breasts for years, since her sister had first started developing and we'd gone bra shopping. Sophie had insisted on her own bras then, and two years later she was working on a healthy collection that included polka-dotted bras, purple bras, and even a few padded bras.

Beyond bras, what she really wanted, oddly enough, was pubic hair. I don't recall ever wanting pubic hair; I'm pretty sure I was horrified at the first signs. But Sophie was obsessed, and had been for some time.

One morning, weeks before the puberty seminar and months before that fifth-grade celebration, Sophie and I were in the bathroom together. This was not unusual; we often found more than one member of the family together in the only functional bathroom in our falling-apart-but-well-loved old house. Ray called it the "his and hers and hers and hers bathroom."

On this particular day, Sophie and I both needed showers, and she was up first. I turned on the water and then turned to Sophie. Much like getting Sophie to put on her shoes, or eat her dinner, or give me back the iPhone she's snagged, this task—getting her into the shower—required a game plan.

I cajoled and bargained her out of her clothes and was insisting that no, taking a shower did not deserve the reward of a shopping spree at Barnes and Noble, when Sophie stopped, grinned, and held up one arm.

"I have armpit hair!" she insisted. "Feel it!"

"Oh, yeah, sure—" I said, distracted by the clock and the day's long "to do" list, running my fingers along her armpit.

"Hey, Sophie, I'm sorry," I said, pulling my hand back and tuning in to the conversation. "I don't feel any armpit hair. You'll get it, but you don't have it yet."

Her eyes welled with tears; her naked little chest started to heave. Shit! I thought. At this rate we'll never get to school.

"I know!" I said. "Let's check and see if you have any hair—you know where."

"Okay!" she said, super-excited.

I crouched down and squinted hard, standing up straight to report my findings. A white lie wouldn't really hurt, right? We couldn't afford another tardy at school.

"I see some!" I said.

You would have thought I'd told the kid we were going to live at Disneyland. She jumped up and down, squealing, her entire body shaking with the kind of pure joy most of us are lucky enough to experience once or twice in life, and announced, "IT'S MY LUCKY DAY!"

❧❧❧❧❧

Clearly, I needed help, and it was on the way in the form of the foremost authority on Down syndrome and puberty, Terri Couwenhoven, M.S., who wrote a book on the topic: *Teaching Children with Down syndrome about Their Bodies, Boundaries, and Sexuality*. The local Down syndrome support group in Phoenix flew her in for the two-day seminar I had received the e-mail about a few weeks earlier.

The first night was parents-only. The PowerPoint about growth and development was a little boring, but Ms. Couwenhoven seemed to know a lot, and it was nice of her to go over the material with us so we'd know what to expect when we brought the kids back. As it turned out, pretty much everything she said was based on common sense. People with Down syndrome are just like everyone else in terms of needing affection and in their sexual behavior—but teaching them to be appropriate is harder because of their cognitive abilities. Everything from how to take a shower to how to handle a crush has to be taught, very slowly and with a lot of repetition.

"So tomorrow," Couwenhoven said, as we were wrapping things up, "I will be showing a video about menstruation. It's pretty outdated, I know you'll all laugh at it, but it's—"

I raised my hand.

"Yes?" she asked.

"*Pink Slip*," was all I could get out. Ray was staring shut-the-fuck-up daggers at me.

"Oh no," she said. "That's not the name. I don't recall it at the moment. You'll love this one. It's about two sisters—"

"Jill and Susie," I said, my face hot.

"Well, yes," the instructor said. "But it's not called *Pink Slip.*"

Oh god, I thought. It has a street name.

"Yes it is," I said.

"How do you know about it?" she asked.

"Let's talk after class," I said.

"Okay, here's the thing," I told her later, as the other parents filed out of the room. "I'm not proud of this, but we used to watch that video at parties and laugh."

Ray chimed in: "I never thought it was funny."

The next day, Sophie and I showed up for the girls-only meeting. We talked about safety and hygiene, and the girls all went into the bathroom to try on pads. When the instructor drew a girl's figure on the board and asked everyone to add a body part, Sophie added a bra—I can only imagine what that instructor thought of me.

And when it came time for the video, the foremost authority on Down syndrome and puberty gave me a funny look and then showed something else. Not *Pink Slip,* but instead an innocuous, modern, but still dumbed-down explanation about getting your period.

ееееее

I still had questions after the seminar. So I called Terri Couwenhoven. She was in a hurry, on her way to several other speaking engagements. She's in high demand. But she agreed to talk to me.

I wanted to know: Was there something I missed? Was there really nothing physical separating Sophie from the rest of us?

No, Couwenhoven confirmed, Sophie would develop just like her peers. "How old is she?" she asked.

"Almost eleven."

"Oh. You've got plenty of time."

Yes. No. I didn't know.

Look, she said, people are not comfortable around sex in general, and that discomfort is magnified when it comes to disability and sex. The only unique characteristic about people with Down syndrome that makes them different in this context is that they don't get the information they need because parents and caregivers avoid the topic with the hope it will never be an issue. When you have an adult son or daughter who still acts like a child, you don't want to think about them having sex.

In fact, it's pretty obvious that as a whole, society is not comfortable with developmentally disabled people having physical relationships, something Couwenhoven documents in her book. And she's not just talking about sex, but any kind of physical intimacy. She writes about marasmus, a mysterious condition that plagued infants and children with conditions like Down syndrome who were housed in institutions in the nineteenth century. *Marasmus* means "wasting away" in Greek. Decades later, scientists learned it was caused by a lack of touch.

"Caregivers were encouraged to pick up, carry, cuddle, stroke, and caress the children—behaviors described as 'mothering'—several times per day," Couwenhoven writes. "At Bellevue Hospital in New York, mortality rates among infants under the age of one dropped from 30–35 percent to under 10 percent by 1938."

Conversely, Couwenhoven writes about her own experience as a Special Olympics volunteer in the 1970s. She was assigned to be a "hugger"—to embrace runners when they finished a race.

"I was uncomfortable with this directive, but did as I was asked," she writes, adding that it gave her a misconception about people with Down syndrome. "I left college believing that they were incapable of learning and understanding how to be appropriate and they hugged everyone."

Many years later (an odd coincidence) Couwenhoven had a daughter with Down syndrome. By then, the Special Olympics had discontinued the hugging practice and Couwenhoven had begun her own education about special needs and interpersonal relationships. Her daughter is now twenty-five.

"How's she doing?" I asked.

Couwenhoven paused, then explained that her daughter did have a boyfriend for about a year, but told her mom she got sick of "doing the work" of having a relationship—talking to him on the phone, going out. Ultimately, she broke up with him.

"She still talks about finding the right guy," Couwenhoven said.

I must have sighed more audibly than I meant to. Live day to day, Couwenhoven told me. (Important subtext: *Quit making this about you.*)

"Separate out your issues and fears and concerns," she said, "and focus on what Sophie needs at the moment."

That made me laugh. In a funny way, I actually felt validated. I had spent so many years doing just what Couwenhoven had told me to do—living day to day, forcing myself to focus on the present. When I finally dipped a toe into the future, I was told to pull it right back.

And yet, as Couwenhoven could obviously tell, I was terrified. Sophie and I had an evening ritual of cuddling on the living room couch, and inevitably, she'd pass out, pinning my arm, burrowed into my side, and I'd stare down at her peaceful little face as my mind raced with questions. Would Sophie get lost the first day of middle school? Would other kids bully her, trample her—not even see her? Would she have a boyfriend, would she go out with her friends to the mall and try on clothes and giggle and get crappy food at the food court? Would she be happy?

I tried to take Terri Couwenhoven's advice, but of course it was too late. You can't unring that bell. I couldn't stop myself from worrying about thumb sucking, sixth grade, or whether Sophie would have a fulfilling life, because my questions extended far beyond middle school.

I know everyone has a different idea of what constitutes "happily ever after," but for me—particularly now that I'm married with kids—

my own personal definition includes having a family. Or at least the right to decide whether to have one.

And here is Sophie—so affectionate, so eager to develop personal relationships. When I picture her grown up, my biggest hope is that she will find someone to love. I'd also like for her to have great sex. I know that sounds bad, and it might make some parents cringe and maybe I'm objectifying Sophie when I say it—but there it is. I want my daughter to fall in love, get married, and have great sex.

That's not a particularly easy thing to say, and I worry it will be even harder to accomplish. Because my biggest fear for Sophie is that she will be lonely. You hear stories from time to time about happily-ever-couples with Down syndrome, but more often, there are sad stories. There is a girl on Sophie's Special Olympics cheer squad who is twenty-four. She recently graduated from high school. She seems fairly capable to me, but her mother says she doesn't have a job. Instead, the girl sits in her room all day watching TV and playing on the computer. Her mother brings her food.

I feel hopeless, thinking about that girl—that sweet, funny, chubby young woman who holds Sophie on her back during cheer routines—sitting alone by herself every day.

And the family part could get messy for Sophie. Men with Down syndrome are usually sterile, and women can have complications during pregnancy. There's a high probability that Sophie's baby would have Down syndrome. And let's face it, who's going to let Sophie adopt? So yeah, there's a lot to work out. But I'm not willing to rule that one out yet. Medical school, okay. I can accept that Sophie won't be a surgeon. But I'm not ready to consider that she will never be somebody's mother.

I'm not sure much of what she learned at the puberty seminar stuck with Sophie, though she remained obsessed with the topic. And so in the morning before school, when she was procrastinating, I would find myself agreeing to let her wear deodorant—which she didn't need—if she brushed her hair first. Mascara if she took her thyroid medicine. And always, a bra from her collection.

One day a few weeks after the seminar, Sophie was about to get in the shower when she announced, "I got my period yesterday!"

"You got your what?!" I sputtered.

"My period!" she said.

"Well, okay," I said. "If you really got your period, then there is blood on your underwear."

We both looked down at the floor, at her crumpled Barbie panties. And we both lunged for them at the same time. A spirited game of keep away ensued.

I held the stain-free panties aloft, feeling victorious. I also felt a little mean.

"I really did get it!" Sophie said.

"You didn't get it yet, but you will—soon," I said, putting the panties in the hamper. "I promise. Now get in the shower."

So she did, climbing carefully into the tub that's still too tall for her. I adjusted the temperature of the water, secured the shower curtain, and made sure she could reach the No More Tears shampoo.

And as I walked down the hall to my bedroom, I could hear Sophie singing a familiar tune at the top of her lungs, a reminder that in so many ways, my little girl hadn't grown up—might never grow up. It wasn't the latest Katie Perry or Miley Cyrus.

It was the ABCs.

ееееее

The false alarms went off so often that when it finally happened, I was completely unprepared—and a little horrified. It had been weeks since the period announcement, months since my pubic hair fib. In fact, as the summer before Sophie's first year of middle school wore on, talk of puberty all but stopped. Instead, both my girls were preoccupied with performances at dance and theater camp, and beach vacations to escape the terrible Phoenix heat.

One morning Ray had already left for work, but the rest of us were piled in the bathroom. Annabelle was in the shower, I was fighting a losing battle with my eyebrows and an old pair of tweezers, and Sophie was peeing. Suddenly she stood up, flushed, and announced, "Mom, come look!"

I don't think she ever really believed me when I told her I'd seen hair the last time. This time I crouched, looked, and stood up to face her.

"Sophie, you have it," I announced solemnly. She did. Not a lot, but it was definitely there.

"Have what?" Annabelle called over the running water.

"Hair!" I said. "She has hair. *There.*"

"Oh boy," Annabelle said, stepping out of the shower to confirm my discovery. "Let me see."

"I KNEW IT!" Sophie shrieked, pulling up her panties and running to grab the phone she'd gotten for her eleventh birthday a few weeks earlier. She proceeded to call my mother, my sister, and several family friends, telling the story over and over, making fast laps around the kitchen table as she talked, gesticulating madly, looking like the world's tiniest business executive ready to make a deal.

"I have vagina hair!" she told anyone who would listen, till I finally told her to stop. We did call Ray on the speaker phone and Sophie announced her news.

"That's hilarious!" he said.

"No, hon," I said gently, my teeth gritted. "It's not funny."

"That's awesome!" he said, clearly wanting to discuss anything but his younger daughter's changing body. I can't say I blame him.

"I'm a growing girl!" Sophie announced just before he hung up.

It's true. The proof was there. And suddenly, just like that, it really wasn't funny anymore. I didn't feel like telling people. I didn't write a Facebook status update or a blog post about Sophie and her "vagina hair."

Life went on as usual. It would be months before Sophie's breasts began to develop in earnest, longer till she got her period. Except for frequent emotional outbursts that somehow weren't like her old temper tantrums, Sophie didn't seem different at all.

But I couldn't stop thinking about how she had changed, how she would change, how in that instant when I saw that hair, shit got real. This was really going to happen. Sophie was going to develop into an adult woman.

I felt like I'd felt when she was born, like someone had knocked me off kilter. I couldn't look at her without thinking about it. I stood at the observation window and stared at Sophie during her swim lesson, as she dove for rings with the six-year-olds in her class, kids the same size as her, with the same swimming ability. But none of them have pubic hair! I whined silently, stressing myself out. Afterward in the locker room, I yelled at Sophie to keep the shower curtain closed.

"You have vagina hair!" I hissed. "You need privacy!"

"You're right," she said, smiling serenely, wrapping the towel tighter around herself, and heading to a bathroom stall to get dressed.

I wasn't smiling.

*I have a daughter who sucks her thumb and has pubic hair,* I thought. Then, *She's still Sophie.* Still my smart, sweet, silly kid.

She was—and she wasn't.

# 12

## THE NEW SEGREGATION

As Sophie approached the end of elementary school, I worried about so many things, from friendships to math skills to puberty. But I wasn't too concerned about where she'd go to middle school. Arizona has one of the most lenient charter school laws in the country, and as a result, more charter schools than just about any other state.

There had to be a perfect fit for Sophie—a school that wasn't exclusively for kids with special needs but was welcoming to all, with small classes and an emphasis on all the things she loved: reading, art, drama, choir, and dance. I put off the search as long as possible, enjoying the community Sophie and I had both worked so hard to build at our neighborhood school.

The summer after fourth grade, with a year left at Broadmor, I began to really think about where she'd go next—particularly after I ran into Jay Heiler, the man who started the charter school movement in Arizona. We knew each other well from the many years I'd covered politics and he'd worked in them.

I spotted Heiler from across a crowded Chinese restaurant on a hot summer night in 2013. It had been a long time since I'd seen him, but he hadn't changed a bit, a head or two taller than the other patrons, a boyish wave in his carefully combed blond hair.

I didn't catch his eye, but I knew he'd come over to say hello, because Jay Heiler is one of the most unfailingly polite people I've ever met. Twenty years ago, he was chief of staff to then-Governor J. Fife Symington, and my colleagues and I regularly beat them both up in the pages of *New Times*. Still, Heiler always returned my calls.

"Amy Silverman?"

I looked up from my chicken and broccoli and smiled.

"Jay Heiler?"

"And this must be Annabelle," he said, remembering her name though he likely hadn't heard it since she was an infant.

"No, Jay," I said, motioning to the ten-year-old across the table.

"This is Sophie."

He took a closer look and for a split second, I thought Heiler might bolt from the table; maybe he'd forgotten that my younger child has Down syndrome. He recovered just as quickly and changed the subject, mentioning that he saw my "Pop" at a golf tournament, wanting to know the gossip at the newspaper.

Business is going well for you, I observed. He beamed. Yes, he said, Great Hearts Academies, the charter school company he founded after leaving Symington, was doing well, expanding into Texas next.

I'm not kidding when I say that Heiler is the godfather of Arizona's school choice movement. During his time with Symington, he tried unsuccessfully to legalize school vouchers and then championed legislation that ultimately made Arizona the second state in the nation with charter schools.

Now Arizona has two different kinds of public schools—
"charter" and the traditional "district." And to this day, Arizona's law
still is considered one of the nation's friendliest to charter operators.
At the time I ran into him, Heiler chaired the Arizona Association of
Charter Schools, an organization devoted to keeping it that way. If
anyone knew Arizona charter schools, it was Heiler. And that gave me
an idea. Why not start my research right then?

"Hey, Jay, I have a question for you," I said, looking over at
Sophie, busily shoveling lo mein into her mouth.

In another year, I explained, Sophie would be done with
elementary school, and I was hoping to find just the right fit for her
for middle school. She'd been in a district school, but I was open to
a charter. And I figured that if anyone would know of the perfect
charter school for Sophie, it was Heiler.

"Have any suggestions?" I asked.

Heiler nodded, not missing a beat. But he didn't mention a
single charter school. Instead, Jay Heiler—the man I'd heard go on
and on for years about the horrors of the traditional public school
system in Arizona—looked me in the eye and told me that he'd
heard there were some very good district middle schools with great
special education programs.

And then he quickly changed the subject.

llllll

I didn't know it at the time, but what Jay Heiler did that night is
known in education circles as "pushing out."

Legally, you can't tell a parent of a kid with a disability that the
child can't attend your charter school. But you definitely can make it
clear that the kid isn't wanted.

It's passive-aggressive, and it's prevalent. It was something I
experienced again and again during the next year as I tried to find a
charter school for Sophie.

I didn't start out pro-charter. In fact, Heiler and I had more than one run-in back in the day over his position on school choice. But parenthood can have a way of changing your politics, and by the time Annabelle was ready for middle school, there were several terrific charter-school options for her. Ultimately, we sent Annabelle to an arts charter school. She loved it. But Annabelle is what's known as a typical kid; she doesn't have a disability.

It was a much different experience with Sophie.

"Don't send her to our school. They'll make her sit in a room by herself all day," a special education teacher at Annabelle's charter school told me.

Several other schools explained that they'd love to have Sophie but just didn't have the right programs in place for a sixth-grader with Down syndrome.

During one school tour, I turned to the education director and asked, "So what do you think about having a kid with Down syndrome at your school?" The color drained from her face, and she sucked wind (really—I heard it). "Well…" she began, clearly stalling.

"Don't say anything," I said before she could finish, mentally knocking that school off the list.

Another special education teacher advised me to pray over my decision.

And after a glance at Sophie, Jay Heiler obviously couldn't think of a single charter school that was even an option for her.

We exchanged pleasantries that night before saying good-bye, but the conversation with Heiler left a bad taste in my mouth. There were more than five hundred charter schools in Arizona. How could there not be one for Sophie?

I set out to prove Heiler wrong.

In many ways, I wanted the same thing for Sophie that we'd found for Annabelle: a school with dedicated, creative teachers, small classes, and an emphasis on both the arts and critical-thinking skills. Both girls wanted to know why Sophie couldn't go to school with Annabelle, but I knew in my heart that Annabelle's school wasn't right, particularly now that more than one staff member quietly had warned me against it.

No worries, I thought. I found just the right school for Annabelle. I'd find just the right one for Sophie, too.

By the time middle school loomed, her math skills weren't so hot, but Sophie collected books like baseball cards. So far, in her almost eleven years, by and large, the challenges she hadn't met were the ones we hadn't given her.

I wanted to keep challenging Sophie.

I also wanted her to be safe and happy. I still have unfond memories from my own middle-school experience.

So as I embarked on this quest to find the perfect school, the thought of tossing Sophie into a big, traditional middle school setting with giant, sweaty boys, snotty, mean girls, and overwhelmed teachers made me crazy.

And I did go a little crazy in my quest.

I called teachers, lawmakers, administrators, lawyers—everyone I knew in the Arizona education system. I stalked other parents at Special Olympics track meets, quizzing them about their kids' schools. I Googled for hours. I hired a consultant. I asked on girlinapartyhat. com. Then I turned to the twenty-first-century water cooler, the surest way to find everything from a handyman to a heart surgeon: Facebook.

"Say you had a kid with Down syndrome in metro Phoenix. Where would you send her for the sixth grade?" I asked in a status update.

Nothing.

Finally, I expanded my Google search to "charter schools" and "special education." And then I realized what was wrong—and how naïve I'd been. This wasn't just a Phoenix issue or an Arizona one. It was a national problem. Practically since the inception of the charter-school movement, complaints have been lodged and research conducted about the lack of special-needs students attending charters all over the country.

First, let's be clear about one thing: charter schools are public schools, and both charters and district schools therefore are required by federal law to provide what is called FAPE, a "free and appropriate public education" to all students with disabilities.

To be fair, district schools aren't without fault when it comes to including special-needs students. School-choice proponents tout Arizona's open-enrollment policies, designed to allow kids to attend school districts out of their assigned boundaries, but the law is written to allow individual districts to make the decision to take a kid or not—and, often, districts cap the number of kids with an IEP they'll take. Also, according to the Arizona Department of Education (but up for debate among civil rights law experts), a school district has a requirement to accept a kid with a disability but has the discretion to place the child at a school in the district, not necessarily in accordance with the parents' wishes.

FAPE means "free and appropriate public education," not best.

But the bigger challenges definitely reside with charter schools, and kids with disabilities aren't attending these schools in numbers proportional to district schools. Not even close. After a year of reporting, I came up with three reasons: money, red tape, and because so few parents were willing to force the issue.

Again and again in my search for a charter school for Sophie, I heard that charters just don't get the same funding for special-needs students that district schools do. That's not true. Both the federal and state governments give both nonprofit charter and district schools money per capita for students with special needs, weighted by disability. For example, a kid with a speech delay will get less money than a kid with a mild-to-moderate intellectual disability (that's what Sophie has). The other area of reimbursement is for therapy—including speech, physical, and occupational, which is covered by Medicaid regardless of whether you are at a charter or district school.

But where a small charter school does have a point about funding is when it comes to economies of scale. A large, established district school can hire special education teachers to deal with their many charges; a newer charter school with just a couple of special ed students will have more trouble working with its resources. Don't get me wrong: On all levels, funding is woefully inadequate. Some studies show that special education is underfunded by 40 percent.

Second, there is the complicated landscape. The charter-school movement was created in direct response to what is viewed as a cumbersome and restrictive public education system. For example, while district schools still employ certified teachers, a charter school teacher in Arizona has no such requirement—until it comes to special education.

Federal special education law requires that special education teachers be certified; this really throws a wrench in it for a charter, since regular classroom teachers do not have to be certified—that's one of the "outside-the-box" perks of running a charter. On top of that, an IEP requires a lot of paperwork, oversight, and often headaches. If it's not done right, the student probably won't be well-served—and the school may be breaking the law.

The National Alliance for Public Charter Schools acknowledges that the special education gap is a significant problem—so much so that it actually created another group, the National Center for Special Education in Charter Schools, to address the issue. In a 2013 report, the center explained why it's important to deal with special education services:

"Based on legal actions in New Orleans and Washington, D.C., and anecdotes from other cities where access and service provision are increasingly under a microscope, charter schools that fail to chart an intentional course related to students with disabilities might be subject to cumbersome regulatory burdens advanced by charter opponents."

In other words, don't do it because it's the right thing to do. Do it because otherwise, you'll have to deal with pesky regulations.

Third and finally, no one has done much of anything to force charter schools to comply with the law when it comes to welcoming special education students. I learned why firsthand. It's true, I probably could have figured out how to push Sophie into any of the charter schools whose staff I talked to during the year I searched (assuming she made it through the lottery process), but I chose not to. Why would I want my kid to attend a school where she's not wanted? To make a political point? I can't do that to my daughter. And what about a parent who doesn't have the time and ridiculous inclination to research the charter school options in a twenty-mile radius? I'm not afraid of an argument or of hiring a lawyer to get my kid what she needs. But even I was left speechless on several occasions during my charter search. I can understand why so many other parents give up early in the process—or never try at all.

So it's become a quiet problem—including in my home state of Arizona, where the charter industry is booming.

Except for a few complaints buried deep in government bureaucracy, I could find almost no research or news stories about the issue of Arizona charter schools failing to serve special-needs students. Repeated requests to public-information officers and education-policy professors at Arizona State University went unanswered.

I decided to crunch the most recent numbers I could find for Arizona. It's impossible to get the exact breakdown, student by student, because of privacy laws, but an analysis of district versus charter state budgets revealed huge gaps in the numbers of special-needs services provided at the two types of schools. In 2012–13, district schools spent about $763 per student on special education and related services. Charters spent $331 per kid during the same period.

I then analyzed the budget for each of the 520 charter schools in operation in 2012–13, looking specifically at four of the most profound disability areas: autism; mild/moderate/severe intellectual disability; multiple disability; and multiple disability with severe sensory impairment. Of the 520 schools, 273 didn't serve a single child with any of those diagnoses during that entire school year.

A General Accounting Office (GAO) study from 2012 also revealed a discrepancy in special-needs students served at charter versus district schools, both nationally and in Arizona. And that research raised another troubling fact. When charters did serve special-needs students, the GAO reported, they served them in disproportionate numbers. The GAO documented that in almost 12 percent of charter schools nationwide, more than 20 percent of the population had a disability that qualified them for special ed services.

By the time I published a story about this in *New Times* in the spring of 2013, metro Phoenix had two charter schools that are designed to pretty much exclusively serve children with autism. And Jay Heiler finally had his vouchers, now called Empowerment Savings Accounts, that go to kids with special needs whose parents can't find public (district or charter) options and want to send them to private schools that serve kids with special needs. Or home school.

There were plenty of schools that educate children with profound special needs and even more, like the school my older daughter attends, that cater to the high-achieving child.

But what about Sophie, who thrived when she was included with typical kids her own age? In a state that prided itself on offering the nation's best in school choice, the options were shrinking in one category—and, increasingly, special-needs kids were educated separately from their typical peers.

I called it the new segregation.

One thing that always stunned me was that Sophie took standardized tests along with her typical peers. For the three years leading up to middle school, she took the state standardized tests. Per her IEP she received accommodations for breaks and extra time, but still, she took the same test the rest of the kids did.

Every time we had an IEP meeting, I posed the question again:

"So Sophie takes the test the same as the other kids, and her test scores are averaged in with the rest of the school's scores, which determine the school's grade?"

Around the table, heads would nod. Finally one day I got bold.

"Why on earth would any school want a kid who brings their average down?" I asked.

The district's lawyer chuckled. "Well," she said, almost under her breath, "Sophie does better than some of the typical kids."

That was nice to hear, I suppose, but it was no guarantee that another school would feel the same way—and make accommodations for Sophie, test scores and all.

I was feeling less and less confident in charter schools. I requested complaints about charters from both the state Department of Education and U.S. Department of Education Division of Civil Rights going back several years. They didn't make for particularly inspiring reading material.

While reading through the federal complaints, I realized how hard it is to make something stick. Take, for example, a complaint filed against Carden Traditional School in Surprise, a bedroom community near Phoenix, in 2011.

By the fourth day of kindergarten, it was clear that things weren't going well for one little boy. According to the complaint filed by his father, he had vomited in class and had behavior issues. The parents met with the assistant principal, special education teacher, and others to discuss it.

From the father's complaint:

"The special education specialist spoke the most, and she simply said [the child] was an 'extreme case,' and that the school did not have the facilities or teachers to meet his needs, and that a public school would be better for him."

In his complaint, the father expressed the opinion that the school had a legal obligation to educate the boy.

In the Civil Rights Division's conclusion, the investigator wrote:

"You identified the assistant principal and special education coordinator as the individuals who stated that the school did not have adequate resources to accommodate your son's disability. When we interviewed them, they both denied that they or anyone else said this during the meeting."

Case closed. The father's complaint was dismissed.

All the state complaints I read, on the other hand, were found to have merit. They included charter schools that held incomplete IEP meetings and didn't fulfill IEP requirements. According to one complaint, a school had listed a special education classroom as a place where services would be given, but the investigation revealed that the school had no such space. At another school, the special education teacher was so frustrated that she filed a complaint herself—saying she was in charge of 350 students (a ridiculous number, obviously).

At another school, IEPs were written with duplicate goals (meaning the same goal was given to multiple children, clearly without personalizing plans), goals were deemed inappropriate by investigators, and in one instance, speech therapy was given over the phone.

Schools went for years sometimes with no special education teacher, and in one case, years when no special education services were given to a child with mild intellectual disabilities.

The most significant case—which had special education lawyers all across Arizona buzzing—involved a finding by an administrative judge that Flagstaff Arts and Leadership Academy denied appropriate IEP services to a girl there, not diagnosing or treating anxiety, reading and learning disorders, and possibly dyslexia. The judge ordered FALA to pay more than $100,000 in tuition at a private school; the case settled for an undisclosed amount, said the family's attorney, Hope Kirsch.

Kirsch wasn't able to discuss the specifics of the settlement, she said, but she could talk about special education and charter schools. She saw a pattern of noncompliance.

"They just don't always have the resources," Kirsch said. "That's no excuse."

She said she'd spoken to a parent recently whose kid hadn't had an IEP in years. Some charter schools don't have attorneys, she said. Other charter schools need training.

"I think that sometimes…they just don't understand their legal obligations," she said.

As for telling a parent a school is a bad fit or doesn't have adequate services?

"It's not legal to say that," Kirsch said. "It's saying, 'We don't want you here.'"

eeeeee

In the end, I took some advice from a friend, who left a comment on Girl in a Party Hat.

"Where are her friends going? It would be so nice for Sophie to go from strength to strength instead of starting over."

How could I have been so stupid? I wondered. For Sophie, the cliché is so true—it had taken a village. And her village consisted of her friends, the classmates she'd literally grown up with. Suddenly, I knew what I needed to do.

I e-mailed Barry Fritch, the principal at Sophie's elementary school, and asked him to put the wheels in motion to get her enrolled at the neighborhood middle school. The principal was delighted— and so kind. He brought Sophie to the new school himself for a tour, helped choose just the right liaison for her transition, and took a separate trip to the middle school to personally introduce Ray and me to the new principal and special education staff.

The school was big and a little scary. But there was a cheerleading squad that Sophie could join, and her classroom aide agreed to follow her to middle school.

There was just one problem. A few years ago, in response to declining enrollment because of charter schools (parents like Ray and me pulling kids like Annabelle and putting them into charters) the school district had begun combating the problem by opening specialized schools and programs designed to hold on to kids.

One of these schools was an "international academy" with small classes, an emphasis on critical-thinking skills, and a requirement that incoming students have As and Bs. There was no special education department to serve a kid like Sophie.

During one of my transition meetings with Sophie's new principal, he admitted that almost the entire fifth grade at her school would be going to the academy, rather than the feeder middle school Sophie was signed up for.

And so Sophie went off to middle school alone. By the night of the fifth-grade graduation ceremony, there was just one other child I knew of who would definitely be going with her.

Tatum, the other little girl in her class with Down syndrome.

# 13

# DON'T YOU FORGET
# ABOUT ME

The scientists were looking for guinea pigs. The parents were looking for hope. The result was standing room only at Global Down Syndrome Foundation's Medical Research Roundtable, held just before the 2015 National Down Syndrome Congress Convention in Phoenix.

Several years ago, when I was first looking at the connections between Alzheimer's and Down syndrome, the topic wasn't so widely known, or developed, and certainly not as well funded. By 2015, the research around the connection had heated up, with top-notch scientists focused on what the brains of people with Down syndrome can teach them about the entire population when it comes to Alzheimer's disease.

I got depressed looking out over the crowd that hot June afternoon; there were a lot of families with toddlers and infants. These parents should be worrying about preschool and playdates, and instead they were here to learn about their kids' death sentence. By 2015, research had shown that 100 percent of people with Down syndrome have the genetic marker that leads to Alzheimer's. Some studies and experts suggest that seventy-five percent or so will actually develop Alzheimer's by age sixty-five. Those are some shitty odds.

(Shitty, but—before we all lose hope—perhaps more complicated than they appear. Dr. Brian Chicoine, medical director of the Adult Down Syndrome Center in Park Ridge, Illinois, told me he's not convinced the numbers are that high. He believes that untreated sleep apnea and insulin resistance, among other things, could account for symptoms of dementia that are often diagnosed as Alzheimer's. Nevertheless, he acknowledged that the numbers are high.)

Worst of all is the revelation that some of these indicators show up on the brains of kids as early as age eight and that a few begin to show symptoms by their teens. That is rare; for most the changes will begin in their thirties and forties.

Not good, no matter how you look at it, for a population that's already had to beg and scrape for every IQ point. Early intervention, therapies, and intense effort from parents, teachers, and others in the life of a person with Down syndrome can result in better cognitive abilities and a higher quality life—which may be dashed before middle age with a diagnosis of early onset Alzheimer's.

I found a wall to lean on, set down my heavy purse, and got out my notebook, ready to learn something. One of the researchers gave a PowerPoint presentation. He began by explaining slowly how Down syndrome was first discovered by an Englishman named J. Langdon Down who ran an institution for people with intellectual disabilities in the 1800s. A photograph of Down appeared on the screen.

Seriously? I gnashed my teeth in silent protest. This was an epic fail in the "know your audience" department, a presentation any parent in that group could have given off the top of the head. Perhaps worst of all were the typos on the slides.

Within a few slides the presentation became hopelessly complicated, jumping from too-basic to incomprehensible, with pictures of brain scans and detailed graphs. I sighed and closed my notebook. After a few speeches and the requisite plea for study participants, the group disbanded and I went up to the front to introduce myself to the PowerPoint guy, who had said he'd just moved to Phoenix to work for Barrow Neurological Institute, a well-regarded hospital and research facility.

Maybe he was nervous, I thought. Maybe this was his first-ever PowerPoint. It might be different one-on-one.

We'd barely started the conversation, when the researcher interrupted me to stop one of the conference organizers walking by.

"Hey, did you get my tax form?" he asked her with a "hint-hint" tone in his voice. He was looking for the payment for his appearance.

I was surprised and a little grossed out; I'd been naïve enough to think that a researcher who lived in town would volunteer his time—or at least consider it part of his salaried job—to appear at a conference like this one.

"Oh yes," the young woman assured him. "I've got your check right here."

While he was pocketing the envelope, I slipped into the crowd.

Research into the connection between Alzheimer's disease and Down syndrome is about money, competition, desperation, and human lab rats. But it's also about the true desire to help people—both people with Down syndrome and those without. And it's shining the spotlight on people with Down syndrome in a way that might just draw them out of the shadows.

The population of people in the United States with Down syndrome was about 400,000 in 2014, although experts say that's a very rough guess. The population of people in the United States with Alzheimer's disease was five million. Given what we know about advancements in prenatal testing and the rapidly aging population, the former figure is set to decline while the latter is growing at an alarming rate.

Alzheimer's disease is named after Alois Alzheimer, a German doctor who described odd symptoms in a patient in 1906. To this day, while much is known about the disease, it is still not possible to definitively diagnose it in a living patient.

The brain has 100 billion nerve cells, which control communication, memory, and other brain functions. Alzheimer's, the most common form of dementia, is caused by damage to these cells, or neurons. Scientists have found both plaques and tangles that cause damage. The gene that causes plaque—protein build-ups called beta-amyloids—has been found on the twenty-first chromosome. This was a breakthrough for scientists and terrible news for people with Down syndrome.

Scientists will tell you that the connection between Alzheimer's and Down syndrome was not discovered until the mid-1980s, when the plaque connection was made, but anecdotal evidence was available for about a hundred years before that. The increase in senility and other symptoms of dementia in people with Down syndrome was first noted just a few years after J. Langdon Down identified it—long before any sort of formal genetic connection was made.

As science has progressed, people with Down syndrome have become increasingly important in research of Alzheimer's disease. Not only do a large percentage ultimately wind up with Alzheimer's, but the onset of the disease happens at a fairly predictable time—which is gold to researchers.

There are only two other groups I've heard of that work as similar research pools—extended families in Colombia and Sweden. They provide much smaller potential research pools than the entire population of people with Down syndrome, but like people with

DS, every member of each of the families has the markers for early-onset Alzheimer's (Alzheimer's in which symptoms appear in the forties or earlier).

I asked Dr. Marwan Sabbagh, a researcher in Phoenix, about his work.

"The field was kind of quiet for a while. I don't know if people knew what to do with it," he said of the connection between Alzheimer's and Down syndrome. "The fields were maturing independently, and now they are converging."

Part of that has to do with life expectancy. A generation ago, people with Down syndrome typically lived into their thirties. Now he was seeing them well into their sixties. That has brought more cases of Alzheimer's within the population and more interest, Sabbagh said.

Sabbagh listed some of his collaborators, people I've been talking to for a long time—Jamie Edgin at University of Arizona, who developed the cognitive test for people with Down syndrome; Matt Huentelman at the Translational Genomics Research Institute, who researches genes and taught me about Mendel. "This is a really, really exciting time to bring the disciplines together," Sabbagh said. The goal is to come up with vaccines and anti-amyloid treatments that will actually precede the onset of symptoms, both in people with and without Down syndrome.

It's mind-blowing stuff. And apparently, the research required to make it happen can't happen without people like Sophie.

Gently, Sabbagh mentioned his need for "patients and samples and biomarkers."

Blood I was okay with. Brain scans not so much. Health concerns aside, I wasn't so sure I wanted to know if Sophie was already showing signs of early-onset Alzheimer's. She hadn't even gotten her period yet. And what if they wanted to enroll her in clinical trials, try medication on her? No, thank you. I thought.

But how do you weigh all that against the possibility of treatment someday, not just for everyone—but for Sophie? I asked the question. Dr. Sabbagh hesitated, then answered strong.

"I think that Sophie is of an age that she could see an effective prevention strategy," he said.

I told him I'd give it some thought.

I've met plenty of people with Alzheimer's disease, and the only thing that terrifies me more than the thought that I'll live to see the day Sophie gets it is the thought that I won't. Who will take care of her if and when she loses the ability to talk, walk, and do the most basic things for herself, things that were hard-won and now taken for granted?

Not her daughter—I cannot bet on that one. Standing in that giant ballroom with all those families hanging on every word from the Alzheimer's researchers, I thought about what an odd sandwich generation the group of us made.

"Just what sort of sandwich is that?" I asked a friend. "Usually it's us between parents and kids. What is it when your kid gets early-onset Alzheimer's?"

"It's an open-faced sandwich—a sandwich you can no longer pick up, or manage, even with both hands," he replied without missing a beat.

Yeah.

I have watched a daughter care for her mother who had Alzheimer's; I saw it up close. In the mid-90s, Ray's parents—who lived near us in Tempe—moved his mother's parents, Bill and Mary Keegan, out from New York City. I remember sitting with them at dinner, looking at wide eyes in wrinkled faces. They couldn't make sense of the heat, the expanses of desert, the long, unwalkable blocks. Both were first-generation Irish Americans, neither had lived outside New York. Neither had ever driven a car and there was no bar within walking distance of their little apartment, a real problem for the couple, who could down domestic beer like it was water.

Bill had been an elevator operator, the kind of guy prone to telling jokes like, "The elevator business is really up and down!" And if I'd heard him tell the story of the time he came to town and Ray's pet tortoise escaped from the backyard once, I'd heard it a dozen times.

So I was surprised when it was Mary, not Bill, who developed memory problems. Over the years, she grew quieter, more fidgety. She ran away from the apartment. She yelled at Bill. Her daughters took her to the doctor: Alzheimer's disease.

Before anyone could figure out what to do about Mary, Bill started turning down the Pabst Blue Ribbon; the family knew something else was wrong. They were right: his abdomen was packed with cancer. He was dead within weeks. No one told Mary at first, and even after they did, she forgot—she'd ask for him, ruining a family birthday party with a cheery, "Where's Bill?" It made Mary's daughters sad to talk about how Daddy was dead, so the sisters started telling her, "Oh, he's out for a bit, Ma." That satisfied her.

I was afraid of Mary. She had long ago forgotten my name, which was understandable, considering our rare visits. Would she yell at me? Hit me? Throw food across the dinner table? No. For the most part, she just withdrew. Little things confused her. One day we had a barbecue at my in-laws' house, where Mary now lived. I sat next to Mary, who carefully chose carrots and celery from a vegetable tray, with each bite asking for the salt shaker—which sat directly in front of her the entire time. I kept handing it to her anyway. Ray's cousins giggled and shook their heads.

But it was hard to be cheery all the time. My mother-in-law, Pat, and her two sisters shared in Mary's twenty-four-hour care, and it was draining. Pat still worked full time doing data input at the police department.

I didn't know what to say around Mary, how to act. Should I just ignore her, or talk baby talk? Ray's family was no help; Pat loved her mother dearly, but she was exhausted. And sad. She missed her mother. Pat's communication with Mary was utilitarian: directions to the bathroom, admonishments about eating too much chocolate. Mary was not interested in television or magazines. She wanted to help around the house and often got underfoot in the kitchen. This further frustrated Pat, who couldn't find anything for her to do—

except for one task: folding paper napkins. Mary would sit for hours, folding each paper napkin perfectly in half, making a pile.

About that time, I had coffee with a friend who happens to be a poet. When she told me she was being sent into nursing homes to write poetry with Alzheimer's patients as part of her studies at Arizona State University, I was intrigued. And befuddled. My first thought was of Mary. She couldn't find her way to her own bedroom without brightly colored signs. What sort of guide would it take to get her to write a poem?

A guide like Karla Elling. In her many years at ASU's creative writing department, Elling had been a big proponent of community-based programs. But while sending poets into classrooms to work with young children made sense to everyone, it took Elling to figure out that it might work with people with Alzheimer's. She knows the disease well; first her father, then her mother died of dementia-related illnesses. Elling had no idea how to handle her father, who was increasingly violent as his condition declined.

"He went through many residences and nursing homes and hospitals and by the time he got out of the last hospital, with his second broken hip, he wasn't allowed to go back anywhere that he'd been," Elling recalled. Finally, she found a nursing home in Scottsdale, near her home, that would take him.

"There he was treated so well," she said. "He could hear little stories from me. He could answer little details about living in the little mining towns in Arizona. I knew his memory was in there."

Elling and her father told his stories together. It brought her peace and appeared to bring him peace, as well.

"After he died I was so filled with gratitude for the people who had sort of saved our family because they had treated him well; I wanted to do something. And what I did was see if they wanted writing students to come into the Alzheimer's unit."

They did. The first poet was a woman named Alice. She could no longer speak, but she could write. One of Elling's students edited Alice's work into a poem called Cloves.

> *A little girl thin year*
> *with some grass amid the house*
> *and dark vegetables getting*
> *further away in the year*
> *for a green thought.*
> *In the spare time,*
> *in the house next*
> *to the spruce and the wheat.*
> *In the urgent house,*
> *the house of cleaning,*
> *the house in the trees*
> *in the time of the heart*
> *amid the fish.*
> *In that place is*
> *a good trip*
> *on this paper.*

I pitched a story idea to my editor and spent months hanging around the Alzheimer's poets.

One of the student instructors was a woman named Carol Smith, an elementary school teacher turned poet. I'd meet her in the parking lot, and she would unload the trunk of her Toyota Tercel, balancing posters and boxes, approaching the locked ward at Scottsdale Village Square. She had her own key.

Inside, the residents were kept clean and warm, with activities scheduled through the day in a large recreation room. But even at the best nursing home money can buy, the residents droop. On one visit a woman fell asleep literally with her head in a jigsaw puzzle.

The poets gathered around a table, and Carol would greet each one by name. They didn't recall her name, probably weren't sure why she was there. But she always proceeded with a big smile and a theme—dinosaurs, the solar system, things that are round. Everything from music to spices was used to try to conjure memories, stimulate thought.

One day Carol Smith showed the residents at Scottsdale Village Square a picture of a forest, a thick gathering of lush pines and asked them, What does it remind you of? Hank, a former farmer, examined the photograph. A curtain of trees.

Smith was stunned. *Curtain of Trees* was the title of the latest book by Alberto Rios, ASU's most celebrated poet and Smith's mentor. Rios later told me that he loved the idea that both a trained wordsmith and a man in the late stages of Alzheimer's disease could come up with the same idea. He was convinced that his process of writing isn't so different from Hank's: both conjure memories and make leaps.

Poetry is "broken narrative," Rios told me. "It subverts the communal narrative. We all agree that we are going to talk to each other and use certain words and cover a certain amount of time and not make leaps that are too big so that we don't understand. Well, poetry doesn't particularly operate that way. We make huge leaps sometimes and talk about things that we don't understand. We search for the mysterious, we try to explore it. And people with Alzheimer's are working much the same way. They make big leaps, but they are leaps that make sense on their own terms."

Like the day Smith and her class talked about windows, which inspired a woman named Ida to write a poem about what it would be like to have an eye in the palm of her hand.

> *It would see the curves in your fingers,*
> *It would see the wrinkles in your hand*
> *And the rings on your fingers.*
> *It would tell you, maybe, how long you're married.*
> *It would see the scar you got when*
> *You were in the first grade and had permission*

*To go through the neighbor's yard to get to your yard*
*Where the lady had a bunch of cats*
*And the cats were turned loose*
*And would come into your yard*
*Usually if you had something in your yard*
*That they could eat.*
*No, the cat didn't scratch me.*
*The lady died a long time ago*
*And it seemed to me*
*They'd already written the story about it.*

This from a woman who spends much of a typical day incessantly asking anyone who will listen, "Are we going to Mass today? Are we going to say the rosary? Are we going to church?"

"Each person is recognized in some way for being intelligent," Elling said about the Alzheimer's poets. "Your intelligence doesn't go away, your connections go away. Your linear abilities go away. But your intelligence is still in there and sort of bright and wonderful. They may be the ultimate existentialists, living in the present at every moment. But memory is only one thing. Life is something else."

I decided to try to write poetry with Ray's grandmother. I borrowed some stuffed animals from Carol Smith. Bought a calendar of kittens—Mary's favorite—and a Koosh ball I thought she'd like to touch. I gathered the materials in a pile in my office, thinking, *Soon.* I was busy, and anyway, she had been the same for so long. She didn't seem sick, just frail.

I knew so little about Alzheimer's disease; I didn't know how quickly death can come. We got a call late one afternoon from Ray's mother. By the next day, Mary was gone.

The next time I visited Carol Smith's workshop, I pictured Mary at the table, playing with the toys, singing the songs, finding meaning in abstract art. Would her poem have hung on the wall? And what would it mean if it had? Mary was dead, and even if she wasn't, she wouldn't likely recognize her words on the page, wouldn't remember the creative moment. I had to ask myself, are we using Alice and

Ida for their accidental poetry? Does it make us feel better to play puppeteer, coaxing pretty phrases from unwitting minds?

Does it matter? I gathered the calendar, the Koosh ball, and the rest of my workshop materials and gave them to Pat, explaining what I had meant to do. She smiled and thanked me, even though I knew she didn't really understand. But I bet she would have loved to have a poem written by her mother.

ееееее

I didn't recall any of the Alzheimer's poets having Down syndrome, and Alberto Rios couldn't recall that, either.

I searched for weeks for a person in metropolitan Phoenix who had both, figuring it would be easy, given the odds. It wasn't. I posted on Facebook, called the Marc Center, reached out to the Alzheimer's association, and asked everyone I could think of. Nothing.

Then I heard about Tracy. She lived just a couple miles away with her older sister. One of Sophie's Special Olympics coaches knew Tracy and said she was starting to show signs of dementia.

I looked Tracy's sister, Blair, up on Facebook and recognized her instantly. Her son went to Broadmor and was a year younger than Sophie. Blair had always taken a special interest in Sophie, stopping to talk to her and mentioning to me on occasion that she had a sister with Down syndrome. But I'd never met Tracy.

Blair Tucker was kind enough to invite me into her home to tell me about her family and their lives, and I got to meet Tracy, who is fifty-two. The first morning I arrived at Tucker's house, Tracy was at a day program, which was good, because the back story was pretty long.

Blair was no nonsense, with pretty, dark hair pulled back, and was wearing a tank top and shorts on this late summer day. As I entered the modest two-story home she shares with her husband, son, and sister, she announced without apology that she's no housekeeper and led me past piles and a full kitchen sink to the small, oilcloth-covered table where she meets with support coordinators and others who provide Tracy's government-funded services.

Fifty years ago, most families didn't keep babies with Down syndrome. Tucker said that the doctors had told her mother to institutionalize Tracy.

"She was livid," Blair recalled.

Growing up, "a lot of people did not know I had a sister with Down syndrome," she said. Tracy went to a school across town for kids with special needs, and the family didn't have guests over much.

Blair didn't recall spending a lot of time with Tracy. She has a memory of rocking her on a rocking horse "for what seemed like hours" and remembered playing school with Tracy and their younger sister. Their mother doted on Tracy, Tucker said, and the little girl was always in her room playing with books.

She didn't read them or even pretend to, Blair said, describing a habit Tracy had of ripping pages out, rolling the paper between her fingers and making little coils or spitwads, "Like a gerbil."

Tracy never had much speech. A word here or there, although Blair said Tracy understood what was said to her.

Tracy lived in her childhood room in their childhood home until their mother died in 2002. Thirteen years later, Blair still teared up, talking about her mother. Tracy then moved in for four years with their younger sister.

And then it was Blair's turn. When we met, she'd had Tracy in her home for nine years. It's not all bad, she said. Tracy could be loving, and Blair had quit her job at America West Airlines to be Tracy's caregiver; the state paid her for those services.

But lately, Tracy had been slipping. "Her mental age was maybe five," when she came to live in Arizona, Blair said. "Now it's like three and a half."

She used to know the alphabet. Now she was down to just a couple of letters. She used to be able to use the bathroom on her own. Now she wore a diaper, and often Blair would find her in the bathroom or by her bed, without the diaper, peeing on the floor.

"She can't take care of herself in any way," Blair said.

Yes, she got paid; yes, she loved her sister—but it was getting too hard, Blair admitted. She couldn't put her son's artwork on the refrigerator because Tracy would take it down and shred it. She had to keep a child lock on the pantry.

"I saw my mom," she said, "and I said to myself, my world will never be that small. But it has gotten smaller."

Today a parent of a young child with Down syndrome would be hard-pressed to avoid news of the connection to Alzheimer's disease. But Blair was only vaguely aware of it when Tracy started to regress around her fiftieth birthday.

Often a personality change is the first sign of Alzheimer's in a person with Down syndrome. Blair said that had not happened.

For the most part, Tracy was still very loving, her sister said. "With me she's always been stubborn, so it's not like that part changed."

I came back the following afternoon to meet Tracy. She was still a "girly girl," loved sparkly things and nail polish, Blair said, leading me upstairs to Tracy's small bedroom. The first thing I noticed was a giant old television set blaring music videos. Apologetically, Blair explained that Tracy does not have cable in her room.

"What are you watching?" Blair asked her sister.

"That," Tracy said after a long pause, pointing.

Tracy was short and trim and gave me a giant hug as soon as I entered the room. She was wearing a T-shirt and cropped pants with knee socks and a backward baseball cap over her bobbed hair. The room was trimmed with faded pink, blue, and purple butterfly wallpaper near the ceiling.

Tracy stopped watching the TV and turned to sift through a big bin on the floor, filled with ripped papers (the coils of paper Blair mentioned were all over the floor), stuffed animals, and Special Olympics medals. Blair pulled out animals and Tracy identified them: "Rabbit! Turtle!" But she couldn't find the word for Barbie, even though her sister said the doll is her favorite.

With her tiny stature and sporty outfit, at first glance Tracy looked young, as young as Sophie, but when I looked more closely I saw fine lines on her face and a few gray hairs peeking out from under the baseball cap. She seemed oddly preserved, protected from the stuff the rest of us worry about.

Blair worried enough for both of them. She had been to the doctor that morning to ask about Tracy's teeth grinding, which had started recently, and to get a referral to a neurologist to see if she has Alzheimer's.

She seemed doubtful that it would do any good, either way.

"How are you going to determine if she has Alzheimer's or dementia if she never knew how to do something in the first place?" she asked.

I told her I saw her point.

"It's very frustrating. It's maddening," she said. Blair said she was making plans for Tracy to live someplace else.

"I have taken care of her for nine years," she said, her eyes wet. For her, Tracy was a daily reminder that her mother was gone, and she couldn't stand it anymore. She wiped tears away. "I feel like she would have been so proud of me for what I have accomplished."

As I was leaving I thanked her and told Blair Tucker that I was sorry it took me so long to find her. Lots of people knew who Tracy was, I explained, but they only referred to Blair as "Tracy's sister."

She nodded.

"That's my identity," she said. "I'm just Tracy's sister. You know what, I don't want to be that anymore. I want to be me."

I got in my car and drove away, and damned if I could think of a single poetic thing about that encounter.

To be honest, all I could think about was Annabelle.

# 14

## GAME CHANGER

In a lot of ways, one of the most interesting things about having a kid with Down syndrome has been discovering where Sophie's participation is welcomed, rather than what she is excluded from.

Like sports. Beginning when she was eight, a whole world of opportunities opened up to Sophie when we received our first newsletter from the city of Tempe Parks & Recreation Department's adaptive services division.

Neither Ray nor I was at all involved with or interested in organized sports as kids, which is probably why we were the king and queen of the nerds. He loved to ride his bike and eventually found rock climbing, but never liked games involving balls. I was the chubby kid picked last every time, the girl who dreaded Field Day all year long, who tried telling the coach I had my period every week to avoid running around the track in gym class. Annabelle ended up at a charter school that didn't even offer PE; she got her exercise in ballet class several hours a day.

Sophie was destined to be the true athlete of the family. The parks & rec newsletters offered a smorgasbord of options for Sophie, whose muscles had been trained by years of physical therapy. I browsed the buffet, picking and choosing sports—speed skating was too hard; bowling was too easy (and stereotypical). Track and field? Just right.

It was the perfect entry point. Sophie loved to run, and it was something she could do alone. We saw other people of varying ages and disabilities at practice each week, but from a distance. It wasn't overwhelming for a family that still hadn't attended an annual Down syndrome Buddy Walk.

Track was only a few weeks each year, and we wanted to get Sophie more involved. That was tough. She was too young for tennis or volleyball and afraid to try swimming the length of the pool.

"And cheerleading's out, of course," I told my mom one day, offhandedly.

She just raised her eyebrows.

Look, if you'd asked me twenty years ago which would be worse—to have a kid with Down syndrome or a kid who was a cheerleader—I'm not sure what I would have said. Speech and debate, newspaper club, Model United Nations—now those were fun, acceptable activities for an empowered young woman. Cheering for boys? No way. Not my daughters—neither one.

My mother is smart. She waited until I least suspected her motives. We were on a family beach vacation—the sun was shining, the breeze was blowing—and it was a rare family-free moment, just the two of us in lounge chairs, relaxing. I was about to nod off when I heard her speak.

"Ames, there's something I have to say," she said, her voice hesitant and serious.

My eyes flew open. Oh god. Oh no. It's cancer.

I sat up and turned to face her.

"Um, what?" I asked, trying to sound nonchalant, my heart racing.

She didn't catch my eye.

"I really think you should consider letting Sophie do cheerleading in the Special Olympics," she said.

I sat back and glared.

"Don't scare me like that!"

"Well, I had to get your attention," she said. "Oh, come on. What do you care? She'll have a blast! Sophie loves to dance!"

She did. She took ballet and jazz and was trying to convince me to let her take tap. But cheer? No way. Not only is it a bitchy girl's sport, I argued, it would literally put Sophie on the sidelines. Isn't the whole point of Special Olympics to make Sophie the one who gets the cheers?

For quite a while, I bored my friends and family with this invented conundrum. Finally, someone asked a really good question—the only important question.

"Does Sophie want to do it?"

I had to admit that I hadn't even thought to ask.

"Hey, Sophes," I said one night before bed. "There's something I need to talk to you about."

"Yes, Mommy?"

"Do you want to do Special Olympics cheerleading?"

"YES!"

And so Sophie cheered. Every Saturday morning, she'd pull on sweatpants and I'd help her with her Velcroed tennis shoes, and we'd head to a fluorescent-lit rec center near our house. For the first few practices, I couldn't really tell what she thought. She was pretty quiet.

Then one evening, Sophie was in the shower and we heard her voice—quiet at first, then getting louder.

"Dribble it, pass it. We want a basket! Dribble it, pass it. We want a basket!" She loved it. Loved the routines—which were admittedly simple—loved the uniform, the pom-poms, her teammates and coaches.

I called my mom to report that as usual, she was right, and then we admitted we'd both always secretly wanted to be cheerleaders ourselves—and had a good laugh.

As it turns out, Special Olympics is more complicated than simply signing up and showing up. There's serious conflict over the mission of one of the oldest organizations devoted to people with intellectual disabilities. I had no idea until Sophie and I attended our first regional cheerleading competition in the winter of 2013.

On a chilly evening, dozens of cheerleaders gathered in an old recreation hall. With some time to spare before the official event, Tempe's team hustled into a side room with fluorescent lights and worn blue carpet to go over the routine they'd practiced for months, a number featuring several simple, traditional cheers followed by a short dance sequence to a medley of pop songs—starting with Taylor Swift's "I Knew You Were Trouble (When You Walked In)" and culminating with "Gangnam Style."

It wasn't easy to choreograph for Team Tempe. Members ranged from my Sophie, who was nine and competing for the first time—so small her brand-new XS uniform had to be pinned at the waist—to a couple of Special Olympics veterans in their fifties. Not everyone was entirely mobile. With all kinds of intellectual disabilities (several team members, like Sophie, had Down syndrome; some were on the autism spectrum or had other diagnoses like cerebral palsy), it was hard to know who would remember what. The rules allowed the coaches to stand in front of the group and remind them of moves during competition.

No aerial handsprings or backflips for Team Tempe; we parents were just hoping this night that everyone would remember to put on sunglasses tucked into uniforms and cross arms over chests in unison at the end of "Gangnam Style."

As Sophie's coaches handed out sunglasses and tied pom-poms onto tennis shoes, my eyes wandered to another team practicing on the other side of the room. These Special Olympians looked much different from the members of our team. I nudged Beth; her daughter, Tatum, Sophie's classmate, was also competing for the first time.

Soon, Beth and I were gawking as the young girls from this other team easily formed a pyramid. A few of them obviously had intellectual disabilities, but others looked like they came out of central casting, vying for the role of "perky young cheerleader," as they leapt into the air, turned cartwheels, and cheered with clear voices.

"What the hell?" I muttered to Beth, pointing. "That one doesn't even look like she has so much as a speech delay! What are they doing here?"

Beth shook her head and went off to investigate. She was back a few minutes later.

"They're part of this other kind of Special Olympics," she reported. "It's called Unified."

Even if you aren't close to someone with an intellectual disability, chances are good you're familiar with Special Olympics—from a story on TV news about an inspiring bowling team or heartwarming images in the newspaper of proud, shivering swimmers lined up to accept medals. Special Olympics gives people with intellectual disabilities of all levels of athletic ability a chance to compete in a variety of events.

Simple, right? Not really. Special Olympics in the twenty-first century is much more complicated. For the pioneers of Project Unify, an offshoot of the original program, it's not just about putting people with special needs in the spotlight and giving them a little exercise. It's also about trying to answer fundamental questions: How do we help these people forge meaningful connections and friendships? How do we teach typical children and adults to be less afraid, to value a person regardless of his or her IQ? And how do we take this off the field and into real life?

Here, perhaps, is the most surprising part. I didn't know it because Tempe was one of the few cities that still hadn't fully embraced a Unified model. But as I found out, out of all the places in the world that participate in Special Olympics, in 2014 Arizona was leading the charge in this ambitious effort. Yes, Arizona—a place that elected hate-filled and ignorant politicians, where people were punished for their differences, where budgets were starved and social-welfare indicators bottomed out on all kinds of rankings.

It wasn't easy, and not just because it was in Arizona. Some fans of traditional Special Olympics didn't want typical peers (called "partners" in Unified) stealing attention from "athletes" (participants with disabilities). One of the biggest challenges was whether to use a competitive model, which was a bigger deal in sports with balls than in track or cheer. Even with rules and referees, it was difficult in some Unified sports to maintain an even playing field that allowed athletes to score—and shine. Some said competition had no place in Special Olympics at all. Others vehemently disagreed.

Either way, I was fascinated and spent the better part of a year interviewing local Special Olympics officials and haunting games and practices.

Earlier that year, officials at a high school in Wichita, Kansas, had made national headlines when they asked a boy with Down syndrome and autism to remove the letterman jacket his mother had bought to recognize his basketball skills.

But at Raymond S. Kellis High School in Glendale, a city on the west side of metro Phoenix, several students with special needs were wearing letterman jackets with the blessing of Special Olympics and the Arizona Interscholastic Association, which had recently amended its bylaws to allow kids participating in Unified sports programs to earn an official letter.

The AIA liked Unified as much for what it does for typical kids as for what it does for those with special needs. These days, officials told me, high school sports tend to draw only super-athletes, leaving most kids in the dust. Kids of average ability made a terrific pool of partners, according to the Special Olympics officials I spoke with—and they were getting in shape emotionally as well as physically, often building truly meaningful relationships through teamwork.

Sounds awesome, right?

My interest in Unified sports grew as Sophie was getting ready to enter middle school. Sophie was the busiest person I knew. She was still cheering for Team Tempe and was on the city's Special Olympics track team. She took swimming and ballet lessons with typical kids and sometimes participated in a drama program designed for people with special needs.

Our neighborhood middle school welcomed Sophie, putting her in general-education classes with an aide, making room for her on the junior varsity cheer team, and starting a Best Buddies chapter and a drama club, in part at my urging.

These classes, clubs, teams, and programs put Sophie in touch with other kids her own age—indeed, Best Buddies is designed specifically to foster relationships between typical kids and those with intellectual disabilities. But as we neared the end of Sophie's first year in middle school, her best friend was her eighteen-year-old babysitter.

Every morning, it was a battle to get Sophie to school. She said it was the dress code, but I worried it was the lack of a social life that kept her in bed with the covers over her head. Every weekend, she begged me for a sleepover date. I kept coming up empty, and it was breaking both our hearts.

Sophie is the most loving, gregarious, engaging kid—and yet she had almost no meaningful friendships with other girls her own age.

It also should be stated that Sophie could be bossy. She was several inches shorter than most of her peers. And while she was working hard to refine her tween tastes, Sophie still sometimes sucked her thumb. If given the choice, she'd watch *The Wonder Pets* and *Peppa Pig*. She collected paintbrushes because they feel soft, and she saw nothing odd about giving one as a gift to a new acquaintance. She was different. And different can be a hard sell anywhere. But particularly in middle school.

Sophie had true, meaningful friendships in elementary school—invitations to birthday parties, sleepover dates, giggle fests—and very little of that had to be manufactured. There were times when she was ignored, but for the most part, the other kids accepted her. As we'd neared the end of sixth grade, no one had been mean to Sophie in middle school (that I knew of), but no one had reached out to her much, either. Even though she was mainstreamed in the classroom, it was as though she was on her own divergent course—one that was taking her further and further away from her peers.

To complicate matters, Sophie had trouble relating to other kids with special needs. She and her cheer teammate, Tatum, had been in school together since kindergarten, and they were friends, but really, the only thing they have in common is that they both have Down syndrome. Tatum is tall and athletic, queen of the monkey bars, reserved and mature. Sophie's more the goofy, girly extrovert. I knew the girls loved each other, but I had a feeling that they wondered why they were shoved together so often, why they wound up eating lunch together every day.

Once, Sophie told me, "Tatum's hard to understand when she talks." The girls have a very similar speech impediment, a by-product of the low muscle tone common in people with Down syndrome—but how could I say to Sophie, "Yeah, well, so are you"?

Sophie was stuck between two worlds, not comfortable in either, and I didn't see that getting better as she got older. With high school looming, I was worried. I didn't want my kid to be a mascot—or a footnote on someone else's college application under "volunteer activities."

I cringed when I saw stories about the "team manager" on the high school basketball team who made the winning shot in a game—relegated to a bench for the entire season, given one moment in the spotlight. Inevitably, that kid has an intellectual disability such as Down syndrome. Inevitably, the whole thing is filmed for the evening news.

High fives all around, right? Meh.

Unified Special Olympics taught me that it doesn't have to be that way.

There was a video making the rounds of a three-point basket made by Mason Rivera, an athlete on the Liberty High School Lions Unified team, during the state championship game February 28 at Gila River Arena. The shot brought the Lions within seven points of the Perry High School Pumas at halftime. In the end, the Lions lost, but that shot was a hard-earned, meaningful moment for Rivera, not just a token.

While Sophie was getting adjusted to middle school last fall, I was all over town—meeting a coach from Gilbert, a special-education teacher in Glendale, a volleyball team in Peoria, and two best friends from Chandler. I heard and saw great examples of teamwork, sportsmanship, and life-changing experiences. I also learned about some Unified experiences that didn't go so well. There were families who preferred old-school Special Olympics, and one mom who didn't care for it at all.

For the most part, I liked it. If there's one thing being the parent of a kid with special needs had taught me, it's that there is no easy fix, no one-size-fits-all solution—for anything. But what these people in Arizona were doing was a real game changer.

In September 2013, when Tim Shriver spoke at the Arizona Special Olympics breakfast, he praised the state's efforts in this new kind of Special Olympics.

In 1968, hundreds gathered on Soldier Field in Chicago for the first official Special Olympics. These, Shriver said, were "the most forgotten people in the country," and his mother had the audacity to call them Olympians.

Thanks to Eunice Kennedy Shriver, the term "Special Olympics" is now a part of the world's vocabulary.

For more history, I turned to Jon-Paul St. Germain, senior director for Unified Sports and Sport Partnerships for Special Olympics, based in Washington, D.C., who told me that the first official "integrated" softball game was played in 1989, a hint of what would someday become Project Unify. But it was many years before Unified really took off. For a long time, simply getting people with intellectual disabilities "out of the shadows and onto the playing field" was an effort, St. Germain said.

Then there was a push to demonstrate that Special Olympics athletes were capable of more—swimming in open water, running marathons, and participating in equestrian sports.

Eventually, St. Germain said, "Within the organization, you started to see that more people were pushing further, and expectations were getting higher and higher, and there was a desire to become more inclusive."

But Unified is not such an easy model. It works best when athletes and partners are equally matched in skill, a particular challenge in sparsely populated areas or when you're gathering participants from group homes instead of community centers or schools. It took time and effort, but eventually, at a global congress in Morocco in 2010, Unified Sports was identified as a priority to keep the games relevant, bring more people in, and overcome stigmas, St. Germain said.

The goal was to reach one million participants by the end of 2015. When I spoke to St. Germain in the fall of 2014, the number already was up to more than 800,000.

Unified started in Connecticut, and Arizona definitely had made a mark in the recent past as a leader in recruiting in the community—but the place where local leaders really have made a difference is the development of programs in schools.

Tim Martin, executive director of Special Olympics Arizona, sounded almost religious in his dedication to the Unified model. For him, it was personal.

As a high school sophomore in Anchorage, Alaska, in the mid-'80s, "I was a kid who made every bad decision you can imagine," he admitted to me over one of many meals we shared. He had no father. But he did have a football coach. One day, the coach ordered him to work on throwing a softball with some kids with intellectual disabilities.

At the time, what he was doing didn't have a name. "What I did was Unified. We didn't get to compete together, but we got to be together," Martin said. "It simply changed my view…I had a responsibility, and I could help others, and they could help me."

Eventually, Martin moved to Arizona and worked at the state Department of Economic Security and then the YMCA. When he joined Special Olympics Arizona in 2009, things were not in good shape. The average athlete's age was forty. Enrollment wasn't high. Neither was the budget.

But Martin knew about Unified, and he was determined to make it "systemic" in Arizona. Today, he chairs the Global Unified Sports Advisory Group, responsible for everything from planning for the world games to training Unified leaders all over the world. In four and a half years, he said, Special Olympics Arizona's annual budget had gone from $2.6 million to $4.5 million. He did it by partnering with groups like the Arizona Interscholastic Association.

In the fall of 2013, several AIA and Special Olympics Arizona staff members gathered around a big conference table at AIA headquarters to tell me about the connection the two organizations have made.

AIA is the 100-year-old organization that governs sports and other extracurricular activities at the 270 high schools in the state. When Tim Martin met AIA director Chuck Schmidt, there was an instant connection, and it was decided that, someday, Unified would be as important to AIA as the state football and basketball championships. Unified became an official designation in the AIA bylaws, which is what allows Unified kids (both athletes and partners) to earn letters. Arizona's the first state to do this, they said.

"It's an official sport; it's the real deal," Martin said. At the time I met them, the men were working on developing national and international training models.

"Tim sold me on it," Schmidt said, adding that what's happening is nothing short of "changing the mindset of what sports is."

Schmidt acknowledged that a very small percentage of high school varsity players in Arizona will go on to become professional athletes. But Unified gives them a different set of tools that they will use for life.

Okay, I said, deciding it was time for a challenge. I never played sports in high school, I told them, explaining that instead, I was on the debate team. And I see that AIA regulates speech and debate. Are there plans in the works to offer a Unified Speech and Debate program? Sophie would love that. (And so would I, I thought to myself.)

Around the table, eyebrows went up. It was quiet for a few moments and then someone chuckled and changed the subject. Later, a Special Olympics staffer told me Tim Martin turned to him after the meeting and told him to figure out a way to make it happen.

*ℓℓℓℓℓℓ*

None of this is easy. Not every attempt at Unified works. After decades in the field, Paula Considine has seen it all. When I met her in the spring of 2015, she was coaching a Unified volleyball team in Peoria, a city on the far west edge of metropolitan Phoenix, and getting ready for the international games that summer.

She'd never consider starting a Unified basketball team or trying flag football again, she said. Both get too competitive, and not in a good way. But when several families approached her in 2013 asking for Unified volleyball, she agreed to give it a chance.

Considine was impressed that a few of her team members were local kids who had participated in Unified in high school and wanted to continue after graduation. Plus, she told me, Unified allowed family members to play together.

On a Monday night in the cafeteria at Sun Valley Elementary School in Peoria, Considine's two teams were practicing for an upcoming tournament. Balls flew across the gym, thwacking white linoleum, and teammates worked together to encourage athletes to keep it in play.

"No matter what, it's always fun," said Haley Iunski, a partner and a senior at Liberty High School who had volunteered with Special Olympics since eighth grade. She took a quick break to talk, her face flushed. "It still gets competitive."

An athlete named Jacob May took his turn serving. Throughout the practice, his teammates admonished him to not hit the ball quite so hard.

"He's strong!" I said, as a ball whizzed by our heads.

"He's showing off," Considine replied, not unkindly.

On a bench nearby, two women were holding court like Statler and Waldorf, the old men in the balcony on the *Muppet Show*. Diana May was Jacob's grandmother. Vicky Mitchell's son, Joshua Fenster, also was an athlete.

The women talked, finishing each other's sentences and eyeing the flying balls. Joshua, who was thirty-five, competed in softball, basketball, and bowling.

"What does he not do?" May asked of Jacob—who plays golf, softball, floor hockey, and more.

Neither woman was particularly keen on Unified, though both admitted that volleyball had been okay.

"The football stunk," May said. Mitchell added that the people with special needs were left out. "They just wanted to win," she said of the partners. She said she told Tim Martin as much. But with volleyball, the coaches were good, and everyone was included. The women were happy.

I have a feeling that even the hardest-core critic would be a fan of Unified after an hour at Kellis High School.

Ten minutes into my first visit to the school, which sits just off Glendale Avenue in the shadow of University of Phoenix Stadium, I started wondering how I could get Sophie enrolled—damn the hour-long commute from Tempe.

I was not alone. Special-education teacher Michael Wakeford said that the program was poised to grow from fifty-five to seventy kids the following school year. Also on the rise: the number of typical kids vying for spots as partners in the Unified Sports class Wakeford offered each semester.

Several years ago, Special Olympics Arizona embedded a staff person in the Peoria School District to write a curriculum that was now used in more than fifty high schools across the state. The result was a model that's been studied by Nike (results are forthcoming) and praised by Tim Shriver, who visited Kellis when he came to Arizona in 2013.

Unified Sports had won a spot on the varsity photo wall at Kellis; when I visited, the school had given out four letters to Unified athletes. Unified athletes routinely spoke at graduation. One day on campus I did a double-take as a kid walked by with an acoustic guitar with a "Spread the Word to End the Word" bumper sticker on it. There was a Unified Dance class, and the woodshop teacher had recently asked Wakeford how he could get involved.

On a Friday afternoon, students gathered in Wakeford's class for Unified Sports, wearing neon-orange shirts with the motto "We Are Able," sweaty and excited from a pep rally. The teacher called roll, then praised the kids for their dance performance. The reaction from the crowd was amazing, he said, rubbing his arms:

"Talking about it right now gives me goose bumps."

In jeans and Converse sneakers with a beard that's the topic of several posters hanging in his classroom, Wakeford clearly is a rock star on this campus. Repeatedly, Tim Martin and other Special Olympics administrators told me that it was the individual people who made Unified work, and this guy was clearly one of them. He took attendance and then Wakeford aimed his large group toward the school's practice gym, where they worked out with volleyballs and soccer balls.

The kids practiced kicking and throwing, cracking each other up and—once in a while—earning a timeout for kicking a ball a little too hard. One young man, a partner, carefully held his teammate's elbow, helping him navigate the busy, noisy gym.

The program didn't get this good overnight, Wakeford admitted. One of the keys to success, he said, is that Kellis uses a training model rather than a competitive one.

"The competitive model asks a lot of things that, on paper, look great," he said. But in many ways, they go against "the reason we do all this."

Wakeford said he'd seen ugly situations, including a particularly bad experience during a soccer game at the national games in Nebraska several years ago. The partner's job is to help the athletes, not show off, Wakeford said, and the problem is that Unified's competitive rules were complicated on purpose, designed to allow athletes to score. He saw both athletes and partners reduced to tears after a poorly trained referee made bad calls, and it was then that Wakeford decided to go in a different direction.

He believed that by eliminating competition, true sportsmanship comes through.

"Competitiveness and Special Olympics aren't words that go together," he said.

The head of Arizona's Special Olympics, Tim Martin, disagrees.

"Every child deserves to fail miserably and have to be picked up and dusted off," he said.

I loved where Michael Wakeford was coming from, but Martin made a good point, too. So many sports programs for kids with special needs (there are others; Special Olympics is just the best-known) never keep score, never make the experience real. The participants never know what it's like to really play a game, what it's like to lose—or win.

All this was on my mind on a clear, sunny Saturday in February 2015, when I joined hundreds of people stuffed in an elementary school gym in Gilbert to watch the state Special Olympics cheerleading competition. As one of a handful of traditional teams that still remained, Sophie's group performed near the end, and I wiggled around on the hard floor, trying to get comfortable, finally spotting an empty chair against the wall and lunging for it.

"There are more Unified teams than ever," the older woman sitting next to me said as Yuma's team took the stage. This woman's daughter was in her twenties, she told me, and was on Mesa's team. Mesa and Tempe almost always competed against each other. Mesa still had a traditional team, too.

What do you think? I asked. Do you like Unified?

"I'm not into it," she said. "I wouldn't mind if they had more normal people doing the coaching, giving personal attention. But not performing."

As I watched group after group take the small stage, I had to agree. I was a fan of Unified in a lot of instances, but not when it came to cheerleading. I'd been watching, and maybe I'd just missed it, but out of dozens of participants, I hadn't seen any partners hanging out with the athletes during downtime. Instead, I saw quite a few perfect little girls steal the spotlight from kids and adults who rarely get a chance to shine.

Finally, it was Team Tempe's turn, and I scurried to the front of the crowd, camera phone ready, to catch Sophie in action. The stakes were high that day. Tempe hadn't won a first place medal in recent memory, maybe not ever, despite adding tricks like (attempts at) somersaults and clumsy lifts. Technically speaking, a win was not such a big deal—teams typically competed in heats of two or three, to ensure that Unified and typical teams did not compete against one another, and this way, every competitor was guaranteed a medal. But a gold was still meaningful, particularly for Tempe. Earlier, one of the coaches had joked with Sophie—still the smallest member of the team as she approached twelve—that the only thing left would be to shoot her out of a cannon. Sophie didn't find that very funny and kept asking about it, a little worried.

Tempe nailed their routine, rocking out to Meghan Trainor's "All about That Bass" and Taylor Swift's "Shake It Off," and then the team settled down to wait for results. Even though I knew it's not supposed to matter, I was dreading the announcement that once again, we'd lost.

But we didn't lose, not this time. Tempe was taking home the gold. It took a few minutes for them to realize they'd won in their heat against Mesa , but when they did, Sophie and her teammates beamed, bowing their heads one by one to receive their gold medals.

Standing there, I realized there really is something to this Special Olympics thing, a magic that you can't always capture. Whether it's a traditional model or Unified, Eunice Kennedy Shriver was on to something with the simple idea of pulling people with intellectual disabilities out of the shadows—and daring to call them Olympians.

I caught Beth's eye from across the gym, and we grinned, our eyes glistening with tears, watching our daughters jump up and down. "Winning matters!" she mouths over the roar of the crowd. "It really matters."

And in that moment, nothing else did.

# 15

# CENTER STAGE

Not every parent of a person with intellectual disabilities is sold on Special Olympics—regular or Unified.

When Sophie was eight, she competed in her first state track meet. I was way more nervous than she was, worried that I wouldn't be able to find a spot in the community college's giant parking lot, let alone find our team, that we'd be late, that she'd trip and fall.

We parked and found the team, put on her shirt, and pinned on her number. I was rushing to get as close as I could to the chain-link fence around the community college track to see her take off, when I saw a familiar face.

Sam. It's just Sam; she ditched the surname a long time ago. Sam is somewhere between my mom and me, age-wise. She has two grown kids, Becky and Christopher. For many years, Becky was a ballet student at the studio my mom runs in Phoenix. Christopher was brain damaged at birth. At first the doctors thought he was deaf, so Sam rushed to learn sign language and became quite accomplished; she later got work interpreting at large theater productions around town.

Turns out, Christopher was not deaf. He is a sweet, giant kid of a man who hugs a little too tightly without meaning to and always catches your eye, asking how you're doing.

Sam was at Special Olympics that day to watch Christopher compete, she told me, grabbing my hands and pulling me in for a hug—it runs in the family. Stepping back and motioning to the field, she made a face. She really hates Special Olympics, she said. Christopher had been excluded from some teams, told he was not good enough, and in any case, these rare opportunities to compete were just not enough.

"That's why I started Detour!" she said.

I smiled and excused myself, rushing off to secure my spot at the fence. "Ugh, Detour," I thought, as Sophie took her mark, ultimately winning a silver medal, racing hard on tiny legs. The race took seconds, literally, and the medal ceremony not much longer than that. We were back in the car and headed home before I knew it—and I was still thinking about Detour.

Detour is a theater company for adults with developmental disabilities, based in Phoenix. Sam started it years ago with just a handful of people and a small space; eventually, she would secure grants and other resources that would put her group on one of the biggest stages in town.

I knew all about Detour, because Sam had drawn my mom in years before—first as an audience member and later by including a few of my mother's ballerinas in large dance numbers. But I had only been to one Detour show when Sophie was very young.

Our nanny at the time had volunteered as an acting coach, and I couldn't say no when she asked if I was coming to the show. But I sat in the very back and squinted my way through it, spending a lot of time studying the program.

Like so many other things—the person with special needs bagging groceries at Safeway, the group home on a field trip to the mall, my own kid on some days—Detour freaked me out.

I couldn't bear the thought of sitting in an audience and staring at people with various disabilities, let alone watching them perform Broadway musicals. I was going to have to get over that very soon.

My mother is a ballerina. Not many people can make that statement, but I can. At five, Susan Sealove's parents enrolled her at the Ballet Academy on Queens Boulevard near their home in Forest Hills. Some Sunday mornings she took the train to Manhattan to perform on NBC's *The Children's Hour.*

She kept dancing as a teen, even after her father uprooted the family in the mid-1950s and moved them to Tucson, Arizona, and she focused on modern dance at the University of Arizona, where she befriended one of her teachers. Years later, when both of them were living in Phoenix and married to lawyers, the two began a studio, Dance Theater West.

Neither my sister nor I took to ballet. As I was the eldest, there were a lot of expectations attached to my birth, and as I mentioned several chapters ago, there's an old family story about how I lifted a dainty leg and pointed my foot in the nursery, gathering a collective "awwww" and pronouncement that I would dance.

Growing up, I loved to be around the studio, the costumes, the music, the dancers—but I never felt right dancing myself. My mother loves to tell people that I announced that dancing gave me a headache and quit at an early age. It's probably true. My sister, who was always very shy, never even made it far enough to actually be able to quit.

And so by the time Annabelle, the first granddaughter, made her appearance, tensions were high. She, too, pointed her toes in the nursery, but she actually meant business. She was barely three when she took her first class, and by the time she was eleven, was taking five classes a week at the studio, another five at the charter arts school she attended, and dancing en pointe, right on schedule. If you had strong feet and took four classes a week, my mother would put you en pointe at eleven.

Things were a little trickier for Sophie. When I'd joked so long ago to my mom that Sophie would simply have to take modern instead of ballet, I never imagined that one day Sophie might actually have an opinion of her own.

Sophie wanted to take ballet.

As a kid I loved to hang around my mother's classes, and being a "dance mom" gave me plenty of opportunity to continue to indulge. I love the philosophy of my mom and her longtime partner. At every recital the two get onstage to make introductions and one of them says, "Ask not what your kid can do for the art of dance, but what the art of dance can do for your kid." As far as I'm concerned, they've got all the right priorities. Dance Theater West isn't too rigorous; the girls aren't required to wear eye-tugging buns or line up like soldiers. From an early age, creativity is celebrated, and girls of all shapes and sizes are welcome.

But until Sophie came along, as far as I know, there had never been a kid with special needs enrolled at the studio.

As Sophie's third birthday loomed, I approached it awkwardly. Sophie would love to dance, I told my mom. My mom offered to teach a class for Sophie and a couple other little girls we'd met who had Down syndrome. It was a disaster. The girls were too young for real ballet steps, and Sophie (and I) knew how different these sessions were from the typical classes.

I kept quiet for a while. I let Sophie's fourth birthday pass. After her fifth, I dropped hints until my mother finally suggested that maybe she was ready. I jumped at the chance, and my mom enrolled her in the three-year-olds' class.

I get where my mom was coming from. We never talked about it outright, but it had to be so hard for her, running a business and dealing with this situation on behalf of a family member. I know that she didn't want it to appear that she was playing favorites, making exceptions, or inconveniencing others. She doesn't teach kids under ten; so another teacher had Sophie in her class. I get that it was awkward.

In any case, Sophie blended in well with her younger classmates. She was still smaller than most of them and needed beginning instruction. She did wander from time to time, and needed extra coaxing and breaks, but she was able to learn the steps—and she loved going to class just like her big sister.

And then suddenly, her first year of dance was over, and it was time for the spring recital. Just days before the end of kindergarten, I dressed Sophie in her navy blue leotard and pink tights, curled her hair and applied the tiniest hints of eyeliner and lip gloss. Annabelle got herself dressed; at nearly seven, she was dancing in her fourth recital.

I swooned when I heard the music for Sophie's number, "Teddy Bear Picnic." I remembered dancing to that song when I was her age. We arrived hours before the show began, ready to rehearse one last time.

In the lobby of the high school auditorium where the recital was held, roses had been wrapped with baby's breath for the parents to purchase. Ray bought a rose for each girl, and I chased Sophie up and down the aisles as we waited for her class to take the stage.

I cried through the dress rehearsal—Sophie knew every step; she smiled and had a blast. There she was, my little girl, onstage with the other tiny dancers. For me, it was a symbol of how far we'd come, of how much Sophie could do.

And then it happened. We were waiting for the show to begin. The auditorium was filling up, and our friends and family had begun to arrive. I was chatting with Trish, who had been there when Sophie was born and continued to show up at just about every important event in the girls' lives. For a moment, I lost track of Sophie, who hadn't yet had to report backstage.

I looked around in a quick panic and found her; she was talking to a woman in a wheelchair. From behind I could tell that the woman was older, with rough skin and short gray hair, and when she turned to smile at me, I saw that she was missing a front tooth. And that she had Down syndrome. Sophie didn't yet understand the concept; she was just interested in the wheelchair.

It was clear that the woman pushing the wheelchair was the other woman's mother.

Both mother and daughter were very interested in Sophie. The daughter was sweet, but she didn't have very many words and clearly had a hard time getting around. Looking back, I wonder if she had Alzheimer's.

As the mother rolled her daughter away, she turned to me and smiled. "Myra took dance class when she was that age, too!" she said. And then she was gone.

I looked at Trish. I didn't have to say a word; she had known me for twenty years.

"Amy, that is not your future," Trish said. I just looked at her, unable to speak.

"Amy, that's not your future. It's not your future. It's not your future." Trish repeated it like a mantra. I blinked a few times, snapping myself out of it. It was time to get ready for the performance.

Sophie danced beautifully, screwing up no more and no less than her classmates. I went home thinking about that woman in the wheelchair and her mother.

*lllll*

Inclusion is so good for so many reasons—for the other kids, for the teachers, for anyone watching, and of course for the kid. Being in dance with her typical peers pushed Sophie to be disciplined and to grow in ways she never would have in another setting. When she was eleven, the fancy ballet company in town advertised a class designed specifically for kids with Down syndrome. I signed Sophie up, just to see what it would be like; she pretty much wound up teaching the class. We didn't sign up again.

There's potential danger in mainstreaming. Not with everything, but with many things, there is an expiration date, or at least a glass ceiling—and that was the case for Sophie and ballet.

Sophie remained two or three years behind her typical peers in class. She stayed small and didn't seem to notice. But as her eleventh birthday approached, she wanted to know when it was going to be time for her to get pointe shoes.

It's not unheard of for a child with Down syndrome to dance en pointe, but it's rare, and my mother had watched videos on YouTube of a few who had tried it and said their form was terrible, which is more than idle criticism—it can mean serious health risks.

I decided to find out just exactly why Sophie couldn't attempt pointe, so I turned to her long-time physical therapist. By the time Sophie was twelve, Dorcas was practically a member of the family. She had begun working with Sophie at three months, and she had borne witness to one of my most embarrassing moments as a "special-needs mom."

When Sophie was born, as I've mentioned, my resource pool was pretty shallow. A coworker of mine knew a woman in Illinois who had a niece in Florida who had Down syndrome. She called her, and reported back with some advice:

"Make sure you get therapy for the baby when she's zero to three."

Okay, I thought, I can do that. I got on the phone and started lining up therapists—physical, speech, occupational.

"Are you sure you want me to come now?" Dorcas Cisnowski asked. "Typically I'd wait till after Sophie has heart surgery."

"Oh no!" I replied. "You need to come now."

After the first session, I thanked Dorcas profusely, adding, "Thank goodness you got here! Sophie is almost three months old, after all."

Dorcas stared at me.

"You know," I said. "That zero to three thing."

Dorcas explained gently that it's zero to three *years*.

Oh.

So really, after that, there were no embarrassing questions. Dorcas came every week for an hour, even though for the first nine months or so, the baby screamed from the moment she saw her to the moment she left.

"Do you want to quit?" I'd ask nervously, as she emerged from the nursery.

"No," she'd say calmly. "She'll get used to me."

And she did—through foot braces, the metal stander, a walker, then running, bending, stretching, and, finally, catching air with two-feet-off-the-ground jumps. When Sophie entered sixth grade, Dorcas finally started making noises about stopping therapy. She typically only worked with tiny babies, she explained, and she had new clients who needed her. Even though Sophie begged her to stay—she loved Dorcas's car trunk full of games and the one-on-one attention—so she phased out her visits till one day I realized that Dorcas hadn't been to the house in months.

But she answered my email about pointe shoes right away, accepting an invitation to breakfast and explaining the physical reason it would be tough to put Sophie en pointe:

"Sophie struggles with sufficient abdominal muscle strength, arched instep, and balance with decreased base-of-support when en pointe. We can talk more specific at our bagel time together."

In other words, her stomach muscles, feet, and balance were all working against her.

My mother echoed Dorcas's comments when I asked her for specifics:

"Currently Sophie's muscle tone and 'line' would not be sufficient for work on pointe....Sure, you could put her in a pointe shoe with lots of gel and stand her at the barre, but it would be wrong in every way, especially that it would give Sophie hope that's not realistic."

Even typical kids sometimes have the wrong feet, my mom reminded me gently. We agreed it wasn't safe for Sophie.

As she got older, I tried to distract Sophie with more cheerleading opportunities, additional Special Olympics events, after-school clubs.

She could still dance, but she'd never make my mom's "elite" ballet company like her sister did. It broke my heart and made me wonder if it had been cruel to put her in class to begin with.

But then I would watch her pirouetting (her version, anyway) around the kitchen to Taylor Swift songs and realize how much confidence ballet had given her. Those recitals gave Sophie some of her first experiences onstage, and they would not be her last.

*lllll*

Sam didn't think Special Olympics was enough for Christopher, and she didn't think it was enough for Sophie, either.

One spring, she asked my mom if there was any way Annabelle and Sophie could take part in a Detour performance of *South Pacific*. Detour is for adults (in recent years Sam had included people with physical disabilities and mental illness along with intellectual disabilities), but once in a while there is a role or two for young children, and Sam wanted to include Sophie, with Annabelle as her acting coach.

Detour includes acting coaches onstage with the actors as shadow cast members. If a coach does his or her job, you don't realize the coach is there—but he or she is essential to the production's success and actors' feeling of safety and well-being. Courtney, our nanny who had been a coach before, quickly offered to drive the girls to rehearsals and be backstage with them at the performances. I agreed.

On opening night, I took my seat in the back of the auditorium, chicken as usual. And something happened. Maybe it was the thrill of seeing both my girls belt out "Dites Moi" in clear voices with giant smiles; maybe it was how comfortable Annabelle was with the cast; maybe it was the quality of the performance. Or maybe I was just ready to grow up. I was captivated.

I attended every performance that weekend, and by the last one I was sitting in the front row.

A couple of years later, when Detour put on a production of *Shrek*, Sam needed three Princess Fionas, in varying ages and sizes.

She asked if the girls would play the younger two, with Annabelle as Sophie's coach. The girls were thrilled, and so was I. I lurked in the back of the room during rehearsals, marveling at how Sam was able to manage a large, incredibly diverse group. She is wiry, with big eyes, black Ray-Bans, and Converse, her signature shoes that she asks each cast member to wear. One day she began rehearsal by yelling, "I'M SORRY!"—and then added that her one "I'm sorry" was going to have to cover any inadvertent slights or voice-raising during the rehearsal session. There were solemn nods around the room.

I even stuck around for the cast party, though I'm pretty sure parents weren't invited. Sam has a tradition at these events. It's not about fancy refreshments or party favors. She asked the dozens of actors to arrange their metal folding chairs in a giant circle on the scuffed linoleum in the church rec room where they rehearse, and she put one chair in the middle. She called it the "Hot Seat."

One by one, each cast member and coach took the seat, and was allowed to ask three others, including their coach, for feedback on their performance. The comments were heartfelt:

"You're really funny. I got to know you a lot during the show and you're a secret comedian!"

"You're awesome. You did a great job."

"I was extremely impressed with the fact that you stayed on script for this show!"

Looking around the circle from my perch against a wall in a far corner, I realized that I knew almost every person by name—and personality. I knew the tall, older man with the stuffed dog that always accompanied him onstage; the tiny, dark-haired woman who worked incredibly hard to get her one line out, and looked so proud when she did; Jenna, who was blind and sounded like she had stepped off Broadway when she opened her mouth to sing. There were several Detour couples holding hands; I loved that part.

When it was Sophie's turn on the hot seat, she pointed to Annabelle and waited patiently for her compliment, swinging her short legs on the metal chair.

"Sophie, I thought you did an amazing job," Annabelle said, "and I love how you can stand up on stage and totally just have all the confidence in the world, and honestly I just really wish that I could have your confidence."

I tried to hide my tears, thinking about what a rare find Detour is. Each individual is gently pushed to his or her limit, celebrated for accomplishments, given meaningful interactions with others with disabilities and those without, and given a place onstage. What more can anyone ask in life? I want Sophie out in the world, mainstreamed in school, taking ballet class, and eventually finding meaningful work and someone to love. But I also hope Detour is always there for her.

After each actor and coach had had a turn, someone pounded out "I'm a Believer" on the piano—the Monkees song ends the movie version of "Shrek"—and everyone sang and danced and Sam's son Christopher played the tambourine. It was a fitting tribute to a fine group of actors, but I am even fonder of "Freak Flag," the other showstopper in Shrek. It's not in the movie, just the stage production, and it features the storybook characters who are booted from their homeland for being weird—only to invade Shrek's swamp, much to the dismay of the equally weird and not very hospitable ogre.

In the end (spoiler alert) Shrek and Princess Fiona marry, they all realize that being weird is more than okay, and they sing:

> *We spend out whole lives wishing*
> *We weren't so freakin' strange*
> *They made us feel the pain*
> *But it's they who need to change*
> *The way they think, that is*
>
> *It's time to stop the hiding*
> *It's time to stand up tall*
> *Say hey world, I'm different*
> *And here I am, stank breath and all. Stank breath and all.*

Shrek's bad breath is a running gag in the show, and that "stank breath" line brought down the house during the performances I saw. The audience was also amused by Sophie, the littlest cast member, who, as luck would have it, had learned how to shimmy just the week before, and managed to get herself a spot center stage, where she, Annabelle, and the rest of the cast belted out the ending:

*We've got magic, we've got power*
*Who are they to say we're wrong?*
*All the things that make us special*
*Are the things that make us strong*

*What makes us special*
*What makes us special*
*What makes us special*
*Makes us strong*

*Let your freak flag wave*
*Let your freak flag fly*
*Never take it down, never take it down*
*Raise it way up high*
*Let your freak flag fly, fly, fly, fly, fly*

# 16

## TRAVELS WITH SOPHIE

It was around the time of her first Special Olympics experience that Sophie started talking about not wanting to have Down syndrome. She was not yet nine, which seemed early, but I got it. Sophie had been mainstreamed her entire life, had only known a couple other kids with Down syndrome. Suddenly she was surrounded by teens and adults with varying degrees of intellectual disabilities. Some were withdrawn; others had trouble moving. Many did not communicate. Most of them looked depressed. To be honest, they scared me a little; I can only imagine what Sophie thought, suddenly tossed into this club.

I was ill-prepared to talk about the existentials of Down syndrome with my child. There is no good response, no right way to handle it. What was I going to say?

Yep, Sophie, as a matter of fact, you're fucked. Your heart doesn't work right, you're going to be short, you will probably get early-onset Alzheimer's, and even though you're one of the kindest, funniest, smartest people I have ever met, most of society will look at your face and judge you immediately—and not favorably.

Oh yeah, and your hair won't curl.

When Sophie complained from time to time about not wanting to have Down syndrome, I tried the usual responses—that we all have things about ourselves we don't like but make the best of it—even though I felt like a giant hypocrite because, let's face it, I couldn't come up with a legit comparison. I changed the subject. It wasn't hard. Sophie was pretty easily distracted, and eventually, she stopped talking about it.

I didn't say anything, but I thought about it a lot, about everything from what it must feel like for Sophie to know she has this "thing" to how she felt about one of the least consequential and most meaningful aspects, her hair.

Over the years, Sophie's desire for curly hair never waned. She looked for women with curly hair on TV and in person, and I've always wondered what a twenty-something African American woman with a giant, gorgeous Afro thought when my tiny girl walked up, twisting a piece of her own hopelessly straight brown strands in her fingers, and complimented her on her "awesome hair."

I knew that finding out why Sophie's hair didn't curl wouldn't change anything, but it bugged me, in this age of instant answers, that more than a decade in I still didn't have the information. While science had unfolded over the years to reveal genetic reasons for everything from childhood leukemia to early dementia, I still didn't have an answer about why people with Down syndrome never had curly hair.

Rather, almost never had curly hair. By the time Sophie was twelve, I had seen and heard of a few people with Down syndrome who had curly hair, but that was the rare exception to a rule documented in even the earliest literature about mongolism.

By that time, I had hit several roadblocks in my quest to find the scientific cause of the fine, straight hair that so often accompanies the almond-shaped eyes, tiny nose, and low muscle tone found in people with Down syndrome. But I wasn't done trying.

In the summer of 2015, I picked up a few threads; none led to my answer. Some scoffed at me—Tom Blumenthal, who runs the Linda Crnic Institute for Down Syndrome in Denver, interrupted before the hair question was out of my mouth. "Can you prove that scientifically?" he asked, dismissing me. Others were kinder—Joel Brenner, the cardiologist from Johns Hopkins, told me that no, he'd never considered the question, but he thought it was a good one and that the answer might even hold some information about why some kids with DS get heart defects and others don't.

Cheryl Maslen, the heart researcher in Oregon, didn't go that far, but she was willing to entertain the notion. In fact, she said, one of her closest friends was researching the genome of the dog, and had figured out why some dogs have curly coats and others straight.

Did I want to talk to her?

YES! Oh my god, yes. I knew enough about genetics to know that dogs don't get Down syndrome (that was one of my earliest questions for Ray when he was holed up at the hospital library), but maybe there was some sort of correlation, maybe certain genes matched up? Certainly if the question had been asked about dogs, it had been asked about humans, right? And wouldn't this person know that?

I looked up Dr. Maslen's friend. She was impressive: Elaine A. Ostrander, Ph.D., Chief and Distinguished Investigator, Cancer Genetics and Comparative Genomics Branch, National Human Genome Research Institute, National Institutes of Health.

If anyone had the answer, it would be her.

~~~~~~

*To: Elaine Ostrander, Amy Silverman*
*From: Cheryl Maslen*
*Hi Amy,*

*This is to introduce you to Dr. Elaine Ostrander from the NIH. She is the geneticist I mentioned who studies the genetics of morphological traits in dogs. She has mapped a gene that determines if a dog will have a curly or straight haired coat. She'd be happy to speak with you.*

*Cheryl*

To: Cheryl Maslen, Elaine Ostrander
From: Amy Silverman

Cheryl — Thank you so much for introduction.

Elaine — I have been wondering about the genetics of curly vs. straight hair since my daughter Sophie was 4 months old. She's now 12. So I am so excited to get to talk to you — THANK YOU!
Do you have any time this week to talk by phone?

Thanks in advance.

Amy

*To: Amy Silverman*
*From: Elaine Ostrander*
*Hi Ms. Silverman*

*So let me first be clear that I know nothing about curly hair genetics in humans. In dogs there is one gene that seems to contribute to curly versus straight. Almost certainly it is not the only one—given how curly versus wavy versus straight that fur can be. In mice there are several genes that contribute to curly hair. I have no idea which of them may or may not be related to genes in humans that contribute to curly hair.*

*Cheryl mentioned that one of your questions related to Down's syndrome.... The counterpart of the genes I mentioned is not on chromosome 21. Certainly there is no obvious correlation from studies of thousand and thousands of children with Down's syndrome and hair type. It is clearly not a diagnostic for propensity to get Down's.*

*What is true is that your situation is far from unique. Lots of parents contact me with children with red hair (mom and dad are brown), eye color surprises, vast differences in height between parents and children and weight. Some children are stunning athletes and have parents who are total klutzes and I have brilliant parents contact me complaining that their children are average and vice versa. There is not a body type or feature for which these examples don't exist. They are everywhere.*

*These examples relate to the fact that we each have 20,000 genes, and each gene comes in many many different "flavors," or as we geneticists say, with many different variants in DNA sequence. Thus, there is an array of about 100,000 different DNA variants that contribute to making us look the way we do.*

*I am guessing if you look back in your family tree far enough you would find a person with curly hair. Their DNA variant has been hiding, masked by stronger variants, and just now has shown up. Do I think it is on chromosome 21? I have no idea. We still have a great deal to learn about the human genome and what all our genes do. Currently this is not an active area of scientific exploration because it is not a marker for any known disease, including Down's. Does that answer your questions?*

*Warmest wishes,*
*Elaine Ostrander, Ph.D.*


To: Elaine Ostrander
From: Amy Silverman
Subject: Re: dog genetics

Thank you for writing! I think you answered some questions, but let me tell you what led me to start asking questions about Sophie's hair and genetics in general….And that might explain what I'm looking for answer-wise. I do understand that there might not be an answer, and that that's one in itself.

When Sophie was born, we waited for four months to get an appointment with a geneticist. By that point the tests were done, we knew she had Down syndrome and not mosaicism. We'd done our basic reading and honestly weren't really sure why we were there. Sophie was about to have open-heart surgery (for the defect that Cheryl Maslen is researching) and to be honest, I was trying to distract myself....My husband and I both have wavy/curly hair and our older daughter's is the same. I wondered about Sophie, and in that moment sitting in the geneticist's office, I realized that I'd never seen a person with Down syndrome who didn't have super straight, fine hair.

Yes, the geneticist said, that's a characteristic of Down syndrome. (He acknowledged that a person who was African American who had DS might be an exception.)

So I've always wondered — how is that? (And here I'll fully acknowledge that I'm no genetics whiz!) Is there a straight hair gene on the 21st chromosome? Are there straight hair genes and curly hair genes, or is it one or the other (and the absence is what gives one straight or curly hair?). Is there anyone out there doing specific research into human hair and genetics?

Did that explain the question?

Thank you again for your help!!!!!

Amy

*To: Amy Silverman*
*From: Elaine Ostrander*

*So I imagine there are people doing human hair genetics, but I have no idea who they are. Frankly I did not know that having straight fine hair was a characteristic of Down's. So you are way ahead of me.*

*Elaine*

I was disappointed, but not deterred. I called on the public relations guy at the Translational Genomics Research Institute in

Phoenix. Was he familiar with anyone who might be able to answer my question?

He did. If anyone knew, he said, it would be Dr. Donna Krasnewich, a program director in the Division of Genetics and Developmental Biology at the National Institute of General Medical Sciences.

I was cautiously optimist, sent off my e-mail, and sighed at the response.

*Hi Amy. Wow, you ask a pretty interesting question that I have absolutely no insight into personally. First, I think most hair traits are probably directed by complex genetics, multiple genes involved in interactive ways to define the traits. With that said, you may want to try Nina Jablonski who, from my quick library search, seems to have an expertise in hair texture.*

Jablonski was a PhD., an anthropologist at the Pennsylvania State University. She wrote back the same day.

To: Amy Silverman
From: Nina G. Jablonski
Dear Amy,

Thank you for your wonderful message.

The short answer to your question is that no one knows much about the genetic basis of human hair texture, period. Downs Syndrome or not, we know precious little about the genetic control of hair form and texture in humans. As you have learned, we know far more about the genetics of hair form in dogs and rodents than we do in humans. One of the few things we do know for certain about human hair form and texture is that the genes that make curly or zigzag hair in dogs and rodents don't appear to have effect on human scalp hair. So, it's back to the drawing board. Who's working on this? Right now, graduate students in my lab and the lab of Mark Shriver in the Department of Anthropology at Penn State are working on this, but we are at the very beginning of our quest. It will be some time (years) before we have a better handle on this. But I am terrifically grateful to you for bringing this interesting issue to my attention because it is often through the careful examination of rare variants that more general mechanisms are revealed.

I'm sorry that I can't be more helpful about answering your question, but at least I can be authoritative about our ignorance!

...I hope to answer your question in a few years.

All the best,

Nina

"Enough," I said to myself, as I closed my laptop. "Enough."

In the summer of 2015, Annabelle really came into her hair. She grew it past her shoulder blades and—her toddler ringlets long gone—coaxed her waves into curls with a combination of layers, hair gel, a diffuser, and sheer will.

Sophie let her hair get long, too, announcing she was growing it for Locks of Love but planned to keep it when it was chopped off, which made no sense to anyone but Sophie.

At twelve, she was most definitely her own person. She DVR'd every episode of the reality show *Dance Moms*, and followed the stars on Instagram. She loved to swim, disliked hiking, and hated wearing the tights that went with her ballet class uniform. She really wanted to go through puberty, although so far all I'd seen were the earliest physical signs and some teary episodes that seemed hormone-inspired. For all the hints of grown-up Sophie, she was still my little girl, always ready for a cuddle, constantly knocking wires loose on her braces by sucking her thumb.

School was surprisingly okay. People were constantly reminding me that middle school is a horror story for pretty much every kid, and I had to admit that in light of that, Sophie was fine. She didn't have any sleepover invitations from classmates, no phone calls or Instagram requests, but she knew every adult at the school, and very slowly, she was making friends among her peers. She was comfortable at this giant institution, proof that it really does take just a few people to make a difference in a kid's life. And she was actually learning how to add integers in math class, coming home with facts she'd gathered about biology and colonial America, memorizing Spanish vocabulary—way more than I accomplished during my own middle school experience.

Sophie was excited for summer—for ballet, drama, and art camps, for time with her favorite nannies, and long afternoons of swimming. Most of all, she wanted to travel. This made me really happy. Sophie liked to go to new places, but most of all she loved to meet people. As a closeted introvert, I'd always used journalism as an excuse to interact with the world. Now I had an even better reason. The previous year, we'd taken the girls to Washington, D.C., for spring break. Sophie had charmed a guard into holding her up for a glimpse of the Oval Office and when she didn't actually see the president, she had done the splits outside the White House, figuring that he was probably peeking out for a glimpse of her.

The following spring break we planned a trip to New Orleans. Ray and I were both worried about taking young girls there, and I wouldn't recommend Bourbon Street after dark, but it was one of the best trips of my life, and remember, I've been to both Holland and France.

Sophie and I both overcame our fear of alligators and loud noises enough to enjoy a swamp boat tour, and she charmed every waiter she met into getting her plain rice with butter. The highlight of the trip came when we stopped to watch a brass band perform in Jackson Square. A large crowd had formed, and we edged around the side. Slowly, Sophie moved her way up to the front and tried out some dance moves. Soon she was front and center, matching moves (or trying to, at least) with a man in high tops and parachute pants who clearly did this for a living. When a number ended and the male dancer dug in the tip jar for twenty dollars and handed it to Sophie, the crowd went wild—and all night long in the French Quarter, people grinned at Sophie as we passed.

So I was looking forward to our summer road trip—to Portland, San Francisco, and Los Angeles. Plenty of things to see and people to meet.

The Ace Hotel in Portland, Oregon, is best known for its role as the capital of hip, inspiration for the first episode of the television show *Portlandia,* but it's also a great hotel for kids. There's a photo booth in the lobby, cool art on the walls, and an incredibly friendly staff.

Within the first ten minutes, Sophie had made such good friends with the bellman that when we checked in, there was a handwritten note and saltwater taffy waiting for her. The front desk clerk overheard Sophie asking me if she could ask for a toothbrush (I was insisting that she had a perfectly good one upstairs already) and handed one over with a grin.

Things were even better in San Francisco, where we were met with hula hoops in the lobby of our groovy Chinatown boutique hotel. Annabelle put her ballerina hips to good use immediately, but Sophie struggled, so one of the lobby employees dropped what he was doing to offer lessons. Then he asked if the girls could have ice cream and then he asked if they could have coloring books and crayons.

When the young man disappeared for twenty minutes, I wondered if I'd misunderstood the offer—turns out, the hotel was out of coloring books and crayons, so he ran a quarter mile to a drugstore to procure them. The next day, I left him a tip at the front desk but really, there was no way to thank him for his kindness. More than the gifts, it was the attention Sophie craved, and she beamed when she finally mastered that hula hoop.

On our first full day in San Francisco, we turned down the line for the vintage cable cars and took a bus to the Castro, where the girls got a taste of multiculturalism as we wandered around the streets. It was unseasonably warm and sunny for June, which is typically the heart of that city's winter.

As long as everyone was fed, they were happy, and I thought back to the last few days and marveled at how nice life was, how comfortable I was with Sophie, how I couldn't imagine life without her. Walking along in the sunshine, I daydreamed a little. I could quit my job and Sophie and I could hit the road, write a blog called "Travels with Sophie," encouraging more people to travel with family members with intellectual disabilities. I was still bothered by how rarely I saw other people with Down syndrome out in public.

We slipped into a little seafood restaurant for lunch, and as usual, Sophie immediately engaged the waitress in conversation. The lunch crowd followed us, and soon every table was packed, and the waitress was juggling more than Sophie's questions about which TV shows she'd liked when she was Sophie's age.

Ray got frustrated and told Sophie to stop asking questions. I didn't think he was being unreasonable—part of learning to interact with society is learning when to stop interacting with society—and Sophie didn't seem to mind. A few minutes later, she announced she had to use the bathroom. We left the table together; I was giggling over the waitress's crush on the Gilmore Girls.

Sophie went first and was washing her hands when she spoke, her back to me.

"Will I still have Down syndrome when I grow up?" she asked.

"Yes," I said, recovering quickly. Damn. It had been so long since she'd brought that up. But I understood why. The waitress, the admonishment, the knowledge on some level that she doesn't act like the rest of us. "You will."

"I don't want to have Down syndrome my whole entire life."

And just like that, like a guest at Mary Poppins's Uncle Albert's tea party on the ceiling, I felt myself slowly lowered to the ground — that fizzy, giddy feeling gone.

Bad enough that she didn't want to have it. Now Sophie was on to the universe. She'd figured out she'd always have it. As usual, I didn't know what to say.

So I pulled her in for a long hug, then together we maneuvered the door and the crowded restaurant, and the four of us walked out into the bright sunshine.

From San Francisco we drove south on the drought-stricken I-5 to Los Angeles, where the girls swam in a hotel pool filled with rubber ducks and Sophie negotiated with the front desk clerk to borrow a book from the tiny library outside, even though she didn't have one to trade. Sophie seemed content, but that moment in the bathroom followed me home, and I started wondering if I needed to look for a psychotherapist for Sophie.

Or maybe, I thought, I am the one who needs a therapist. I couldn't decide, so I never made an appointment, letting the recommendations languish in my e-mail inbox.

We ended the summer with more travel—this time to La Jolla, a beach town north of San Diego, for our annual trip with my sister Jenny and her family. This trip is sacrosanct. In several decades, I can recall missing it only a handful of times: the summer I backpacked through Europe, the year Annabelle was rude enough to be born on the exact week of the trip. We didn't skip the year Sophie was about to have heart surgery for the first time; I flew with the baby, feeding tube and all, despite protests from the pediatrician.

Jenny and I had spent countless hours tanning on this beach when we were kids; now we brought our own children here, dousing them with sunscreen every half hour and yelling at them to wear hats and sunglasses. I remember spending hours in the water, boogie boarding, and now I sat under an umbrella and watched Annabelle and her cousin, Kate, catch waves. Sophie refused. She sat with me under the umbrella, afraid to dip more than a toe in the water, instead asking to play gin rummy or go to the pool.

Kate and Sophie are just weeks apart in age, but Kate is most definitely Annabelle's peer, not Sophie's. She was unfailingly kind to her cousin, who adored her, but she was bonded to Annabelle, and one night I watched the two of them—my older daughter's long blonde curls blending with my niece's dark ones as they lay awake at night, telling secrets—and wondered if that's how Annabelle and Sophie would be if Sophie didn't have Down syndrome.

The next morning, Annabelle and Kate were signed up for a surf lesson. Jenny and I walked them down the beach, trailed by Sophie and her younger cousin, Sam, who was nine. I had asked Sophie earlier if she wanted to take a surf lesson, knowing the answer would be a quick no, which it was. But when we met up with the surf instructor, a young woman named Jo, Sophie joined the girls on the sand, listening to the instructions intently—then sat quietly and watched the lesson once they were in the water.

I pretended to take pictures. It was hard to look at Sophie; I know she wanted to be with the other girls, to do what they did, to be them. I really understood how Sophie felt. I didn't want her to have Down syndrome, either.

I also knew, in that moment, that this pity party wasn't helping either of us.

After the lesson, I pulled Jo aside. "Do you think it would be possible, I mean, could Sophie ever take a lesson? Would you do that?" I asked, stumbling over my words. Jo didn't hesitate. Yes, she said. But Sophie needed to get comfortable in the water first. She recommended that Sophie start by boogie boarding on her own. "It would help if you told her that yourself," I muttered. So she did, and I reiterated, explaining to Sophie that if she got some experience boogie boarding, next time she could take a surf lesson with the other girls.

Sophie nodded, clearly not committing to anything. No way, I thought to myself, and rounded up playing cards and other distractions, the editor in me guiding the end of the story without even realizing it.

Two hours and several games of Go Fish later, Sophie was playing with the iPad under an umbrella; the other kids were in the water. I settled into a lounge chair and closed my eyes, lulled by the sounds of families playing and waves crashing.

"Hey Amy!" my brother-in-law Jonathan called across the beach. I sat up with a start, not knowing how much time had passed. Jonathan was grinning.

"Check it out!" he said, pointing to the water. "Sophie's boogie boarding."

It's funny. In the photos I looked at later, Sophie's got a death grip on the board, the only kid on the beach wearing goggles, her jaw set hard and her mouth crinkled in concentration. But all I remember when I think back is the kids, Sophie included, cracking up with joy. And how as soon as she washed ashore, Sophie was back in the water, ready to catch another wave.

# BIBLIOGRAPHY

Abraham, Willard. *A Time for Teaching.* New York: Harper & Row, 1964.

Abraham, Willard. *Barbara: A Prologue.* New York: Rinehart & Company, Inc., 1958.

Blatt, Burton, and Fred Kaplan. *Christmas in Purgatory: A Photographic Essay on Mental Retardation.* Syracuse, NY: Human Policy Press, 1974.

Couwenhoven, Terri. *Teaching Children with Down Syndrome about Their Bodies, Boundaries, and Sexuality: A Guide for Parents and Professionals.* Bethesda, MD: Woodbine House, 2007.

Cowan, Ruth Schwartz. *Heredity and Hope: The Case for Genetic Screening.* Cambridge, MA: Harvard University Press, 2008.

"Crispin Hellion Glover's Feature Film *What Is It?*" Accessed December 17, 2015. http://www.crispinglover.com/whatisit.htm.

Fairman, Christopher. "The Case against Banning the Word 'Retard.'" *Washington Post,* February 2010.

Gabrielson, Ryan. "Police Ignored, Mishandled Sex Assaults Reported by Disabled." *California Watch,* November 2012.

Irwin, Megan. "Home Invasion." *Phoenix New Times,* May 2008.

Kingsley, Emily Perl. "Welcome to Holland." Copyright 1987.

Larson, Kate Clifford. *Rosemary: The Hidden Kennedy Daughter.* New York: Houghton Mifflin Harcourt Publishing Company, 2015.

Marcus, Amy Dockser. "New Hope for Treating Down Syndrome," *Wall Street Journal,* April 2005.

Miller, G. Wayne. *King of Hearts: The True Story of the Maverick Who Pioneered Open Heart Surgery.* New York: Broadway Books, 2002.

Milne, A. A. *Now We Are Six.* London: Puffin Books, 1992.

"Retarded." In *Oxford English Dictionary.* Accessed June 10, 2015. http://www.oed.com/viewdictionaryentry/Entry/164191?p=emailASh/fGPDQwecc&d=164191.

Rhim, Lauren Morando, and Paul O'Neil. "Improving Access and Creating Exceptional Opportunities for Students with Disabilities in Public Charter Schools." National Center for Special Education in Charter Schools, October 2013.

Ruhlman, Michael. *Walk on Water: The Miracle of Saving Children's Lives.* New York: Penguin Books, 2004.

Shriver, Timothy. *Fully Alive: Discovering What Matters Most.* New York: Sara Crichton Books, 2014.

Vanesian, Kathleen. "Chris Rush Retrospective at Mesa Art Center Forces Us to 'Stare.'" *Phoenix New Times,* April 2010.

White, E. B. *Charlotte's Web.* New York: Harper Collins, 1952.

*Wikipedia,* s.v. "List of Disability-Related Terms with Negative Connotations." Last modified November 24, 2015. https://en.wikipedia.org/wiki/List_of_disability-related_terms_with_negative_connotations.

Wilkinson, Amber. "What Is It." Eye for Film. January 30, 2005. http://www.eyeforfilm.co.uk/review/what-is-it-film-review-by-amber-wilkinson.

## ACKNOWLEDGMENTS

Thank you to my agent, Jenny Bent, for believing in this book, and to my editor, Susan Stokes, and everyone at Woodbine House, for making it a reality.

Thank you to Laurie Notaro and Claire Lawton. The three of us are not big huggers—but you have each held my hand through this entire process, and I am forever grateful.

Everyone should be lucky enough to have a friend who doubles 24/7 as a personal editor. Thank you, Deborah Sussman. And thank you to other friends who were kind enough to read versions of this book, including Tricia Parker, Kim Porter, Elizabeth Naranjo, and Tricia Theis Rogalski.

For wise and honest advice, cheerleading, attendance at secret writing parties—and, mostly, for listening—thank you to Sativa Peterson, Brad Snyder, Cindy Dach, Shannon Wilkinson, Terry Greene Sterling, Kristin Gilger, Tom Zoellner, Paul Rubin, John Dickerson, Eric Schaefer, Gayle Shanks, Tim McGuire, Ando Muneno, Judy Nichols, Timothy Archibald, Paul Morris, Judith Riven, Liza Dawson, Kathleen Vanesian, Suzanne Perryman, Betsy Sokolow Sherman, Rebecca Fish Ewan, Jude Joffe-Block, Stacy Pearson, Denise Resnik, Jennifer Longdon, Cynthia Clark Harvey, and Tania Katan.

I am lucky to have had (and to continue to have) amazing mentors and coconspirators at school and work. Thank you to Michael Lacey, Robrt Pela, Lisa Davis, Sarah Fenske, Laura Laughlin, Rick Barrs, Andy Van De Voorde, and Christine Brennan. To Dan Horowitz, for making me a lifelong American Studies major; and to the late Steve Isaacs, who first taught me the value of a really good story idea.

Thank you to the Mothers Who Write students (past, present, and future), who inspire me every week with their bravery and talent; and to Jessica Hill, Katie Johnson, and Charlie Levy for starting the Bar Flies reading series with me. Thanks to the kind people at *This American Life,* including Julie Snyder, Zoe Chace, and Ira Glass, who let me tell Sophie's story more than once; and to Mark Moran, Jon Hoban, Kelly Madison, and others who've given me so much air time at KJZZ in Phoenix.

There is not enough space in the world to recognize every person who has made a difference in Sophie's life—in our family's life—but here's a start. Thank you to Lynn Wright, Jennifer Zamenski, Courtney Funk, Jeanine Cardiello Gleason, Sarah Case, Abbie Parker, Rachel and Sarah Trim, Beth and Tatum Wiley, Frances Cohen, Rachel Cohen, Janice Coggins, Dorcas Cisnowski, Barry Fritch, the delaGarza Crouch family, Sarah Hales, Bobbie Schorr, Amy Segal, Maddy Wilkinson, Raimie Manch, and Sam.

Thanks to my online support group for everything from IEP advice to pie recipes to the concept of IEP Day Pie.

Thank you—in ways it's impossible to express in words—to my sister, Jennifer Lurie, and brother-in-law, Jonathan, and to my parents, Susan and Dick Silverman.

No one has taught me more about journalism, parenting, and love than Ray Stern.

And finally, thank you to Annabelle and Sophie. Each in your own way, you show me every day how to be a better person. I love being your mom.

# ABOUT THE AUTHOR

Amy Silverman is managing editor at *Phoenix New Times* and a commentator for KJZZ, the National Public Radio affiliate in Phoenix. Her work also has appeared on the radio show *This American Life* and in *The New York Times*. Amy holds a master's degree in journalism from Columbia University. She lives in Arizona with her husband, Ray, and daughters, Annabelle and Sophie. For more information, visit www.myheartcantevenbelieveit.com